THE PAST SPEAKS

A woman, touching a legendary megalith said to move down to the river at evening to wash off the blood of its sacrificial victims, becomes dizzy in its presence, and she senses strong vibrations. *What is happening?*

Year after year, people report faintness, visions of the past, or irresistible attractions to certain stones or places such as Stonehenge—as documents on file with the British Government's Department of the Environment clearly demonstrate. *What do they mean?*

These reports may bear witness to a power of tremendous magnitude—the power of megaliths constructed thousands of years ago—*a power that reaches across the centuries into our own time.*

"A probing, speculative look into the hidden world of man's past"—*Science News*

Maple Grove
Healing Awareness Center
149 Main Street
Ravena, New York 12143

Earth Magic

Francis Hitching

A KANGAROO BOOK
PUBLISHED BY POCKET BOOKS NEW YORK

Published in Great Britain in 1976

POCKET BOOKS, a Simon & Schuster division of
GULF & WESTERN CORPORATION
1230 Avenue of the Americas, New York, N.Y. 10020

Published by arrangement with William Morrow and Company, Inc.
Library of Congress Catalog Card Number: 76-44438

ISBN: 0-671-81815-5

First Pocket Books printing April, 1978

1   2   9   8

Trademarks registered in the United States and other countries.

Printed in the U.S.A.

CONTENTS

INTRODUCTION

IN THE HIDDEN WORLD OF MAN'S PAST, 5,000 YEARS
ago and more, extraordinary things were happening. All
over the world people were developing, unprecedentedly,
into human beings whom we today would readily recognize as cousins rather than distant ancestors; and as different kinds of societies emerged, nowhere was there a
more fascinating and enigmatic one than along the fringes
of northwest Europe. From as far north as the Shetland
Islands, Jutland, and the Baltic, to as far south as the
Mediterranean coastline of Spain, unlettered farming
communities were working out a complex, mathematically advanced society whose achievements we are only
just beginning to appreciate. It culminated in the final
version of Stonehenge, and it is even possible that its
people colonized part of America. It is perhaps the largest and most important lost civilization on earth.

Yet it is also one of the world's great mystery stories.
What sort of people were the megalith builders? What
sort of life did they lead? What could have persuaded
them to manipulate into position their great chunks of

stone? Something compelling, certainly—but to an outsider trying to discover just what, the picture is confusing. On the one hand there are the archaeological findings, often dry, cautious and inconclusive. On the other hand are the unorthodox prehistorians, bubbling enthusiastically with theories of a golden age of precivilization, when the world lived in peace and plenty. And the two sides mistrust each other with a quite exceptional vehemence.

A typical 1972 editorial in *Antiquity*, a highly respected British archaeological journal which reaches a wide readership of scholars, inveighed against the "world of the New Diffusionists, Black Horses, Atlantis, Pyramidiots, straight-trackers and the rest of them, the world which every student of antiquity recognizes, with an embarrassed smile, as a danger only to those whose weak and muddled heads prefer the comforts of unreason to the difficult facts of archaeology."

This world is in turn reflected in the cyclostyled pages of the *Ley Hunter*, a fringe publication dealing with speculative theories of prehistory, one of whose contributors recently reviewed a book on Druids by Stuart Piggott, professor of archaeology at the University of Edinburgh, and one of the most highly regarded figures in his field. Piggott, said the reviewer, "treats as plain fancy anything which is not plain fact as exhibited by the archaeological viewpoint . . . carries his archaeological straitjacket with its corpus of agreed knowledge and method into the foreign field of semi-philosophy and semi-religion in a disastrous oil-and-water emulsion account . . . a strange and wild book by a scholar whose head appears buried in the sand of nineteenth-century physics."

Well, both sides can't be right—or can they? Are they each describing opposite sides of the same coin? After many years of more than casual interest in the subject, I found myself with the opportunity of turning detective. At first, as I read my way into the published material, the mystery deepened. There seemed no way of penetrating the lost life and motives of megalithic man from the few ruined clues he had left behind. But then, as my search took me into folklore and divination, into the distant history of the early Christian church, across America to explore the legends and customs of native Indians, up hillsides to talk to farmers who use the stones today, to physics laboratories and theories of electromagnetism, and into libraries to unearth the forgotten findings of early scholars, the first glimmerings of a solution began to appear.

As with any mystery story, I have left my tentative conclusions to the last chapter. Otherwise, I have presented the evidence as it came: first of all what is known from archaeology, and then from more unorthodox sources. As the clues emerged, I have tried to remain dispassionate and weigh their worth. But perhaps we shall never know the whole truth. Something magical was happening in the time of the megaliths, and good magicians don't reveal all their secrets.

My appreciation is extended to the work of all those quoted in the text, many of whom have been kind enough to offer their helpful comments. I should also like to thank my friends John Hopkins (librarian at the Society of Antiquaries), Tony Couch, Patrick Dromgoole, John Green, Colin Ronan, Marje and Norman Runnion, and—especially—Michael Bakewell, who discussed with me the mysteries of the megaliths on many occasions and at many sites.

London 1976

PART

I

1

WORLD OF STONE

Either Stonehenge and Avebury and all such are temples of a race so ancient as to be beyond the ken of mortal man, or they are the sepulchral monuments of a people who lived so nearly within the limits of true historic times that their story can easily be recovered.

—JAMES FERGUSSON, *Rude Stone Monuments Throughout the World*, 1872

SCATTERED OVER THE FACE OF THE EARTH LIKE PEBBLES on a sandy beach, the rough remains of man's lost past lie there to baffle and haunt us. No continent is without its lingering traces of a time before writing or metal or the wheel: humps and hollows arranged in mysterious geometric patterns; massive stone monuments erected with stubborn effort; paintings, carvings, and obscure symbols; underground chambers and tombs that carry, even today, echoes of primitive ritual. They mark the time when man began to place his life into a settled order, and they are clues to one of the world's last great archaeological mysteries—how did man, as we would recognize him today, emerge from the thick forest of prehistory?

It was an age of stone, and the word *megalithic* (which, strictly, should refer only to monuments using large and heavy stones) has come to describe generally the huge number of these clues which can still be widely found. For each country has not only its major and justly famous attractions for tourists and scholars, but many thousands of smaller, deeply intriguing sites that hint at the variety of ways in which man, everywhere, began to discover civilization. Britain has not just Stonehenge, but a whole landscape marked by prehistoric earthworks, man-made hilltops, giant hill figures. America's vast, undeciphered runwaylike patterns on the ground in Peru, or the renowned serpent mound in Ohio, may ultimately be less important than the many uninvestigated stone structures in New England. France has uncounted thousands of burial chambers, and mysteriously aligned stones pointing to the sky. Spain, Portugal and the Mediterranean islands abound with stone monuments, richly decorated with mystifying designs. The empty countryside of Ireland and Scotland is dotted with the half-ruined remains

5

of arrangements of stone that at first appear to be circles, but upon examination turn out to be elegantly designed ellipses or egg-shaped outlines. From northeastern America, through all of northern and western Europe, north Africa, the Biblical lands, the Middle East, and as far as southern India, there are apparently identical megalithic tombs constructed laboriously by men who, thousands of years ago, heaved and levered great slabs of stone and rested them with infinite precision in their chosen place. In China and Japan there are underground man-made chambers uncannily similar to their counterparts on the other side of the globe.

Over vast distances, prehistoric man seems to have behaved in a strikingly unified way. Of course, it may be facile to imply that, because a freestanding megalithic lump in China looks like a freestanding megalithic lump in Scotland, there must therefore be a connection between them, and a scholarly archaeologist of today's disciplines is justified in warning that "there is a latent fallacy . . . which accepts that similarity of form and building materials as denoting a fundamental unity over enormous tracts of time and space."

Yet sometimes first impressions, when you see the wood and not the trees, are the most vivid and the most real. Victorian archaeologists, uninhibited by later intel-

Dolmen (known locally as a cromlech) at Pentre Ifan, Wales. Probably once covered by a mound 130′ long.

lectual doctrines, were quick to see the parallels in the worldwide development of man, and their findings still have the capacity to astonish. In 1872, when James Fergusson made the first universal catalogue of known prehistoric antiquities in his *Rude Stone Monuments Throughout the World,* the list he came up with was colossal. After devoting his early chapters to England, Ireland and Scotland, he noted comparable discoveries in Scandinavia and North Germany; in France; in Spain, Portugal and Italy; in Algeria and Tripoli; in the Mediterranean islands of Malta, Sardinia and the Balearics; in Palestine, the Sinai, Arabia, Asia Minor; and in north, central and southern America. Archaeology had been in existence for only half a century, but it is still the most comprehensive list compiled. Today, he would be able to add chapters on China, Japan, and the Pacific, all showing the extraordinary similarity throughout the world of the ways in which ancient man used stone. In 1901, the *Archaeological Journal* printed some sketches showing the "similarity, and almost identity, of rock sculpturings on Clydeside discoveries to those on rocks and objects discovered in Central Australia," which are still as much of a puzzle today as they were then. Perhaps more, since similar markings have subsequently been found cut on rocks in many other places.

In the hundreds of thousands of years that led him to the Pyramids and Stonehenge, man became extraordinarily adept at working with stone. His axes could clear forests (in an experiment in Denmark, using reconstructed stone axes, it took two men only eight minutes to cut down a sizable tree), his arrows slay wild animals. But stones took on a deeper significance for him, and became far more than mere weapons. They became monuments and symbols. He became obsessed with them—with their shape, size, weight and arrangement—and the feeling that he had for them has never quite been lost. The Old Testament is punctuated with such references as "And Joshua wrote these words in the book of the law of God, and took a great stone and set it up there under an oak that was by the sanctuary of the Lord. . . ." The Greeks revered the *omphalos,* a sacred stone of a rounded conical shape in the temple of Apollo at Delphi, which they believed to mark the central point of the world. In churchyards and on roadsides all over western Britain and

France, there are many hundreds of "Celtic crosses"—age-old standing stones marked with the sign of the Cross, a fusion of different eras of worship and veneration.

Throughout history, the stones of megalithic man have inspired emotions of reverence and fury totally out of keeping with the humdrum facts of their geological make-up. At Avebury, in many ways a greater engineering achievement even than Stonehenge, the Middle Ages saw the introduction of a ceremony in which, every twenty-five years, one of the great stones was ritually dislodged and attacked, under the auspices of the Church, in order to symbolize the conquest of the Devil. After the monument was discovered and popularized in the seventeenth century, the attacks increased in frequency and intensity until, by the eighteenth century, a local farmer known as "stone-killer Robinson" organized weekly parties of destruction, watched desolately by the great antiquarian, the Rev. Dr. William Stukeley:

> The barbarous massacre of a stone here with leavers and hammers, sledges and fires, is as terrible a sight as a Spanish auto de fé. The vast cave they dig around it, the hollow under the stone like a glass-house furnace or a baker's oven, the huge chasms made through the body of the stone, the straw, the faggots, the smoak, the prongs, and squallor of the fellows looks like a knot of devils grilling the soul of a sinner.

But equally, some stones retained their ability to excite awe and wonder. Locally, all over the world, they were believed to have healing properties, and villagers took part in rituals whose origins went back thousands of years. Covens of witches held their ceremonies in stone circles, believing that it brought them a supernatural power. Today, there are some people who believe in a hidden earth force that can be physically felt through the stones, and many more who can sense, as when touching a great sculpture, a tactile response as described by J. R. L. Anderson in *The Ridgeway:* "The texture is oddly exciting, thrilling to the fingertips like a small electric shock. One can, and, to get the sense of them properly, one should, walk up and touch these stones: unlike

STRIKINGLY SIMILAR ROCK MARKINGS FROM
SCOTLAND AND AUSTRALIA NOTED IN *ARCHAE-
OLOGICAL JOURNAL* (1901).

1. Churinga Ilkinia, or sacred rock drawings of a group of
the Honey Ant totems of the Warramunga tribe of Australian aboriginals. 2. Cup-and-ring marks from Cochno, Scotland. 3a. Warramunga tribal design. 3b. Slate carving,
Crannog Dumbuck, Scotland. 4. Cochno, Scotland. 5a and
5b. Warramunga designs. 5c. Plum tree totem design. 6a-
6d. Cup-and-ring marks at Auchintorlie, Scotland. 7. Cochno
rock carving. (N.B. only four toes.) 8. Design from rocks
at Emily Gorge, Australia. 9. On rock at Quinrupa, Australia. 10. Cochno, Scotland.

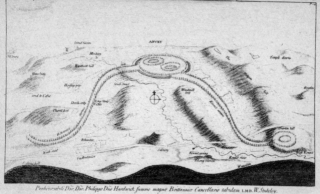

Prohononbile Die Dio Philippo Dio Hardwick Summo magnæ Britanniæ Cancellario tabulam I.M.D. W. Stukeley.

The Rev. William Stukeley's portrayal of the once-serpen-
tine shape of Avebury. Because of optical distortion, it has
not yet been established whether the avenues in fact existed
like this, or if Stukeley's visionary qualities led him to this
conclusion.

so many other antiquities they will not suffer from the
touch of many hands."

And yet for centuries, scholars and historians have
largely ignored these monuments to our lost past. No
Roman writer mentioned Stonehenge, though many must
have known of it. Avebury lay unknown except to locals
until on a January morning in 1649 the antiquarian John
Aubrey galloped past the huge stones while fox hunting
with the Wiltshire hounds. He was struck with the sudden
revelation that he was gazing at a monument of enormous
antiquity and significance, and he started a fashion for
megalith hunting that, ironically, led to many of them
being mutilated and destroyed. It was less than 100 years
ago that anybody suspected stone monuments and megalithic man of being capable of astronomical observation,
and only in the last decade have archaeologists come to
believe the evidence of their advanced geometry. And
perhaps this is not surprising. A tumbledown collection
of stones in a field, a shapeless malformation that might
as well be an abandoned chalk pit as a sacred prehistoric site, the ruined and partial remains of an ancient
monument—all these are at the same time so puzzling
and so commonplace that it is natural enough to pass

on to more recent and more understandable historical
events.

Yet they are important not just because they are witnesses of the time when man took his first steps toward
civilization, but because collectively—enigmatically—
they give tantalizing hints of something magical that was
going on, and that we have lost. Anybody looking for
the first time at pictures and accounts of megaliths in
various countries notices not only their superficial similarities, but any number of coincidences. For instance, in
continents thousands of miles apart, local languages use
the same word for "stone." The word—oddly enough—
is written phonetically *man* or *men*. Thus in Celtic, Europe's most ancient language, a dolmen is a table stone;
a menhir is a standing stone (once known in England
as a hoar stone); in Wales, Pen-maen-maur means the
hill of the big stone; in Cornwall, Men-an-tol is the stone
with the hole. Yet go away as far as southern India,
where rough stone tombs were still being built by hill
tribes as recently as this century, and in Khasi *mansmai*
means the stone of oath; *manloo* the stone of salt; and
manflong the grassy stone. It is enough to intrigue even
the most skeptical.

The search for what went on in the mind of megalithic
man is strewn with clues like this, sometimes leading on
to false trails, but also sometimes clearing a new path
through the undergrowth of prehistory. Each type of
megalith contains its own enigma, and each place where
they are found poses a variation of their riddles. But
one thing they have in common is that in an age before
metal and before writing, they are today's solid and lasting
reminders of man's first efforts at solving the mysteries
of the universe. Their challenge now is to find meaning
in their Sphinxlike ambiguities.

The starting point for many archaeologists is to examine the burial practices of our lost past. Partly this is
because, through them, the philosophical development
of man can be dimly traced—they let us look at his
emerging belief that he needed more in life than food,
drink and shelter. Animals do not bury their dead;
nor, as far as has yet been discovered, did earliest man.
But at least 50,000 years ago, in Europe and the Middle
East, a form of ritual burial began to be practiced, and
by the time the megaliths were built, burial was a com-

plex and widespread ceremony. Burial sites have a practical value to archaeology as well. Without written evidence, ideas about what happened in prehistory have to
be interpreted largely from the things man used—his
weapons, his food bowls, his ornaments—and these were
often buried with him. Thus the steady improvement
in the quality of stone tools gives us an insight into how
he became physically more expert and adept, and the
development of his burial practices provides some of the
clues to his spiritual growth.

Interest has been concentrated on the megalithic
tombs of northwest Europe because of their huge number
(more than 6,000 in France alone), their variety, and
above all, their distinctiveness. But the more they are
examined, catalogued and classified, the more mysterious
they become. For although many skeletons and human
cremation ashes have been excavated, suspiciously few
grave goods accompanied them. Yet they are collectively
the most substantial body of megalithic evidence that
exists, and a chronological look at the way they were
built, and the shapes they took, raises a question that
is fundamental to understanding those times: were the
megaliths meant just for burial, or did they once have
another, more important, purpose? And was this purpose
the same in all the other places of the world where
they are to be found—for instance, in the New England
stone chambers, which are at first glance almost identical to megalithic tombs in Spain and Portugal?

The earliest mounds erected, obvious on the skyline
to any tourist in western Europe, were long earthen barrows. They are not all that numerous—perhaps only 400
of them in all—but they are of an impressive size, and
give the first indications of how megalithic man regarded
huge movements of earth as a necessary part of his life.
They are usually from 100 feet to 300 feet long, though
the biggest are nearly 500 feet, and they were built and
used over a very long period—certainly for a thousand
years, and perhaps for much longer. Nearly always, they
are built on conspicuous sites, from which the countryside can be viewed for miles around, and are higher
and broader at the east end, where the burials took place.
To build them, a wooden enclosing wall was often constructed, with a "house" at one end in which the bones
of the dead were placed and covered with flints. Over a

period of time the house collapsed, and earth silted up over the bones.

The number of dead varied enormously, from as few as one or two to more than fifty. The average was six, and the skeletons of men, women and children have been found in the barrows in roughly equal numbers. Sometimes the corpses were buried whole; sometimes the skeleton fragmented; sometimes long after death, so that exposure to the elements had removed all the flesh from the bones; sometimes with a jawbone or thighbone missing, apparently deliberately taken away. Sir William Colt Hoare, who in 1812 recorded his excavation of thirty-seven long barrows in Wiltshire, noted that all the bodies were lying "strangely huddled," or "in a confused and irregular manner."

The first puzzle to be noted from these archaeological findings is that the barrows are far larger than they needed to be, perhaps in much the same way as a mausoleum is too big for a coffin. The burial area in a barrow is often no more than a twentieth of the total. And for a small community, preoccupied with gathering and farming enough food for existence, the effort involved in making a barrow was remarkable. It has been calculated that at least 5,000 man-hours were needed to move the earth in a typical barrow—say, ten men working every day for three months.

Secondly, far fewer burials took place than one might expect—half a dozen funerals in more than a thousand years seems very odd. Nor does the act of burial itself seem to have been of very great importance. Not only were the dead buried higgledy-piggledy, almost casually it appears, but they were not accompanied by their belongings, or the trappings of power and wealth, as in the Bronze and Iron Ages to come. So there is at least a possibility that the mound itself was more important than the interment; its size and shape, where it was placed—these things may have had a special significance, as they did with other megaliths.

Of course, technically, long earthen barrows are not megaliths at all, since they use no stone. But they are unquestionably part of the same society, overlapping with the most easily recognizable megaliths of all—dolmens, sometimes called cromlechs. In their most distinctive form, these stand exposed to the air on some bleak moorland, a slop-

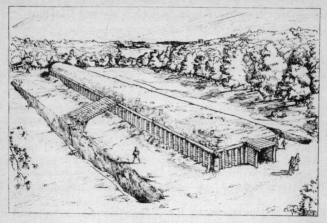

Reconstruction of Fussell's Lodge long barrow (after Paul Ashbee).

ing capstone of immense weight (often fifty tons or more) supported by three or more upright slabs. Nobody is sure how many years they were in use. Burial evidence suggests at least 2,000, and if there was an earlier time before they were used as tombs, it could be at least double that period. Equally, archaeologists argue whether they were all once covered with earth, which has now (somewhat improbably) been removed by natural erosion or farming, or whether the ones that today stand gauntly naked on the hillsides were always intended to look like that.

The same sort of puzzles emerge as with long barrows. Not all dolmens contain evidence of burial, although the vast majority do—but this may be because of grave robbers in the past. Nor can we be sure that the burials took place at the time of construction—a typical cremation urn is often of a much later period than the dolmen itself. But they are certainly evidence of a widespread belief in something extraordinary or supernatural. More than 15,000 of them are to be found in Europe, most of them partly underground, and many thousands more in other countries. The scale of the building enterprise is daunting: when covered with earth to make a barrow, or stone to make a cairn, as much as 15,000 tons of material was used. Perhaps there is a parallel with medieval cathedral-building, in which burial was only part of a wider religious function. Some archaeologists have compared the effort of constructing them, taking into consideration the difference in size of the population, with the effort required by Egyptian society to build the Pyramids.

How they were constructed has long been a subject of fascination. King Frederick VII of Denmark, a keen antiquarian who called them "giants' houses," gave a lecture in 1853 which he illustrated with drawings of rollers and ramps that could have been used. Sir Joseph Hooker, in his presidential address to the British Association in August 1868, called attention to a "tribe of semi-savages" in India who regularly erected stones weighing up to sixty tons to commemorate their dead. He wrote: "The method of removing the blocks is by cutting grooves along which fires are lit, and into which, when heated, cold water is run, which causes the rock to fissure along the groove. The lever and rope are the only mechanical aid used in transporting and erecting the blocks." Professor Richard Atkinson, the archaeologist who has made the definitive excavation and account of Stonehenge, has calculated that it needs at least two men to move one ton. Therefore a fifty-ton capstone would need 100 men, with another 100 as a back-up gang to shift the rollers and steer the sled. Up a slope of one in 6½ (nine degrees), nine men per ton would be needed. Thus, with strenuous difficulty, he calculated that the stones were moved.

The explanation does not satisfy everybody. Rear Admiral Boyle Somerville, writing in 1923 of a large dolmen in County Donegal, Ireland, pointed out: "There is no space for the necessary leverage—if levers were used—nor for men to manipulate them, for the ground falls away steeply on both sides. We must also wonder how, besides being lifted, the great stone was directed, as is the case, towards the summer solstitial sunrise."

His point about the orientation of the tomb is very important. There is much evidence that a large proportion of all megaliths were sited with great geographical care, and built with an engineering precision which is extraordinary. In many cases, a dolmen built an inch or two out of line would have collapsed within months, rather than millennia. Even more magically, there are still today some twenty "rocking stones," where slabs as huge as the biggest capstones on a dolmen have been placed with such infinite

The Tolmen in St Mary's Scilly p.174.   *The Tolmen in Northwethel Scilly p174*

Rocking stones in Isles of Scilly. Similar stones have been
found in northern Vermont.

care that they are balanced perfectly, and their great mass
can be moved with no more than the pressure of one hand.

The grandest of dolmens is an architectural variation
called the passage grave. Often to be found under a circular mound rather than a rectangular one, the chamber
itself does not open directly on to the outside of the mound
as with the more usual underground chambers, but is connected by a passage sometimes as long as seventy feet.
Some of the chambers are the oldest stone monuments
made by man, and in their way they are marvels of construction. Their roofs are vaulted, the stones carefully laid
one on top of another, leaning inward until they join at a
central point. Inside, they are big enough for several people to move about.

The most celebrated examples are at Maeshowe in the
Orkneys; in northern Brittany, where they are older than
anywhere else; and at Newgrange in Ireland, where the
stones are richly engraved and the passage exactly oriented
on the midwinter sunrise, whose light fleetingly illuminates
the twenty-foot-high chamber. But they can also be found
at different dates in Southeast Asia and Japan, and many
writers have noted their similarity to the *mastabas* of the
early Mediterranean civilizations.

As with the dolmens used as tombs (or indeed with the
cave in which Christ's body was placed after the crucifix-
ion), the entrances are often sealed off with a large upright
stone slab, perhaps to mark the end of the tomb's use after
a certain number of burials had been made. The way in
which they were sealed is another of the puzzling clues

about the nature of early man, and about whether, at different times, the same primitive spiritual beliefs were held in many separate countries, over many thousands of miles of the earth's surface. The unifying element is a "porthole" formed in the slab that seals the tomb, and its almost universal distribution has been noted by archaeologists since Victorian times. It can be found widely in western and northern Europe, in Spain, France, Sardinia, Sicily, Palestine, Algeria, Bulgaria, Persia, Iran and India.

The final category of grave evidence bequeathed to us from megalithic times is the familiar round barrow—the circular enclosures classified as disc-barrows bell-barrows and so on, that pockmark the face of the countryside around Stonehenge and elsewhere in that part of southern Britain known as Wessex. Here there are fewer of the mysteries of earlier megaliths. Though they vary in size and shape, they have always and undoubtedly been graves, each excavated to be the tomb of a single important person who was often buried with rich belongings—amber beads, gold ornaments, bronze daggers, archery equipment. On the ground, round barrows look as if they belong with the rest of megalithic culture, and in a sense they do, because they were there while megaliths such as Stonehenge were still being built. But they were significantly different. They were put there by a new race of people— the Beaker People—who arrived in Britain from Europe and seem to have taken over the megalithic sites. They brought with them metal, and a love of elaborate richness; the Stone Age had become the Bronze Age. For the nature of megalithic life, the clues lie in earlier monuments.

Of all our legacy from megalithic man, the simplest yet most enigmatic is the single standing stone, known in Celtic countries as a menhir. The distinguished French archaeologist, Professor P. R. Giot, has written of menhirs that "whether isolated or in groups, they remain enshrouded in mystery. This is no doubt why their study has, unjustifiably, been comparatively neglected. . . . With the very limited evidence at his disposal, the interpretation of single menhirs is one of the archaeologist's nightmares, and has given rise to far too much speculative literature."

Sometimes associated with dolmens and stone circles, sometimes not, they are mysterious because at first glance they seem to serve no useful function. One stone may stand alone in the middle of a field, the crops growing

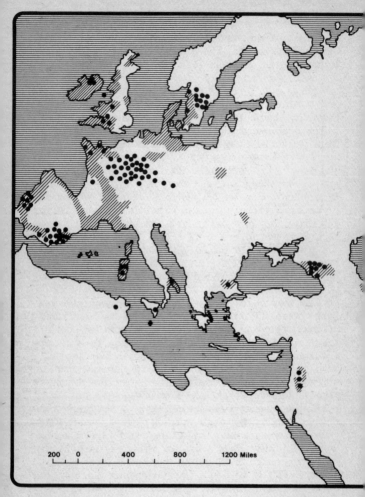

Distribution of Porthole Graves in Northern Hemisphere (after V. G. Childe). In New England, megalithic structures of similar shape usually have a vent in the roof.

Distribution of Megalithic Tombs

• With port-hole

Indian Dolmen

IRAN

INDIA

around it; another may be built into a church wall; another mark a hilltop, perhaps just away from the summit. The largest one known—the Grand Menhir Brisé at Locmariaquer in Brittany—now lies on the ground broken into four pieces. But once, like Cleopatra's Needle, it stood fifty-seven feet high, weighed around 380 tons (six times the weight of the largest stones at Stonehenge) and could be seen ten miles out at sea. Near by, at Carnac, are the most renowned menhirs in the world: 3,000 of them, in rows nearly a mile long, a section of them associated with the dolmen and mound at St. Michael's Mount—unquestionably a sacred megalithic site for 2,000 years or more.

Once again, and with all due caution about a too-facile acceptance of universality, it is extraordinary how, in continents many thousands of miles apart, they stand incongruously from the earth, their shape and patterns so similar. Professor G. N. Roerich, in *Trails to Inmost Asia,* noted the megaliths of Do-Ring in the highlands of Tibet. They consisted of eighteen rows of standing stones, aligned east-west, with a stone circle or a cromlech at the western end of each, "precisely the same arrangement as Carnac." In Vermont and New Hampshire, among the profusion of boulders which colonial farmers cleared from the fields and made use of as boundary walls, there are individual stones, which by their placement or by their size seem out of context, erected there in some long-forgotten time. One such, ten feet six inches high, stands isolated in a field near South Woodstock, Vermont, its mass and form identical with stones on the Celtic coast of Europe. Another, similar but a little shorter, stands at the entrance to a disused farmyard a few miles away. A colonist had once used it as a gatepost, and the marks of his metal chisel-drills can still be seen; but so can earlier inscriptions from a much more distant past, tantalizingly eroded by the years of weathering.

If the scholarly world of archaeology is reluctant to make guesses about their purpose, others have not been so shy. They have been interpreted as boundary posts, landmarks, gravestones for warriors. They have been compared with similar stones, objects of a phallic cult, in Africa and Asia. People with psychic and sensitive faculties claim to be able to recognize a hidden force in them, and to experience sensations ranging from giddiness to pins and needles when they approach or touch them

Scale of stone
to man.

Standing stone, central Vermont: at 10'6", probably the largest in the state.

(there is a standing stone in Gloucestershire known as the Tingle Stone). In Brittany, many stones were used until recently in ceremonies that were supposed to help fertility: girls slid down them on bare bottoms, couples danced naked around them in the moonlight and then made love beside them. Over the imagination at least, menhirs still retain an ancient power.

Megalithic man's preoccupation with the arrangement and placing of stones can perhaps be best seen in the multitude of circles that he made with them on the ground. In most places in the world they are scattered, and seemingly put together without great precision—surrounding a dolmen in India, for instance, or attached to a tomb in Japan. But here and there, and particularly in Britain and Ireland, they are built in such a way as to throw new light on his life. For what emerges is his deep fascination with the movements of the universe, and a marvelous knowledge of high mathematics.

This is a very recent archaeological discovery, and until about ten years ago, stone circles were as impenetrably baffling as menhirs, noted chiefly for their quaint local names: Long Meg and her Daughters, the Hurlers, the Merry Maidens, and so on. But now it seems as if not just Stonehenge but hundreds of stone circles could be used for extremely accurate astronomical observations: certainly of the sun and moon, probably to predict eclipses, and possibly involving movements of the stars as well. So could the alignments and standing stones in Brittany. As far away as the African state of Gambia, stone circles known to archaeologists since the 1890s were shown seventy years later to be aligned with outer standing stones on the midsummer sunrise. In 1974, a series of stone circles and cairns was noted nearly 10,000 feet up in the mountains of Wyoming, similarly able to provide early Americans with astronomical calculations.

What is more, throughout a 1,000-mile-long swathe of northwestern Europe, the circles and alignments have been found to be constructed to a common unit of measure—the "megalithic yard" of 2.72 feet; and this measure was then used to lay out on the ground complex geometrical designs more than 1,000 years ahead of their time. For a society that had no written language, and no obvious form of communication over long distances, it seems little short of miraculous. Yet some experts think the megalithic yard spread even farther. Statistical analyses of the New England megalithic sites indicate that it may have been used there as well, which would suggest a communication of early mathematical practice of a truly extraordinary degree.

But once again, the more that is discovered about the prowess of megalithic man, the more baffling he becomes. For, given that stone circles are related to astronomy and geometry, why did he build so many of them? And why were some of them on such a gigantic scale? Stonehenge would have worked just as well as an astronomical observatory if it had been smaller. Yet it was built and rebuilt at least five times, and at one stage the massive bluestone inner circle of stones was floated and dragged more than 100 miles from Prescelly in South Wales.

The same is true of Avebury, which John Aubrey wrote "doth exceed Stonehenge as much in grandeur as a Cathedral doth an ordinary Parish Church." Even today, after

most of the stones have been destroyed, and roads built
through its great earthworks, there is still an unmistakable
atmosphere of wonder and achievement in what is left:
the huge, circular earth bank, more than 400 yards in diameter, that would have taken a hundred able-bodied
men more than three years to build, and, according to
the calculations of a Victorian archaeologist, could have
held an audience of 250,000; inside, the circles of stones
twice the height of a person, none less than forty tons; the
mile-long avenue of menhirs leading up to them; and the
whole design once, as seen by Stukeley, part of an enormous serpentine pattern that encompassed the surrounding hills and landmarks. All this—what is left above the
surface and what has been found by excavation—has
been surveyed to discover that it could indeed have been
used both as an observatory and as a mathematical model.
But the scale of the undertaking leaves no doubt that it
must have had a metaphysical function as well.

The stones at Avebury, like most megaliths, are "rude"
in the Victorian sense of being unshaped and unadorned.
But mystifyingly there are a few designs, that seem to
have been generally known, which are used on a small
proportion of stones in many countries. The markings on
the Newgrange passage grave give a good selection—spirals, zigzags, diamonds, circles. In an age before writing,
any symbol is important. But the difficulty is to know
which are ornamental and personal, like graffiti through
the ages, and which ones portray a significant part in the
life of megalithic man.

There is one class of carvings—so-called "cup-and-
ring" markings—which is so distinctive, so widespread,
and at the same time so obscure, that it has been the subject of endless archaeological debate. It consists of a number of small concentric circles gouged apparently at
random intervals over the face of the stones, and sometimes joined by wavering lines that lead outward from the
center of the circles. They vary in diameter from two to
four inches, and can be found on dolmens and passage-
tombs in Palestine, North Africa, Corsica, France, Germany, Scandinavia, Great Britain and Ireland. On other
monuments, they can be found in Asia, Africa, America
and Polynesia. They have been known to scholars for well
over a century—Professor Daniel Wilson, touring America in the 1870s researching his book *Prehistoric Man,*

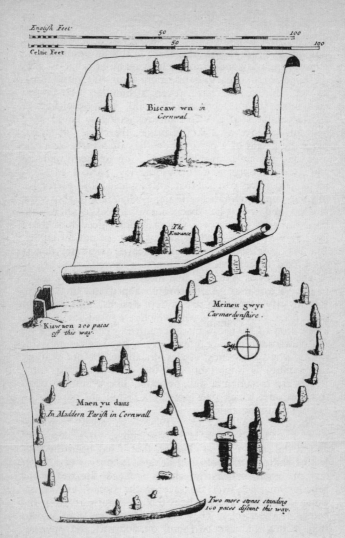

From Stukeley's *Roman Prints* (about 1758). The upper circle, at Boscawen-noon near Lands End, still stands undamaged today.

found an extremely vivid example on a piece of granite standing stone nine feet high in Forsyth County, Georgia.

Dozens of possible interpretations have been put on the markings, ranging from the severely practical to the mystic: that they were mortars where food could be ground up, or the basic units of length for the megalithic yard, or that they were breasts of the Mother Goddess, or even representations of flying saucers. The design is so readily identifiable, and at the same time unusual, that it is extremely hard to imagine how it can have been conceived independently by so many different tribes and races so many thousands of miles apart, and over such a long period of time. Another puzzle is that within each territory, it can often be found only locally. In Scotland, for instance, the Clava group of dolmens, near Inverness, has a distinctive collection of cup-and-ring markings. It happens that these dolmens are the only ones known in Scotland which face southwest instead of east, and also the only ones which are surrounded by a stone circle. It is a reminder that the broad picture of megalithic life is complicated by local variations—as if the Clava builders were a breakaway sect determined to experiment with their own forms of design and symbolism, which happened to coincide with similar experiments elsewhere in the world.

But of all the evidence that has been left behind to observe and analyze, the most extraordinary is the most huge: megalithic man's determination to reconstruct the countryside around him. In Britain, large tracts of the landscape are dotted with tumps and mounds that fall into no category of barrows, dolmens or graves. The largest is Silbury Hill, 130 feet high, covering four and a half acres, and representing ten years of work for at least 500 men. Archaeologically, absolutely nothing has been found that gives a clue to its original purpose: no burial lies beneath it, and no stone chamber. All that is known is that as well as being the result of immense effort, it was designed, like the Pyramids, with a geometric and engineering skill that made it last indefinitely. To prevent it changing shape, it was built with interior reinforcing walls of chalk.

Equally distinct are the flattened hilltops of Britain, their coils of earthworks ringed beneath them. For years, history books and maps have described them as hill forts

or castles—and it is true that many of them were used as
such, much later, in the Iron Age and by the Anglo-
Saxons and Romans. But when megalithic man first built
them, they must have been for some different and utterly
mysterious function. As forts, they are indefensible—some
of them have five or six big gaps in the top earthwork,
and they often cover so many acres that a population of
thousands would have been needed to keep an enemy at
bay. But of this population, there is as little evidence as
there is of burial at Silbury Hill. Antler picks, stone axheads and charcoal from small fires show that megalithic
man was there, and flattened the hilltop in the first place.
But there is none of the detritus to indicate large numbers
of people, and in any case there is usually no source of
water to sustain long periods of community life.

Yet he deliberately changed the face of the countryside, as did other races in other places. The mammoth
"runways" on the plains of Peru have been photographed
and unsuccessfully interpreted often enough. A century ago
Professor Wilson, after noting similarities between many
prehistoric features of North America and the Celtic coast
of Europe, announced his discovery of great earthworks
at Newark, Ohio, "so stupendous that we have nothing
like them in our islands." He went on to describe them:

> Broad levels on river terraces . . . groups of sym-
> metrical enclosures, square, circular, elliptical and
> octagonal; with long connecting avenues suggesting
> comparisons with the British Avebury or the Hebrid-
> ean Callernish, with the Breton Carnac, or even with
> the temples and Sphinx avenues of the Egyptian Kar-
> nak and Luxor. . . .
>
> Overhung as it is with the gigantic trees of a prim-
> itive forest, the surveyors describe their sensations on
> first entering the ancient avenue as akin to the awe
> with which the thoughtful traveller is impressed when
> entering the portal of an Egyptian temple, or gazing
> upon the silent remains of Petra. In the centre of the
> enclosure is a remarkable structure, apparently de-
> signed to represent a gigantic bird with expanded
> wings. . . .
>
> There are avenues upwards of a mile long and
> 200 feet apart, parallel and beautifully level, and
> ending in an octagonal earthwork . . . there is a cir-

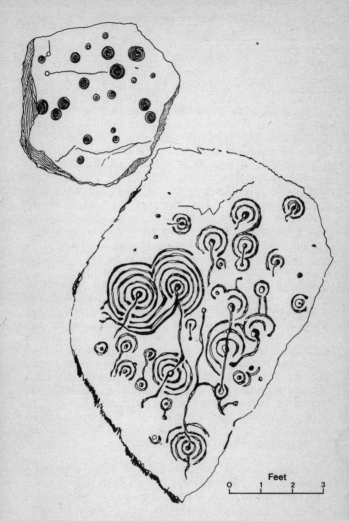

Feet

0   1   2   3

Cup-and-ring markings found by Professor Daniel Wilson in Cincinnati, Ohio (above), and typically at Clava, Scotland.

cular work 2,880 feet, or upwards of half a mile in circumference, *a true circle*.

In Britain, the evidence is very strong that the scattered distributions of mounds, ditches, stones and other megalithic sites may often not be random at all. Quite the opposite: over many miles of the landscape, some prehistorians claim to be able to trace precisely straight lines that pass over the marks and relics of prehistoric times— lines that seem to crisscross and converge over certain key points in much the same way as a national power grid. The existence of these lines is challenged by most traditional archaeologists, and the evidence for them is examined more fully elsewhere in this book. But when giant triangles can be found on the map, their angles exactly marked by ancient stones and settlements, when megalithic sacred centers many miles apart are aligned on each other and on a significant astronomical bearing . . . then, at the very least, these lines may turn out to be yet more clues to the mysterious civilization that once existed.

Modern archaeology, with the immense amount of material available to be catalogued and compared, and the new range of highly sensitive geophysical devices with which to explore the past, has perhaps been going through a phase in which the detail of prehistory has become overwhelming, and the minute ways in which various tribes and societies differed have seemed more important than the way in which they are broadly similar. In the late nineteenth century, the emphasis was often the other way around. A learned West Country clergyman, the Rev. W. H. E. McKnight, read a paper to the Wiltshire Archaeological and Natural History Society in 1887 that today would be regarded as dangerously simplistic:

> Primitive temples like Abury are scattered over the face of the earth, witnessing one common religion for its inhabitants . . . that of the sun, as witness in circular megalithic temples in every quarter of the world. . . . The religion, whatever it was, was once the religion of India, China, Southern Europe, Arabia, North Africa.

In the wilds of Tibet is a "Druid Temple," in a perfect circle in the bottom of a valley remote from

Circle and menhir in Persia, from an 1845 picture history of antiquities which described them as "druidical."

all intercourse with the rest of the world . . . witnessing not only to a common worship but to a strange *level* of existence of the human race throughout the world at the time they were building.

If we enlarge the time of man's existence since the deluge by several thousand years, we can imagine a state of things in which it would have been possible for the human race to have remained long undeveloped—in one sameness of existence, with habits of life but little varied, and with one common worship symbolized by the common temple, found almost everywhere.

Of course, it was an oversimple view—but at the same time he may have been groping toward a central truth. To find out, we have first of all to establish just when this supposedly universal society began, and then look at the physical remains of this past age to discover what kind of life was lived. The Rev. McKnight knew it was important to place a date on what he was discussing, but he could do no better than "far back in the distant ages, when mankind were dwellers in caves and earth burrows." But then the puzzle of man's antiquity has not been the least of the megalithic mysteries that have occupied scholars over the years, and as it turned out, the Rev. McKnight was a great deal more accurate than some of his contemporaries.

2

THE RIDDLE OF ANTIQUITY

Everything which has come down to us from heathendom is wrapped in a thick fog; it belongs to a space of time which we cannot measure. We know that it is earlier than Christendom, but whether by a couple of years or a couple of centuries, or even by more than a millennium, we can do no more than guess.

—RASMUS NYERUP, DENMARK, 1806

THE IMPORTANCE OF ACCURATE DATING IS THAT, WITH-
out it, we cannot know how any particular society or culture fits into the overall pattern of world prehistory. The
purpose of archaeology is to trace the development of
civilized man, and this is achieved by studying the relics
of our past and placing them in their proper order. The
tools he used, his ornaments, the structures he built, the
bones of man himself—none of these are of much value
if we do not know their date.

But dating an ancient chamber or mound is full of
snags. Were the contents put there originally, or later?
And if there are no contents, it becomes even more difficult. The usual way is to compare the site with a similar
one elsewhere. But how can anyone be sure that a particular menhir is like another? They may have been
erected thousands of years apart. Nevertheless, the effort
has to be made, because the period of prehistory
concerned is absolutely crucial. The time when most of
the familiar stone monuments were built in their various
continents was also the time when civilized man, as most
people would recognize him, finally emerged.

It is exceedingly difficult, living as we do from day to
day and with the life-span of threescore years and ten
built into our thinking, to conceive just how enormously
long the story of mankind has been. Perhaps the most
vivid analogy is to imagine oneself standing at the end of
a year, and to pretend that all the history of man took place
in the last twelve months, so that each day equals about
5,000 years. Back in January, perhaps earlier, and probably in Africa to begin with, a sort of ancestor known as
homo habilis lifted himself onto his two hind legs, and
began to communicate with his fellows, thus marking himself apart from the animal kingdom. By June (about one
million years ago) he had taken a fundamental step for-

33

ward—he was making crude stone tools. Around August,
he learned how to light fires and cook meat. Imperceptibly,
eon by eon, he moved on, his tools slowly improving and
his numbers increasing. In late September (about 500,000
B.C.), our forebears *homo erectus* brought to Europe the
first crude hand axes, before being driven back to Africa
by one of the great glaciations of the Ice Age. During
December, Neanderthal man (classified as *homo sapiens*), with his short, stocky build and heavy brow-line,
was living widely in Africa, Europe and the Middle East,
housing himself in caves and wearing animal skins for
clothing.

And then, quite suddenly, our progress accelerated dra-
matically. About ten days ago—50,000 B.C.—our direct
ancestors *homo sapiens* had their first glimmerings of
immortality, and began to bury their dead. Eight days
ago, Neanderthal man vanished from the face of the
earth, and perhaps about the same time the first travelers
set foot in the Americas. Within the last week we learned
to count and to paint, and three days ago the great cave
paintings of France were being executed; people's skills
as hunters can be seen in the variety and technique of
the delicate stone tools and weapons that were being made.

For all our ingenuity, however, we were still, during this
last period of the Ice Age, hunter-gatherers. We had not
yet turned ourselves into farmers, could not control our
environment. But two days ago (around 11,000 B.C.) the
glaciers began to retreat, the climate became steadily
warmer throughout a broad belt of the northern hemisphere, and conditions became right for us to take our
most important step toward civilization—to cultivate crops
and to breed livestock. In that last accelerating dash toward modern times, something extraordinary was happening. For to complete the analogy: yesterday we learned to
read and write, nine hours ago Christ was born. The significant advance of man took place only during the last
forty-eight hours of the whole year.

STONEHENGE DATING

The questions of where he took this step, and when,
have been a puzzle ever since antiquarians began to be
interested in man's origins, and until the second quarter

of this century the dates above would have seemed ludicrously ancient. Throughout the centuries of speculation, the most common errors were to underestimate both the antiquity of man and his intelligence, all species of prehistoric man being traditionally pictured as ignorant savages. Antiquarianism became archaeology, a more exact and scientific discipline, little more than a hundred years ago, and since that time its scholars have only slowly—almost reluctantly—accepted that early man must have been both more ancient and cleverer than had been assumed. Certainly, they derided the findings of those who supplemented traditional dating techniques with unconventional methods—even though some of these findings have now turned out to be much more accurate than their own deductions.

The late T. C. Lethbridge had taught Anglo-Saxon archaeology for many years, and had been Honorary Curator of Anglo-Saxon antiquities in the Cambridge Museum of Archaeology and Technology. But in spite of these credentials, he was never felt to be quite part of the mainstream of archaeology. An obituary by a fellow scholar after his death in the autumn of 1971 reads: "Perhaps, for a short while, Tom Lethbridge was a semi-professional." He lived his life among archaeologists, and he had a major discovery to his credit, of the Gog and Magog giant hill figures hidden beneath the turf some three miles to the south of Cambridge. Nevertheless, he was always regarded among his friends as something of a maverick, stimulating them with ideas and theories that had little hope of being tested by normal scientific procedures, and one of the unscientific methods he used was the dating of prehistory by dowsing.

The ability of some people to divine water, or other hidden substances below the soil, by means of dowsing is widely established, and there is a great deal of current research which attempts to discover the physical principles that make this possible. What is much less widely accepted (except by dowsers themselves) is the uncanny use of dowsing so as to make a discovery about other objects or people many miles distant. There are numerous published accounts, for instance, of criminals or missing people being located by dowsing with a pendulum over a map of the area where they are thought likely to be. Nobody knows how this works, but somehow—sometimes—it does.

Lethbridge himself believed it "must somehow be in the operator's mind," and he discovered that, in the same mysterious way, his pendulum let him work out the date of any object, were it a Victorian clock, an Elizabethan chest, or an ancient monument. The method he used was to hold a dowsing pendulum exactly thirty inches long over either a map or the object itself, and count the number of gyrations of the pendulum, each gyration representing ten years. When the pendulum stopped, he had arrived at the date. In 1965, Lethbridge decided to try to date Stonehenge in this way, and obtained some samples of the inner circle of bluestone rocks. At the time, it was confidently held by official archaeologists that this part of Stonehenge could not have been built earlier than 1600 B.C., and that the earliest date for the original Stonehenge was 2000 B.C.

Lethbridge's results were surprising—so much so that he said disarmingly that he did not really believe them himself. Held over the bluestone chippings, the pendulum came up with a date of 1870 B.C. Over a map, where he was concentrating on the site as a whole, the answer was 2650 B.C. "Since one can see no reason why the pendulum should give any sensible answer at all, this seems remarkable," he wrote. Just how remarkable was only proved afterward. Recent, scientifically based datings for Stonehenge, which have a degree of accuracy previously not possible, give a date for the bluestone circle of 2000–1800 B.C.; and for the earliest earthworks of c. 2700 B.C. Thus the dates now generally accepted by archaeologists are to all intents and purposes identical with those obtained by Lethbridge's mystifying process of dowsing.

These scientific advances in archaeological dating during the last ten years—the "radiocarbon revolution"—have shattered the accepted pattern of prehistory so comprehensively that the archaeological world is now in a turmoil. An immense amount of scholarship had been devoted to cataloguing and comparing the achievements of preliterate man, and to "proving" that civilization began in the Middle East, and that every significant discovery was made in that area. The scientific bombshell is that the dates on which this theory was based are now known to be wrong by anything from a few hundred years (Stonehenge, for example) to many millennia (early

America). Megalithic society in Europe is far older than was thought, the first Americans arrived in the New World much earlier and achieved much more than was thought; every textbook written before the 1960s is having to be fundamentally revised. It is as if a team of outstanding academic minds were painstakingly nearing the end of a difficult jigsaw puzzle, only to be told to incorporate another, even more difficult one, from which most of the pieces were still missing.

In fact, the whole story of how the archaeological world gradually came to learn about man's antiquity is a revelation of how the ability of early man has been consistently underestimated.

THE FIRST GUESSES

The earliest speculations go back as far as the eighth century B.C., in ancient Greece, where tradition lingered on that there had been a previous age when bronze was used, and iron not yet discovered. Later Herodotus, in Rome, divided the history of ancient man into four phases: first, when he used for tools only his own teeth and fingernails; second, when he learned how to work stones and make fire; third, when he could smelt copper; and finally, when iron was the basis of his life—categories that anticipated by some 2,000 years the Victorian prehistorians who divided the past into the Old Stone Age, the New Stone Age, the Bronze Age, and the Iron Age. But generally, the Romans and their successors took remarkably little note of the monuments of the forgotten past—Julius Caesar does not mention Stonehenge, although the structure was almost certainly known to him (nor, incidentally, does the Domesday Book). Saxon legends ascribed stone circles and the like to "the work only of malicious or evil genius, belonging to the devil," and in the ninth century A.D. the *Historia Brittonum* of Nennius stated that Britain's first inhabitants were the followers of Brutus, son of Aeneas.

But history as written in those times is a melange of gods, myths and romance. It is not until the twelfth century A.D. that we have the first precise suggested date for early Britain. Geoffrey of Monmouth (A.D. 1100–1154) decided it was the arrival of Brutus, a Trojan Prince, in

1170 B.C. which began the inhabited history of these islands.
His *Historium Regium Britanniae* also gives the first written account of the origins and date of Stonehenge. According to this version, which was repeated often during the
next 400 years, Stonehenge was built by the British King
Aurelius Ambrosius soon after A.D. 470, to commemorate
the 460 English chieftains massacred in that year by
Hengist the Saxon. A rival view, which became popular
toward the end of the sixteenth century, was that Phoenicians, coming to Cornwall to look for tin, were Britain's
first colonists. Certainly, there was never a suggestion that
an island race could have developed on its own.

In the New World, too, scholars and travelers were
equally baffled about the origin of the native American
Indian. Who was he? Where did he come from? Their
wrangles and false guesses mirrored the European squab-
bles about the nature of primitive man; and for fully 300
years, until the middle of the nineteenth century, the study
of prehistory was in a straitjacket of religious dogma.
The literal truth of man's beginnings as described in the
Old Testament was not allowed to be questioned. Thus
it was "known" that Adam lived for 930 years, his sev-
enth son, Methuselah, for 982 years, Methuselah's grand-
son Noah for 600 years, after which came the Flood, or
the Great Deluge, which covered the earth. Many attempts
were made to work out the chronology implied by these

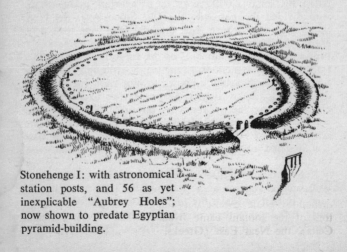

Stonehenge I: with astronomical
station posts, and 56 as yet
inexplicable "Aubrey Holes";
now shown to predate Egyptian
pyramid-building.

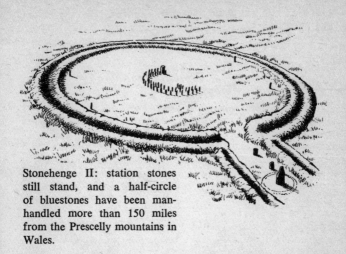

Stonehenge II: station stones
still stand, and a half-circle
of bluestones have been manhandled more than 150 miles
from the Prescelly mountains in
Wales.

figures, and finally one was successful (that is to say, it
was accepted by the Church). The date for the Creation of
man was calculated by Archbishop James Ussher at 23
October 4004 B.C., at nine o'clock in the morning, and the
year was inserted in the margins of the Authorized Version of the Bible. The entire history of the world was
therefore peopled outward after that date from the Biblical lands. Civilizations, it was known, had flourished in
Palestine, Egypt, Greece and Rome, and at some point in
time the British Isles must have been colonized by either
Trojans or Phoenicians.

But how did man get to America? There was considerable argument about whether the Indians should even be
regarded as human, so difficult was it to imagine them
being descended from Adam and Eve. Many of the first
Spanish settlers treated them as beasts, literally, and it
took Pope Paul III's Papal Bull of 1537 to admit them
formally to the ranks of humanity. The Indians were now
assumed to be descendants of one of the Ten Lost Tribes
of Israel—a view quite widely accepted right through to
the nineteenth century, and still believed by Mormon
churchgoers today. Those less spellbound by religious
orthodoxy could choose between theories that the ancestors of the Indians came from Europe (Scandinavians,
Celts), the Near East (Greeks, Trojans, Egyptians, Car-

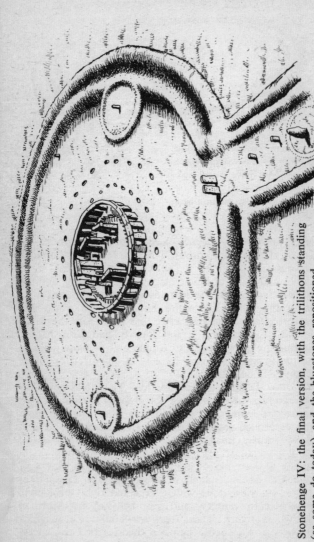

Stonehenge IV: the final version, with the trilithons standing (as some do today) and the bluestones repositioned.

Grave Creek Mound, West Virginia: a nineteenth-century picnic place.

thaginians), the Far East (Chinese Buddhists, Koreans), Asia (Scythians, Mongols), Africa (Mandingos), Atlantis, or the land of Mu.

For many overlapping reasons, there was a scholarly reluctance on both sides of the Atlantic to believe that great works could have been achieved by primitive man. Some writers gave up in despair, such as Francis Wise, who in 1742 ascribed the White Horse in Berkshire, the Giant of Cerne Abbas, and other hill figures, to Saxon origins, and lamented: "Where history is silent, and the monuments do not speak for themselves, demonstration cannot be expected, and the utmost is conjecture supported by probability." He was right about conjecture. The next 100 years saw a flowering of academic theorizing, in which armchair speculation concentrated on two areas that excited both awe and bewilderment: Stonehenge; and the great earthen mounds in the valleys of the Mississippi and the Ohio.

STONEHENGE AND THE DRUIDS

From the seventeenth century onward, Stonehenge-guessing was a fashionable intellectual pursuit (other monuments being as yet unnoticed and therefore unexplored). King James I visited the site, and commissioned his architect Inigo Jones to write an account and make drawings of its original construction. Voicing a prejudice that was repeated in many books on prehistory even into the present century, Jones said that it could not possibly have been built by early Britons, "a savage and barbarous people, knowing no use at all of garments," and quite incapable of erecting "stately structures, or such remarkable works as Stonehenge." He believed instead that it had been built by the Romans in honor of the god Coelus, some time after the time of Agricol (*d.* A.D. 79). In 1611, the cartographer John Speed published his *History of Britaine*, and confidently drew pictures of naked early Britons, their skins painted with elaborate designs. In 1624, the historian Edmund Bolton wrote that Stonehenge was a monument to Queen Boadicea, built after her defeat by the Romans. Other people preferred to believe Dr. Walter Charleton, physician to Charles I and II, who published a scholarly work putting its date as "the beginning of the reign of that excellent Prince, Alfred." He said it was erected by the Danes "to be a Court Royal, or a place for the inauguration and election of their Kings."

In the same year, Charles II commissioned the Wiltshire antiquary and biographer, John Aubrey, to make a survey there. Aubrey started with the advantage of having known Stonehenge since childhood, and his work begins the long archaeological process of pushing the date of ancient man back to where it belongs. He says that both Stonehenge and Avebury were constructed before Saxon or Roman times, and that since the Druids were "the most eminent order of priests among the Britaines, 'tis odds, but that these monuments were the temples of the priests of the most eminent order, viz., Druids, and it is strongly to be presumed that they are as ancient as those days."

Aubrey's suggestion that Druids were responsible for Stonehenge was taken up avidly in the eighteenth century. In 1740, Dr. William Stukeley published *Stonehenge, a*

"The portraitures and paintings of the ancient Britaines" from John Speed's *History of Britaine* 1627; Speed has made no attempt to create a scenic background different from his own time.

Temple Restored to the British Druids, an immediate success. He was both a fanciful and a romantic man, and because of this his books and calculations have been held suspect by later critics. But he was the first person with the insight to see that there were links and similarities not only between Stonehenge and Avebury, but with other stone monuments as well. By his own account he "spent every year a month or two at Abury and Ambresbury in Wilts., and by innumerable drawings and measurements made myself master of the nature of the two great temples of Stonehenge and Abury, with many lesser"—the lesser including Silbury Hill, Stanton Drew, and the Rollright Stones. He was also enough of a visionary to be the first to spot the fact that Stonehenge is aligned to the midsummer sunrise. He put the date of Stonehenge at around 460 B.C., with Avebury much older.

Whether the Druids ever used Stonehenge (most archaeologists nowadays say they didn't), it is an idea that has caught the public imagination ever since, and its echoes can still be heard even today in the midsummer rites performed there each year by a sect making use of the same name. Their "sundrie kinds of magicke," their skills in

William Stukeley's depiction of "a British Druid"; his association of Druids with the mounds and circles such as those in the background started a myth.

Victorian representation of "Arch Druid and Druids" in their sacred oak grove; the oak grove is fact, the costumes fancy.

astronomy and mathematics, their sun-worship, their bloody ceremonies of ritual sacrifice, their awesome nobility—these things first reported by Julius Caesar—fit naturally, if mistakenly, with the unsolved majesty and mystery of the site. Stukeley's work became a textbook in its time, and remains an inspiration for many investigations today.

THE LOST MOUND BUILDERS

It was at least partly this kind of romantic speculation that led to a century of similarly mistaken detective work on the nature of the Mound Builders of North America. Early travelers were understandably impressed by the earthworks, tens of thousands in number, the biggest up to 100 feet high and 500 feet in diameter, the most complex having several miles of immense geometric squares, circles and octagons laid out in furrows or banks on their surface. They were—and are—truly a wonder to compare with the Pyramids or the megaliths. Random excavations, or rather treasure hunts, revealed the existence of rich belongings far beyond the grasp of the few uncommunicative and nomadic Indians who currently lived in the area. On one site, skeletons were found completely enclosed by coils of pearls, weighted down with pounds of copper, and accompanied by precious works of sculpture, pottery and ceremonial artifacts.

Book after book came from the pens of visitors to the sites, many of them best sellers, and what they described contrasted so sharply with their observations of the day-to-day life of contemporary Indians that it seemed inconceivable for the ancestors of these poor people to have created such monuments. There was, too, a psychological need to create an heroic or mythical past for the New World. For if it could be shown that a race of great people, giants even, had lived in the Americas in the ages past, then there was no need to feel the continent inferior in its history to the glory of past Mediterranean civilizations. Perhaps, too, such evidence would justify the colonists' shabby treatment of the Indians, who could then be regarded as invaders or usurpers, rather than the original inhabitants.

Thus fancies about a lost race began to pour out, exaggerated by the fact that the mounds were at first called "barrows," and a link between them and their megalithic counterparts in Europe and the Biblical lands was readily assumed. Robert Silverberg, author of the definitive history of the subject, wrote: "Learned men came forth to suggest that our land had been visited long ago by Hebrews, Greeks, Persians, Romans, Vikings, Hindus, Phoenicians—anyone, in short, who had ever built a mound in the Old World. If the Israelites built mounds in Canaan, why not in Ohio? And what had become of the builders of the mounds? Why, obviously, they had been exterminated by the treacherous, ignorant, murderous redskinned savages who even now were causing so much trouble for the Christian settlers of the New World."

By 1820, the weight of published theories was heavily on the side of those who believed in some noble, vanished

Mid-nineteenth-century portrayal of burial mounds in the Mississippi Valley: cf. Silbury Hill p. 1001.

society, which had created the mounds and disappeared, and although some thought it might be a different and more elegant kind of Indian (e.g., the Toltecs of Mexico), the newly acceptable idea of the New World's first inhabitants having arrived via the Bering Strait simply increased the list of possible Mound Builders to include Hindustani, Chinese, and Scandinavians.

On both sides of the Atlantic, the years until 1850 marked the peak of speculation and obscurantism. In general, the Church's view of history still held sway, and as late as 1833, the President of the Royal Society of Great Britain, together with the Archbishop of Canterbury and the Bishop of London, asked writers to contribute treatises proving that "the creation story of Genesis was literally exact and that Noah's Ark and the Flood were facts of prehistory." Various reverend gentlemen added their mites to the myths of our distant past. The missionary John Heckelwelder made popular a legend he had heard from the Delaware Indians about a previous race known as the *Alligewi*, who were said to have "built to themselves regular fortifications or intrenchments," to have been "remarkably tall and stout," and to have included giants among their people. In 1846 the Reverend E. Duke accidentally guessed right by putting Stonehenge as contemporary with the Pyramids, and at the same time described "seven circular planetary temples, representing the planets, revolving round Silbury Hill," which, so far as is known, have not been seen by any other person before or since.

But saner and more cautious voices were already beginning to be heard. Thomas Jefferson, later to become the third President of the United States, carried out what has been described as "the first scientific excavation in the history of archaeology" on a mound in Virginia, and afterward wrote to a friend: "It is too early to form theories on those antiquities, we must wait with patience till more facts are collected." In England, Sir William Colt Hoare finished a series of less well-conducted excavations on the barrows of Wessex, and concluded in his two-volume history of Wiltshire in 1812 that he was in "total ignorance of these sepulchral memorials . . . we have evidence of the very high antiquity of our Wiltshire barrows, but none respecting the tribes to whom they appertained, that can rest on solid foundations."

Such was the state of archaeology in the mid-nineteenth century. It was clear that in the hidden world of prehistory, something mysterious had been going on—but what? And when? So far archaeology had been carried out without the benefit of scientific method—in fact, "antiquarianism" would probably be a better word to describe the activities that had taken place. The story of the next 100 years is very largely the story of how science challenged and quite soon destroyed the religious dogma on which the study of prehistory was at this time based; and how at the time two new errors—diffusionism and faulty dating—came to be incorporated and in their own turn discredited.

THE END OF GENESIS

The new science of geology was the major weapon in the fight against the Genesis-view of the Church. By 1830, it was possible to dig and discover as many as thirty-two different strata—geological levels—in the ground, each with its own range of fossils. This fact was hard to square with the Biblical record of one catastrophic flood, but a tortuous effort of "logic" persuaded the weight of religious and academic opinion to accept the geologists' findings. Another puzzle for Biblical scholars was that flint axes and spearheads had been discovered buried in undisturbed ground, twelve feet below the surface, near to the bones of extinct animals. "The situation in which these weapons were found may tempt us to refer them to a very remote period indeed, even beyond that of the present world," wrote their discoverer, John Frere, in 1797. In the 1820s, even more startling finds were made, both in France and in Britain, this time of human bones associated with flint implements and extinct animals such as rhinoceros and mammoth. It was altogether too much to comprehend. The findings were completely unacceptable to the combined establishment of Church and geologists. In spite of all evidence to the contrary, the bones were dated "of the Romano-British period."

But the new enthusiasm for excavation ensured that sooner or later there would be more discoveries. A French customs official, digging forty feet deep in the gravels of the river Somme in the 1830s, discovered flint axes and arrowheads in conjunction with—therefore contemporary with—the bones of elephants and rhinoceroses. It took a further twenty years for his work to be accepted, by which time a Devon schoolmaster, excavating in a cave in South Devon, had made similar finds. Two Englishmen, the geologist Joseph Prestwich and the antiquarian John Evans, scrutinized both discoveries, and were convinced. In the summer of 1859, Evans told the Society of Antiquaries in London: "This much appears to be established beyond doubt, that in a period of antiquity remote beyond any of which we have hitherto found traces, this portion of the globe was peopled by man." His judgment was accepted. In the same year, Darwin published his *Origin of Species*, and science was triumphant. Freed from its straitjacket, archaeology could begin to look at the true nature of man's past.

The framework for investigation was already there. Denmark had set up a National Museum of Antiquities, and appointed as its first curator Christian Thomsen. Echoing Herodotus, he divided prehistory into three ages—Stone, Bronze and Iron, the Stone Age subsequently being further divided into two parts by the British archaeologist Sir John Lubbock. He wrote a best-selling book, *Prehistoric Times,* which went through seven editions during forty-eight years, and his simple pattern of phases has served as the basis of scientific archaeology until very recently. He summarized the progress of man thus:

> From the careful study of the remains which have come down to us, it would appear that Prehistoric Archaeology may be divided into four great epochs:
> I. That of the Drift: when man shared the possession of Europe with the Mammoth, the Cave Bear, the Woolly-haired Rhinoceros, and other extinct animals. This I have proposed to call the "Palaeolithic" Period.
> II. The later or polished Stone Age: a period characterised by beautiful weapons and instruments made of flint and other kinds of stone: in which, however, we find no trace of the knowledge of any metal excepting gold, which seems to have been sometimes used for ornaments. For this period I have suggested the term "Neolithic."
> III. The Bronze Age, in which bronze was used for arms and cutting instruments of all kinds.
> IV. The Iron Age, in which that metal had superseded bronze for arms, axes, knives, etc.: bronze, however, still being in common use for ornaments, and frequently also for the handles of swords and other arms, though never for the blades.

However, valuable though this was as a basic system for cataloguing excavated finds, it is, of course, very limited. While you can find out the order in which things happened, you still cannot put an absolute date on when they happened. So disputes about Stonehenge continued unabated. James Fergusson, in *Rude Stone Monuments,* put it in post-Saxon times. Edgar Barclay, saying that "we have no reason to believe that the ancient Britons were capable of adjusting their buildings with a knowledge of geometry," put it at A.D. 79.

EARLY AMERICA

In America, the same approaches to archaeological method led to a comprehensive demolition of all theories of "lost people" as the original Mound Builders. A long series of reports on excavations published in the annual reports of the U. S. Bureau of Ethnology in the 1880s and 1890s, showed that however superficially similar the mounds might have been, their disparate contents showed them to have been built by many different tribes over a long period of time. But here again, stratigraphy was only of partial help in suggesting just when that time was.

Because of the bronze in the mounds, they belonged in Sir John Lubbock's third epoch. But was that epoch contemporary with the European one? Cyrus Thomas, who headed most of the major excavations, did not think so. Many of the "lost people" theories, which he was in the course of destroying, were also associated with supposed dates of 10,000, 20,000 or even 100,000 B.C., and perhaps he felt that these were also automatically discredited. Perhaps he was overinfluenced by forgotten accounts of early settlers, recently rediscovered, which showed conclusively that some mounds were still being built by Indians in historic times—the sixteenth century A.D. Perhaps a millennium of mound building was as much as his imagination could encompass. Whatever the case, he went on record with his belief that the earliest mounds had been created in the fifth or sixth century A.D. He was certainly not alone in his reluctance to believe in a long prehistory for the inhabitants of the New World; the pendulum, after many years in which prehistorians were assuming a great antiquity for early man on that continent, was about to swing in the other direction.

The two men responsible for this were William Henry Holmes, appointed chief of the Bureau of American Ethnology in 1902, and Aleš Hrdlička, appointed to the United States National Museum in 1903. Both were determined to set new standards of professional excellence in archaeological techniques, and were ruthless in refusing to accept results from sites that had been poorly excavated or tampered with. They rapidly (and rightly) dismissed the findings of those who thought they had found stone tools or skeletons to match the discoveries of Europe—

that is to say, dating back 100,000 years or more. But having cleared the ground of bad evidence, they then reached the illogical conclusion that man's arrival in America happened no earlier than about 2000 B.C. Their reasoning, if one can call it that, seems to have been that because all the evidence so far for great antiquity was unsatisfactory, therefore it was their duty to deny even the possibility of such antiquity.

Hrdlička, particularly, tyrannized his less eminent colleagues. According to the archaeologist Frank H. H. Roberts, his scathing attacks led to the position where:

> The question of early man in America became virtually taboo, and no anthropologist, or for that matter geologist or palaeontologist, desirous of a successful career would tempt the fate of ostracism by intimating that he had discovered indications of a respectable antiquity for the Indian.

At another time during the peroid in which Hrdlička held court, the geologist Kirk Bryan told his fellow students: "If you ever find evidence of human life in a context which is ancient, bury it carefully, but do not forget about it."

It was 1926 before a significant dent was made in the position Hrdlička had established. Near Folsom, New Mexico, a black cowpuncher casually mentioned seeing an unusual flint arrowhead stuck in the whitened ribs of some longhead beast sticking up from the ground of an arid river bed. Jesse Figgins, Director of the Colorado Museum of Natural History in Denver, heard about it and immediately investigated. The site turned out to contain exactly what American archaeology needed: a man-made projectile point of a previously unknown nature, unmistakably embedded in a long-extinct bison. Without doubt, man had been in America for 8,000–10,000 years. For a while, Hrdlička maintained his argument, and Frank Roberts believes his discouraging influence lasted until about 1940. But by then, there had been some thirty similar "Folsom" finds in other parts of North America, and most archaeologists happily settled for the conclusion that the earliest inhabitants of the continent arrived via the Bering Strait not earlier than 10,000 B.C.

Although we know now they were wrong about the date,

they were almost certainly right about the route. Whereas at the same time in Europe, archaeologists were wrong about the megalith builders on both counts.

DIFFUSION AND THE NEAR EAST

The direction of European archaeology went off course when it began to reject the idea that man may have developed in many places, in much the same independent way. In the latter half of the nineteenth century, this was a concept that greatly appealed, and when the Frenchman Gabriel de Mortillet wrote a guide to the first major exhibition of prehistoric material drawn from the whole of the Old World at the 1867 Paris Exposition, he suggested there were three basic and unalterable laws that governed prehistory: 1, The Progress of Humanity; 2, The Similar Development of Mankind; 3, The Great Antiquity of Man.

But as more and more archaeological discoveries were made, this became seen as a too-simple framework that simply could not contain all the facts. If humanity was ordained to progress, and mankind to develop similarly, what was the explanation for the various regressions that had taken place—the vanished peoples such as the Mayans, the fall of the Roman Empire, the barbarism of Europe in the Dark Ages? And what had happened to the glories of Babylon, Egypt and Greece, whose civilizations flourished in ancient times, and whose triumphs were now bewitching the European scholars?

These societies had demonstrably faded from their earlier supremacy, and although the time of these past achievements was not yet exactly known, they were generally thought to be earlier than anywhere else in the world. And so the view grew up that societies were destined to rise and fall, and that the spark of civilization was struck at a single point—the Near East. At this central source, all principle inventions and all the first significant steps of progress were made, and from here the ideas and innovations spread outward like ripples on a pond to colonize and civilize the savage world, taking on local variations as they went. The process was called diffusion, and such difficulties of distance as it presented—how did it spread to China? to America?—were little dis-

cussed. Far more effort was devoted to rediscovering the
societies of ancient Mesopotamia, Egypt, Greece and
Rome, than to the prehistory of all the other places in the
world put together.

It was understandable. The monuments were more
widespread, more obvious, more sophisticated. There
were written records that could be deciphered and translated. These records in turn revealed an absolute time
scale—a chronology which at last could begin to establish
the length of man's antiquity. Among the documents deciphered were a number of lists of Egypt's kings. Carefully
interpreted, they suggested a date of 3100 B.C. as the
founding of the First Dynasty—now recognized as the
oldest time in the world that can be calculated solely by
written records and calendrical studies. Similarly in Mesopotamia, the Sumerians and then the Assyrians made
lists of their own kings and dynasties that go back to before 2000 B.C. Written Greek records can be found as
early as 1000 B.C. Painstaking cross-references among the
three gradually gave archaeologists their first certain table
of pre-Christian dates.

But until the last quarter of the nineteenth century
there was still no way of accurately dating events (such
as the construction of Stonehenge) in countries that did
not have written records. Excavations in the Aegean—
Greece and Crete—were uncovering civilizations far older
than 1000 B.C. How much older was only guesswork until
the Egyptologist and antiquarian Sir Flinders Petrie made
two historic discoveries. In Egypt, in surroundings that
could safely be dated as c. 1900 B.C., he found unmistakable Cretan pottery: therefore, the Cretan civilization
must have been in existence at that point of time. He
confirmed his method amid the excavations of Mycenae
on the Greek mainland, where he found Egyptian pottery
known to have been made c. 1500 B.C. Petrie gave archaeology its first means of testing dates simply by looking at
the evidence of objects found in similar geological strata,
and the method, known as cross-dating, is still in use today.

By the end of the century, historians were confidently
placing the bronze age of the Aegean at around 3000 B.C.,
and they were beginning to relate their findings to the
remains of prehistoric man as found in Europe. In 1908
the Swedish scholar Oscar Montelius proposed a dating of

2500–2000 B.C. for the use of copper by prehistoric man in countries north of the Mediterranean: and 2000–1650 B.C. for the first pure Bronze Age. With the benefit of our modern knowledge of radiocarbon dating we know that he was more nearly right in these dates than many of the archaeologists who revised his work in the years to come. But equally, we can see how wrong are the assumptions which he and others made. With the possible and rather suspect exception of little blue "faience" beads found widely in Britain (including Stonehenge) and elsewhere, there is simple no evidence of any direct imports or trade from the Near East to Europe, nor vice versa. All that can be said is that certain Egyptian vases, for example, are "like" certain Scandinavian vases. Nevertheless, it was assumed with a bland confidence that prehistoric Europe was savage, the prehistoric East cultured. Montelius wrote:

At a time when the people of Europe were, so to speak, without any civilization whatsoever, the Orient and particularly the Euphrates region and the Nile were already in enjoyment of a flourishing culture. The civilization which gradually dawned on our continent was for long only a pale reflection of Oriental culture.

He was wrong, but it is not hard to sympathize with the state of mind that led to this point of view. The "rude" dolmens, standing stones, circles and chambers were rough and insignificant compared to the complex buildings and the glittering treasures of Egypt and the Aegean. What is more, they were as baffling as they were coarse. What on earth was their purpose? It was beyond comprehension. So archaeology, at the turn of the century, entered a period when speculation about the meaning of the monuments, and the nature of the men who built them, was kept to a minimum. Instead there was a massive cataloguing of his pottery and tools, and a bewildering number of guesses at his gradual and interrupted progress toward civilization. The various kinds of burial chambers were identified, excavated, and plotted. The grave goods, such as were found, were compared and categorized. The Four-Age system was broken down into a complex number of overlapping subdivisions—the "Beaker People," the "Wes-

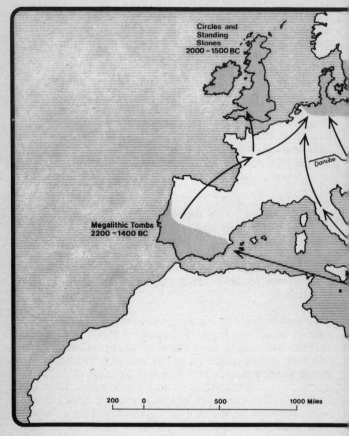

Circles and
Standing
Stones
2000 – 1500 BC

Danube

Megalithic Tombs
2200 – 1400 BC

200   0   500   1000 Miles

How diffusionist theory depicted the spread of civilization outward from the Middle East and Egypt (bottom right corner) to remainder of the world.

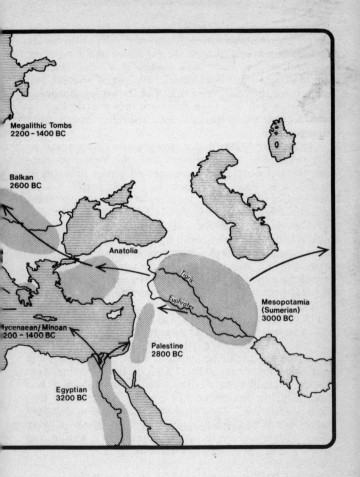

Megalithic Tombs
2200 – 1400 BC

Balkan
2600 BC

Anatolia

Tigris

Euphrates

Mesopotamia
(Sumerian)
3000 BC

Mycenaean / Minoan
200 – 1400 BC

Palestine
2800 BC

Egyptian
3200 BC

sex Culture," the "Corded Ware People" and dozens more.

But even though the mass of detailed discoveries made the picture ever more complicated and difficult to see as a whole, it was still hung in the old frame of diffusionism. Archaeological research was dominated by the figure of Gordon Childe, whose prodigious amount of research and publication included, in 1925, *The Dawn of European Civilization,* and it is from this work that most of us have been brought up to believe that civilization began from Mesopotamia.

In his book, Childe traced two voyages in the spread of culture westward and northward from the Near East. Recognizing the early date of chambered tombs in southern Spain, he supposed that these were built under Aegean influence, and that the practice of constructing them spread northward through France to the British Isles and Scandinavia. The advance of metallurgy, he suggested, took a different course. Starting from Mesopotamia and Crete, it spread through Greece and eastern Europe before arriving on the Atlantic seaboard. In later publications, he refined his chronology. The neolithic age in eastern Europe, he said, began around 2700 B.C. and in north and west Europe around 2400 B.C. Except in detail, the established world of archaeology accepted these findings almost as it had accepted the Biblical datings a century before. As late as 1958, Professor (then Dr.) Glyn Daniel could put a date for the construction of most passage graves in northern France at 2000–1700 B.C. In the same year Childe was still convinced that European prehistory was essentially "the irradiation of European barbarism by Oriental civilization." But what had happened a hundred years before happened again. Scientific advances were about to demolish the theoretical framework which he and others had so painstakingly constructed.

THE RADIOCARBON REVOLUTION

The breakthrough had been made in 1949, by an American chemist named Willard Libby. Although surrounded by a maze of statistical, geophysical and other complications, Libby's central discovery had the simplicity of genius. He took as his starting point the long-known fact that all living things are composed partly of carbon, and that carbon itself contains a tiny but fixed proportion of a radioactive element called Carbon-14. He also knew that as soon as the living thing dies, Carbon-14 decays at a fixed and measurable rate. So that after about 5,600 years, the proportion of C-14 to carbon is only half of what it originally was; after a further 5,600 years only one-quarter; and a further 5,600 years only one-eighth, and so on. Libby's breakthrough was to realize that this could be applied to samples taken from excavated sites—preferably a piece of charcoal, or burnt seed, but if necessary bones, shells, or wood. Simply by measuring the amount of C-14 in them, and checking this against the standard C-14-to-carbon proportion, an absolute date could be fixed for the sample.

His discovery was without question a revolution, and like all good revolutions it was hard fought. But steadily over the years, as results mounted up from chemical laboratories all around the world capable of making the calculations (today, nearly 100), a pattern of dates emerged, and by 1960 the archaeological world had largely accepted Libby's techniques. Indeed, those first results did little to disturb the existing framework of archaeology. Radiocarbon dating confirmed the results of pollen analysis and geological research to put the end of the Ice Age around 8000 B.C. Radiocarbon dating also seemed to match up tolerably well with the known calendrical dates of the Near East stretching back to 3000 B.C. It was only in between these dates that the new method was more controversial. Almost everywhere, the age of early settlements was being pushed back by up to 1,500 years. A farming community in Jericho was dated as *c.* 6000 B.C., compared with the *c.* 4500 B.C. that was expected. Dates in northern Europe, similarly, were 500 to 1,000 years earlier than had been anticipated. But by a certain judicious back-dating of the Near East, and by treating a few strangely early radiocarbon results as minor and isolated oddities which would doubtless be sorted out in due course, it was still just possible to fit prehistory into the existing framework. The first radiocarbon revolution was absorbed—only to find that another revolution was about to take place.

Until 1966, it was possible for archaeologists to cast doubt on the validity of radiocarbon dating in a number of ways. They could point to the inaccuracy or inconsistency of similar samples taken from the same site. They queried how free from contamination many of the samples were. And when Libby's supporters pointed out that the above criticisms might be true of individual results, but not of the broad mass of dates that was emerging, a further query was raised. For although radiocarbon and calendrical dates had seemed to match up well enough in the early days of the revolution, it had been apparent for some time that the radiocarbon dates were now consistently too young—i.e. too recent. Building on the Great Pyramid of Cheops, for example, was known to have started *c.* 2600 B.C. But radiocarbon dating said the date was *c.* 2200 B.C. Critics asked why, if a supposedly unerring scientific method was provenly wrong in this case, it should not equally be wrong in other centuries or millennia?

Their answer came in 1967 when Professor Hans E. Seuss told of dating experiments with one of the world's oldest trees, the bristlecone pine of the White Mountains of California. Some of these trees are nearly 5,000 years old, growing, as do all trees, one ring on their trunks each year. Carefully dated samples from the tree rings were checked against the radiocarbon datings that emerged from the same samples. Because the calendrical age of the tree-ring sample is known, any deviation from the predicted radiocarbon age can be plotted on a chart, and a graph made. What emerged was confirmation for the critics of Libby, but the consequences were traumatic. The corrected dates—usually now called the calibrated dates—differed substantially from previous radiocarbon findings. The corrections, on the whole, grew larger the further back into history they went: up to 1000 B.C., the radiocarbon datings were perhaps 200 years too young: at 3000 B.C., they were anything up to 1,000 years too young.

The findings caused a furor. If they were correct, they constituted a wind of change as strong as a typhoon, blowing away all preconceived notions about the development of man in prehistoric times. Seuss's graph was submitted to unrelenting statistical examination, and the dates it showed were so unbelievable that they were held to be, by at least one scholar, "archaeologically unacceptable." But after Seuss's first calculations, many more tests were made, using different trees and different laboratories, and they are still going on. There are, certainly, justified doubts about the detailed precision of the graph which Seuss first drew. But it is impossible to dispute its general accuracy. Professor Colin Renfrew, of Southampton University, the most prolific of a new generation of archaeologists and an ardent proponent of the revised radiocarbon dating, summed up in 1974: "The calibration is here to stay, and its magnitude is now clear."

Renfrew also said that the effect on all previous patterns of prehistory was "dramatic," an adjective which, if anything, failed to do justice to the shock waves that calibration sent through the world of archaeology. New C-14 results were pouring in, the vast majority of them confirming an antiquity for prehistoric man that nobody had even suspected. The chambered tombs in northern France, which Professor Glyn Daniel had placed 2000–1700 B.C., were now 4400–4000 B.C., much older than the Pyramids or the round tombs of Crete, which had previously been thought the oldest stone monuments on earth. The ditch at Stonehenge (the foundation for the astronomical laboratory built within it) was at its latest contemporary with the building of the Great Pyramid of Cheops, and might well be earlier. The early Balkan metallurgists, supposedly taught by the master craftsmen of Troy, were working with copper 1,000 years before them.

Even more astonishing was a discovery in 1974 concerning the great decorated chamber at Newgrange in Ireland. Radiocarbon dating had placed it at 3300–3000 B.C., contemporary with many other dolmens and tombs in Europe. Now it was found that it had been built with an unimaginable degree of mathematical sophistication for a structure of that date. The light from the midwinter sunrise was found to come from a precisely designed stone "roof-box" so that it could pass down the twenty-yard-long covered passage to the central chamber. It had been a solar laboratory at least 500 years before the Pyramids, and more than 1,000 years before the completion of Stonehenge.

As in Europe, so in the rest of the world. Now that prehistoric civilizations were being investigated in their own right, both their great age and the knowledge of their people became apparent. Decorated pottery could be found in Japan before 7000 B.C., in Africa before 5000 B.C.

Callanish

Skara Brae

Maes Howe

Ballynagilly
4500 BC

Newgrange
3300
BC

Jordhøj graves
3350 BC

Hembury Camp
4200 BC

Lambourn barrow
4340 BC

Stonehenge
2750 BC

Barnenez 4400 BC

Carnac

Danube

Vinca
7000–4500 BC

Los Millares
3300 BC

Troy 6000 BC

Çatal Hüyük
6000 BC

Mycenae
2000 BC

Maltese temples
3300 BC

Knossos
2000 BC

Great Pyramids
2600 BC

Nile

0   500   1000 Miles

Jarmo 6000 BC

Tigris

Euphrates

Jericho
?500 BC

Europe as the latest calibrated radiocarbon datings show its prehistoric development; independent communities develop over a wide area (although farming and the growth of cities still seem to have spread from the East).

There were flourishing stone industries in Australia in
10,000 B.C. The great Harappan civilization in India,
more widespread and more complex than anything in the
Mediterranean, was found to have begun independently
c. 3000 B.C.

In the Americas, the impact of radiocarbon dating was
only slightly less spectacular to begin with because the
framework of prehistory was more soundly based than in
Europe. C-14 results proved, finally and conclusively, that
man had reached the New World more than 10,000 years
ago. But most of all, the results made it possible for archaeologists to adjust the order and the length of life of
the various societies and cultures that had been so painstakingly traced out with the old archaeological techniques. The Mound Builders, for instance, had long been
thought to consist mainly of two types: the Adena, who
came first, and the Hopewell, with their greater riches,
the two cultures living alongside each other for an undefined period of time. Now, after some early mistakes with
contaminated samples and laboratory errors, calibrated
C-14 dating was able to provide a set of dates which
showed the start of Adena between 1000 and 400 B.C.,
and the start of Hopewell around 500 B.C.; both cultures
seem to have faded away by c. A.D. 500, although other
types of mounds continued to be built by different tribes.

The main impact of the new dating techniques on
United States archaeology came subsequently, with more
than 1,000 finds from all parts of the continent to indicate
the restless paths of early man as he discovered new
places to hunt, and later to farm. The archaeologist
Richard S. MacNeish has summarized: "Not only have
dated finds become more numerous, but older and older
dating of Man in the New World has become acceptable."
MacNeish himself has substantially contributed to this
with excavations in a cave near Ayacucho, in the highlands of Peru, which have provided C-14 datings of bones
deposited by man as far back as 20,000 B.C. Elsewhere,
in his study of caves in the valley of Tehuacán in Mexico,
he has illuminated our knowledge of man's progress with
an almost uninterrupted record of prehistory in the area
from about 10,000 B.C. to A.D. 1500. It is clear that plants
were being domesticated by 5200 B.C. (when a primitive
form of maize also appears), that settled farming existed
by 3400 B.C., and complex villages by 1500 B.C.—all,

evidently, without Gordon Childe's "irradiation of Oriental civilizations."

The radiocarbon upheaval is excitingly able to allow a new generation of archaeologists to go back and look again at some of the clues to our past which were discarded or ignored during the last hundred years, and to ask some different questions. As Colin Renfrew puts it: "In the long term the real significance of radiocarbon dating will not be to allow us to talk more about prehistoric chronology, but to encourage us to talk less. For chronology will be removed from the field of general discussion: radiocarbon dates will be among the basic factual data."

It means, in fact, being able to take a fresh look at the emergence of civilized man in his different ways in different places—to look at his society as a whole: what he grew and ate, how he organized his life, what part religion or magic played, how he traded and with whom. And this sort of embracing survey of megalithic times in Europe already suggests that they are even older than the earliest radiocarbon dates. So far, for instance, the oldest megalithic settlement we know is at Ballynagilly in County Tyrone, where charcoal from a hearth, and other material, make it certain that a kind of farming community lived there about 4500 B.C.; turves of grass, presumably growing in forest clearings, were found in the Lambourn long barrow dated at 4340 B.C.; and the huge causewayed camp at Hembury in Devon was in use—for whatever purpose—by *c.* 4200 B.C. But the scale of these undertakings, and the evidence of trade in flint axes and pottery, means that there must have been an extended period of time previously while the communities built themselves up.

In America, too, many people feel that radiocarbon dates are only beginning to hint at man's antiquity on the continent. While most archaeologists would now accept an early date for man's arrival of around 25,000 B.C., there is already a disputed date for a skull found at San Diego, California, of *c.* 29,000 B.C.; and MacNeish thinks there is also evidence, from cross-dating of stone tools and weapons between South America and Asia, of the earliest arrivals between 40,000 B.C. and 100,000 B.C., thus taking us neatly back to the speculative dates of nineteenth-century believers in the lost peoples of Mound Builders.

For an outsider peering at the argumentative world of
academic prehistory, perhaps the best attitude is to re-
member that there is no significant advance in archaeological thinking that has not been bitterly disputed at the
time; that no theory of prehistory is either complete or
unarguably correct; and that in spite of the immeasurable
tons of stone and bone artifacts dug up from where they
have lain for 5,000 years and more, there are huge gaps in
the canvas painted by archaeologists.

Where did the Adena and Hopewell Mound Builders
emerge from, and where did they disappear? Nobody
knows. If the antiquity of man in America is really so
great as is now being suggested, where are the indisputably ancient skeletons? To date, only one camp site on
the crucial Bering Strait immigration route has been found,
and the earliest C-14 date there is *c.* 8000 B.C. Does this
leave open the possibility of immigration from elsewhere?
Similarly in Europe, during the whole 4,000–5,000 years
of the mesolithic era that preceded the megalith builders,
we so far know of only one grave with a skeleton to suggest what man was like in those times. Just how old may
the oldest standing stone be?

However, we now have a much better time scale than
ever before. Man's settlements and monuments are much
older than was thought, and the older they are shown to be,
the more mystifying and exciting they become. There is
an extraordinary paradox in the seeming incompatibility
between the quality of everyday domestic life, as represented by excavations, and the giant intellectual and physical achievement represented by the megaliths. Stuart
Piggott wrote of Skara Brae, a settlement in the Orkneys
used toward the end of the period, and built with walls of
stone:

> Within the dark interiors of the huts, the air thick
> with acrid peat smoke, there seems to have been, at
> the time of their use, a state of indescribable filth
> and disorder. The floors are found stained with sew-
> age and strewn with bones and shells discarded from
> successive meals; in the beds there fell down among
> the loose bedding not only personal possessions such
> as bone pins or beads, but oddments such as a calf's
> skull or a shoulder-blade shovel.

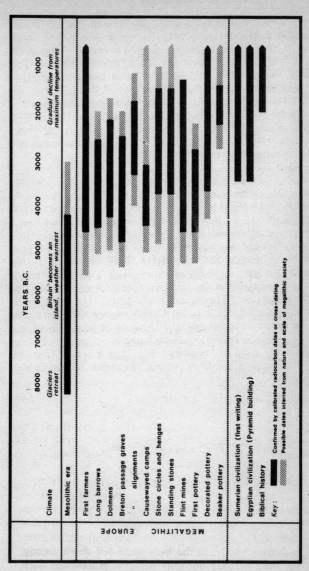

Date chart of the megalith builders.

Yet these same people were the contemporaries of the
megalith builders of Carnac, of whom Stuart Piggott and
Glyn Daniel, after many years of skepticism and disbe-
lief, wrote in 1974 how the Grand Menhir Brisé in Brittany was capable of foretelling the rising and setting of
the moon in eight critical positions: "[It might be] controversial, but it begins to look as though the people of
prehistoric France who were responsible for the dolmens
and alignments and menhirs were not only skilled architects and builders, but had considerable mathematical
and astronomical knowledge as well."

This cautious acceptance that (as another archaeologist
put it) "barbarians, too, had brains" still sits uneasily
with the evidence that 100 years of archaeology has produced from the ground and put in the museums for us to
examine, and perhaps it is time to examine a little more
closely the "indescribable filth" of day-to-day life. It is
hard, looking at a tiny razor-sharp flint chipping in a glass
case, to imagine that the sickle blade of which it once
formed a part represented as much of a leap forward in
man's imagination as, say, Newton's formulation of the
law of gravity. The world over, during a few thousand
years preceding the birth of Christ, men and women somehow found in themselves the capacity of independent and
imaginative invention. At the same time, many of them
found the need to build megaliths and mounds. Both activities contain magic of a kind, and each is inextricably
linked.

3

LIVING WITH STONE

This globe of earth hath, according to the process of its nature, existed under a successive change of forms, and been inhabited by various species of mankind, living under various modes of life, suited to that particular state of the earth in which they existed. The face of the earth being originally everywhere covered with wood, except where water prevailed, the first human beings of it were Woodland-Men living on the fruits, fish and game of the forest. To these the land-worker succeeded. He settled on the land, became a fixed inhabitant and increased and multiplied. Wherever the land-worker came, he, as at this day, ate out the scattered race of Wood-men.

—GOVERNOR POWNALL OF MASSACHUSETTS, 1773

ARCHAEOLOGISTS HAVE LONG ARGUED TO FIND A DEFINI-
tion for civilization. Some said, as did the Greeks and
Romans, that it was impossible for man to be civilized
without being able to write. Others added that he must be
able to organize and run a town of 5,000 people or more.
Professor Gordon Childe identified the criteria of civilization as: the plow, the wheeled cart, animals trained to
harness, the sailing boat, the ability to smelt copper ore,
knowledge of the solar calendar, standards of measurement, writing, processes of reckoning, specialized craftsmen, city life, and a surplus of food large enough to support those people who were no longer producing their
own. Glyn Daniel summarized: "When we speak, then, of
the origins of civilization we mean the origins of the first
literate town-dwellers."

It was not until later than 3000 B.C. in southern Mesopotamia, the area nowadays covered by Iraq, that man
was able to achieve the whole of this somewhat imposing
list. By then, he was set firmly and irrevocably on the
road that led to high learning and the flowering of the
great civilizations of Egypt, the Mediterranean, Greece and
Rome, and because there are written records of his progress during this period, it is possible to picture life in these
cities with fullness and precision.

More relevant to megaliths, although the evidence is
harder to interpret, is the portrait of everyday life before
man reached this stage. For in the time before he learned
to write or use the wheel—a slow and by no means certain development—he achieved altogether different kinds
of skills. They may not have added up to civilization as
basically defined, and they did not always lead directly
to the growth and sophistication of cities, but these new
accomplishments were not just remarkable: they were
unique.

One of the world's leading experimental archaeologists, Peter Reynolds, who runs an Iron Age farm on the southern chalk hills of Britain laid out identically to its counterpart 3,000 years ago, has said of the quantum jump from hunting to farming: "I put it at no less a human intellectual achievement than the discovery of the theory of relativity." Certainly, the farming revolution was as important to mankind as the industrial and scientific revolutions that were the other, later changes of a fundamental nature.

The big difference is how long it took for early man to make the jump. Today, we are used to believing that anything more than ten years old is out of date, and objects more than fifty years old are officially classed as antique. But for early man, change was imperceptible. Not only did one generation live in exactly the same way as the generation before it, but many thousands of years could pass with no apparent development whatever, the only movement being imposed by the changing weather as the various phases of the Ice Age advanced and receded; and hunting man moved to follow his prey. This period of prehistory, from 70,000 B.C. to around 10,000 B.C., is usually known as Palaeolithic, and the most vivid picture of life in its later stages can be seen in the magnificent cave art of southern France. If one of the attributes of civilization is leisure, then this at least must have been available during the thousands of years when the caves were decorated, for the art shows the vigorous confidence of men who knew exactly where their next meal was coming from.

But they were not just living in caves. A palaeolithic site at Dolni Věstonice in Czechoslovakia was inhabited between about 27,000 and 23,000 B.C., and its excavation gives proof that the enormous herds of mammoth provided early man not only with meat and clothing, but with a primitive form of shelter as well. The tusks were used as a framework for huts, with the dried skins stretched over them to keep out the cold and snow—in the coolest periods of the Ice Age, the temperature there averaged around freezing point. As many as 100 people seem to have lived in the community, and the debris of their discarded mammoth bone and ivory covers several acres. It was a hard and wayward life. Sometimes food was available in abundance—animals to be hunted, berries and wild foliage to be picked and eaten. But man was at the mercy of the elements, the seasons, and the migrations or movements of his prey.

It was almost certainly this, rather than some restless spiritual urge for discovery and adventure, which led to the peopling of the New World. The great glaciations locked up vast quantities of water, dropping the level of the sea from 150 to 300 feet during various phases. Thus a land bridge was created across the Bering Strait, which by a meteorological freak missed the worst of the snow and ice. On occasions, this bridge may have been as much as 1,300 miles wide, with freshwater lakes and lush pasture to water and feed the herds of mammoth, bison, ox, ground sloths, and wild horses that crossed eastward from Asia. On their trail came tribes of men and women, classified in the textbooks nowadays as Palaeo-Indians. Just how they killed their prey, or how they lived, is not known; compared to finds in Europe, there are not even any indisputably old stone spearpoints, let alone early camp sites with the wealth of evidence such as provided by Dolni Věstonice. But, as was shown by Richard Mac-Neish and others, long before the Ice Age ended, man had spread throughout the Americas.

Neither here, nor anywhere else in the world, had he yet learned to farm. He had no conception that it was possible to control his environment, no understanding that work done this year might bear fruit the next.

His chance came as the climate warmed, and the ice sheets began to move back northward. It was not uninterrupted, nor evenly spread across the continents. But broadly, the warming that ended glaciation is put at around 11,000 B.C., followed by the reappearance of glaciers between 8800 and 8300 B.C., and after that another gradual warming to the optimum period of 6000–5000 B.C. And just as the map of disappearing glaciers is variable, so too was the development of farming. This so-called "neolithic revolution" required man's discovery, by cross-fertilization, of cultivated wheat (or maize, which has to be sown by man). Its greater yield, and its annual harvesting, together with the domestication of animals, meant that man could at last cease his roaming, nomadic life, and become independent of the need to hunt food.

EUROPEAN FARMERS

It seems certain now that the first place this happened
was in the Near East, where, in what is now Israel, the
changing climatic conditions seem to have brought a relatively quick response from the hunters who lived there. By
about 10,000 B.C., a people called the Natufians are
known, from the smooth polish on their stone sickles, to
have been reaping cereals—grain and grasses—though
whether they also cultivated them is debated. The first
major brick-walled settlement in the world, Jericho, was
inhabited at about the same time. By 9000 B.C. there is
evidence of animal-herding in northern Iraq, and by 7500
B.C. Jericho had become a city with walls and thirty-foot-
high towers. Some of the first pottery in the area comes
from Çatal Hüyük in Turkey a little before 6000 B.C.

A settlement in Jarmo, midway between the Mediterranean and Caspian seas, has now been thoroughly excavated. Around 6500 B.C., it consisted of twenty-five houses,
each with a few small, rectangular rooms, made of baked
mud. Barley, wheat and peas were harvested, and bread
baked in clay ovens. Sheep and goats were bred. No more
than 5 percent of the diet came from wild animals. With
many more marvelously preserved sites in the dry air still
to be excavated, the map of man's emerging civilization
in the Middle East can be carefully traced, culminating
in the invention of both writing and the wheel in Sumeria
some time shortly before 3000 B.C. And it was from the
simple agricultural beginnings there, according to diffusionist theory, that the knowledge of farming spread outward to the rest of Europe, Asia, and North Africa.

It does not now seem as straightforward as that. At a
1968 seminar in Sheffield on the domestication of plants
and animals, at which papers were read by many of the
world's experts in this field, it became clear that the
evidence for a uniquely Middle Eastern origin of all agriculture was very thin. Introducing the report of the seminar, two noted archaeologists, Peter Ucko and Graham
Dimbleby, wrote that the earliest agricultural activities
"varied greatly in extent, specialization and sophistication. . . . Domestication was a process extending over
several thousand years [with] its own special characteristics in different areas of the ancient world."

It seems likely that wheat and barley may indeed have first been bred and harvested in the broad band of lush farmland—as it was—which constituted the Middle East. According to the latest evidence from the excavation of a cave in Nahal Oren, Palestine, it may also have happened quite suddenly, around 6500 B.C. But similar break-throughs happened elsewhere: in eastern Asia, perhaps in the fourth millennium B.C., rice was discovered independently; and in Mexico in the sixth millennium B.C., maize.

Again, it is even less certain that all domestication of animals originated in the Middle East. The first traces of the domestic dog are at Star Carr in Yorkshire, and at Idaho in the United States, both of which are radiocarbon dated to before 8000 B.C. Cattle seem more likely to have come from eastern Europe or Turkey than the Near East; a variety of wild boar in the Crimea was probably the first to be captured, domesticated and bred for pig meat; some of the earliest evidence of bones of sheep and goats (it is difficult to distinguish between them when they are this old) comes from Ireland.

So what emerges is a number of different cultures that developed not so much through the force of invasion as from the local circumstances of the climate and the soil. In one area there would be a group of settlements—not yet a "nation" or a "country"—which had developed the use of the plow; in another, cattle-rearing would have provided meat and milk, but the harvesting of grain was still at a primitive stage. And between the various places, for the next 3,000 or 4,000 years, there must have been sporadic contacts and a cross-fertilization of ideas and developments.

Some idea of man's long and halting progress during this period is shown by the fact that, unnoticed and unrecorded in most history books, there was time for an entire society to rise and fall.

In the area now approximately described as the Balkans, from Greece in the south to Czechoslovakia and southern Poland in the north, from part of Germany in the west to the Ukraine in the east, a widespread farming community grew up, and developed almost all Gordon Childe's criteria for civilization. They had small townships, specialist craftsmen, their own religion and institutions of government. They used copper and gold for ornaments and tools, and were even at the beginnings of creating an alphabet. It

Key

A. Egypt, 3600BC –
B. Sumer, 2900BC –
C. Indus, 2500 – 1700BC
D. Andean, c.2500 – 1250BC
E. Minoan, 2200 – 1400 BC

F. Megaliths, 4000 – 1500 BC
G. Huang-Ho, 1760 BC
H. Mayan, 1200 BC – 900AD
J. Aztec, AD 1300 – 1500
K. Megaliths of New Guinea, New Caledonia
 and Fiji c. 1000 BC
L. Moundbuilders, 1000 BC – 500 AD

World Map of Discoveries
Approximate radiocarbon dates

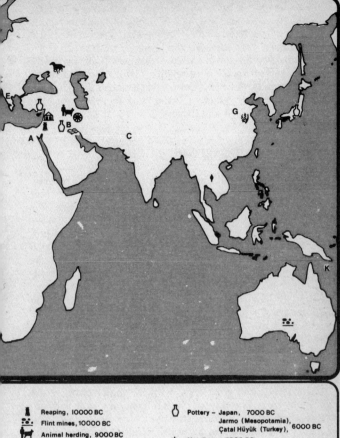

🏺 Reaping, 10000 BC		🏺 Pottery – Japan, 7000 BC
⚬⚬⚬ Flint mines, 10000 BC		Jarmo (Mesopotamia), 6000 BC
🐴 Animal herding, 9000 BC		Çatal Hüyük (Turkey),
🐕 Dog – Yorkshire, Idaho, 8000 BC		† Metallurgy, 7000 BC
🏛 City – Jericho, 7500 BC		∗ Proto-writing, 5000 BC
🌽 Maize, 5200 BC		🌾 Rice, 3500 BC
💀 Skull– San Diego, 29000 BC		✏ Writing, 3000 BC
♦ Bronze spearhead – Thailand, 3600 BC		⚙ Wheel – Netherlands, Sumer, 3000 BC
		🐎 Horse, 2500 BC

started around 7000 B.C. and was at its richest around
4500 B.C., when it grew all the crops then known to man,
bred all the animals, and had widespread trade and communications, including sailing boats. Had it continued, it is
highly likely that the Balkan people, rather than the
Sumerians, would have had the distinction of becoming
the first fully fledged, unmistakable civilization. But bands
of seminomadic hunters, both savage and aggressive, in-
filtrated from the wilds of Asia, and by 3500 B.C. the
society was enfeebled and dispersed.

MEGALITHIC EUROPE

Meanwhile in north and western Europe, local communities were developing in their own way, and of the three
great areas of neolithic man in the Old World at this time
—the Atlantic coast, the Balkans, and the Middle East—
the society being created by the megalith builders is perhaps the most enigmatic and absorbing, and about which
least is known. Its efforts were concentrated in a quite
different direction from the other two. It didn't learn writing; but it became astonishingly knowledgeable in mathematics. It didn't invent the wheel; but it moved
monumental quantities of stone. Its beginnings can be seen
in the long transitional prefarming period known as the
Mesolithic age. It marked the time when climatic changes
were bringing simultaneous botanical and zoological
changes—as Stuart Piggott describes them, "from the
stunted sub-arctic flora of the tundra to the beginnings of
the woodlands and grasslands, with the hardy birch as the
dominant tree. The day of the reindeer, in what was becoming temperate Europe, was over, and in its place the
red deer and the elk (in natural conditions animals of the
woodlands), were establishing themselves as the main
source of meat, together with wild cattle."

Although not farmers, communities developed significantly. Man became skilled at exploiting the new conditions, inventing barbed spearpoints to catch fish and
birds; the bow and arrow to hunt the more elusive game;
paddles with which to move primitive canoes for lakeside
fishing; hafted axes to chop down the encroaching undergrowth and trees. At Star Carr, the best preserved of sites
so far excavated, dated around 8000 B.C., artificial rafts

of birchwood were built on the lakeside. Four or five families joined together each summer in an organized, communal life of hunting and fishing, and collectively producing tools and weapons made of flint, bones and antlers. Masks made out of the front part of the skulls of deer have been found, used for rituals or for disguise. Their dogs helped in the hunt for game. They adorned themselves with necklaces made of deer teeth or bird bones. From evidence so far found, it looks as if the population was very thinly scattered; some archaeologists say as few as 10,000 people—men, women and children—for the whole of Britain. There was plenty of food for all.

Then, into the lives of these self-sufficient, slowly developing people, came the techniques of farming. It probably happened before 5000 B.C., but just how and why is much debated. By now (from about 6000 B.C. onward) Britain was an island, so that free passage of game and hunters across the bed of the North Sea had long since ceased. But whether the first neolithic farmers came across the sea in boats at this time—as they certainly did a little later— or whether they emerged locally as a result of the increasing warmth and scarcity of game, nobody is quite sure. In any case, the communities of the mesolithic and the neolithic overlapped for many hundred years. Their differing stone tools have been excavated side by side, the neolithic axes being much heavier, polished, and a great deal more efficient at clearing the thickly wooded countryside. Another uncertainty for archaeologists is the climate. Certainly it was warmer, by an average of about two degrees centigrade. But periods when it was moist seem to have alternated with drier times, so that nobody today is sure exactly what the weather was like at any given moment.

In any event, it was a time of rapid ecological change. In order to survive, man had himself to learn to adapt, and enough is known about how he managed this to be able to draw a reasonably accurate picture of life then. The people were generally light-boned, graceful, quick in movement, and seem to have been spectacularly skillful with bows and arrows. The men averaged about five feet three inches in height, the women two or three inches less. They had long, narrow faces, and are thought to have had dark skins. Only about one-third could expect to live to the age of forty. Life was centered around a community of twenty-five to fifty people, mostly interrelated.

As nomadic habits changed to more settled farming, the first job of any family was to clear a site for itself. Today, when visiting the places where they made their farms, the eye and the imagination have to fill in the valleys with endless dark forests stretching into the distance and up the hillsides. They were not like a modern tended forest, with its paths and openings beneath broad trees. Instead they would be inhospitable and often dangerous places, where wild boars and cats lived in an almost impenetrable mass of briar and undergrowth.

To clear the bigger trees—oak (predominantly), elm and plane—the farmers cut rings of bark around the trunk of the trees in springtime, so that by summer they would be dying, dry from lack of sap. Then, using the heavy stone axes, the men would clear the undergrowth of birch and shrubs. In a Danish experiment, three men cleared 600 square yards of silver birch in four hours. To cut bigger trees to provide branches for building and fencing, the axes were equally efficient: a man could fell an oak tree with a one-foot diameter trunk in only half an hour, using short, sharp cuts from the elbow. Having saved what timber they needed, the farmers burned the brushwood where it lay, and the remaining trees where they stood. In the soil, enriched by ash, he planted his selected wheats and barley—einkorn, emmer and spelt—much as Finnish peasants did until recently.

As the grain came through and the young animals grew, fences were needed to keep off scavenging animals and birds—wild cattle, pig and deer, rooks and pigeons—and no doubt the children of the family were used during daylight hours as guards and shepherds. Children, because of their affinity with young animals as pets, are now widely thought to have been a key factor in the domestication of animals. First came the dog, which developed into a common breed standing eighteen inches high at the shoulder, with a head much like that of a foxhound. Then came goats, sheep, pigs and cattle, followed by the ass, known in Mesopotamia in 3000 B.C. Last of all was the horse, domesticated on the steppes of Asia and not brought to Atlantic Europe until well into the Bronze Age.

Gradually, as generation succeeded generation, and communities moved on from farmstead to farmstead, initially because the soil became worn out, the face of the landscape changed until by the fourth millennium B.C. there

Barbarian fishermen, depicted mid-nineteenth century.

would have been many aspects of it that we today could recognize. Although the forests would still be there in much of the valleys, the hilltops themselves, cleared along the great swathe of chalk that lies in a broad belt across southern England, might not look unfamiliar. Heavy, angled branches of trees were shaped and sharpened to make a primitive form of plow that tilled the ground. Shoulder-blade spades from deer and cattle were used to pile up the earth on the long barrows that were being built, their sides raised more steeply than now. Around them were the first fields, sometimes enclosed by stone walls, where animals grazed to keep the forest at bay, and the corn grew. The great causewayed camps reared high above the surrounding fields and trees.

There must have been established trackways, because trade, and specialization in certain skills, had by now begun. Complex flint mines deep beneath the chalk hills provided flint tools and weapons that were distributed hundreds of miles away. There is evidence that people took a considerable pride in the aesthetic as well as the practical nature of these tools. A polished axe cuts down trees no more efficiently than a rough-flaked one of the same weight and size—but it is more pleasing to the eye and the hand. Many of the delicately shaped spear- and arrowpoints have been flaked by craftsmen so that ridges and grooves follow each other in a symmetrical pattern.

But what impresses some archaeologists most is the sheer creative imagination of inventing, say, a sickle when there was nothing at hand but trees and rocks. Dr. Mark Newcomer, an American specialist in flint-knapping at the Institute of Archaeology in London, who has a large collection of stone tools of all sizes, made by him from flints dug out of the same mines used 5,000 years ago, told an audience in 1976: "Flint blades are sharper even than razor blades. When they are put together along a curved piece of wood so as to cut grass, they are more efficient than the best modern sickle. Not only do they cut better, but they stay sharp longer, because minute fragments of flint come away from the blade and make it self-sharpening."

Substantial houses were built, the timber structure filled in with smaller branches, sods of earth, and mud; often, there was a division between the family living space and the animal barn. Inside, a certain amount of craftwork went on—weaving, pottery-making (though not on a potter's wheel), basket-work, the tanning and shaping of leather for clothes, thongs, skins, bags and jugs. Modern experiments re-creating these conditions have shown that life in megalithic farms, more than 5,000 years ago, was considerably further advanced than in many tribes of South America, Africa and Asia even today—indeed, much the same kind of plowing still continues on the peasant hill farms of Mediterranean France. As Professor Richard Atkinson said in 1974, it was in its essentials "a pattern of life at a peasant level which persisted without substantial change until the end of the medieval period in Europe."

For land transport, sleds and rollers were used. The wheel is usually thought to be a Sumerian invention, unknown before 3000 B.C., although in northern Europe, the first examples of wheeled carts came from the Netherlands and Denmark at approximately the same time. They are heavy and solid, and in the forested and mostly hilly areas of Britain they would have been of very limited use.

Diet for megalithic man need not have been monotonous. Although meat, taken from the cattle, sheep and pigs they bred, and the deer they still hunted, formed much the major part of any meal, it could be amply supplemented by the vegetarian offerings of nature—berries, fruit, nuts and herbs. Apples, superior to the crabapple, were grown. A form of beer was probably brewed. Bread, without yeast, was baked in lined pits, milk curdled in pottery urns and turned into cheese. Peas and beans were grown as vegetables. All manner of fish could be caught in the streams and lakes, and pigeons and crows shot and roasted. Shellfish added to the variety, although there is evidence that it tended to be an addition to the diet only when times were hard and other foods in short supply. Snails were widely eaten. The French gastronome Raymond Oliver has deduced that even before pottery was used, highly palatable hot dishes were possible. Here is his recipe for Neolithic Broth (which more accurately should be named Palaeolithic or Mesolithic Broth), published in his book *The French at Table:**

Scrub with dry hay or grass a hollow in a rock and fill it to a third of its capacity with spring or rain water. Allow a quart per person. By its side, where the wind cannot blow its ashes into the broth, light a very hot fire. Heat round stones, preferably balls of sandstone, in its center. When they are very hot, take one and drop it into the water. Remove it and replace with another and so on until the water boils. Have a bunch of twigs ready to cover it between operations. Prepare the vegetables: onions, beans, carrots, wild asparagus, beech nuts, peeled acorns, rue, nettles, dandelion, coleseed and herbs. Add these to the water with salt and wild rose petals. You may also add the hips. Continue with the stones until the vegetables are cooked. Then add grated animal fat (such as mutton tail or kidney fat) and add one last very hot stone to complete the blending of fat and liquid. Eat with a scallop shell held with a wooden fork.

AMERICAN FARMERS

Such, so far as archaeology can show us, was the state of neolithic farming technology *c.* 3500 B.C. in megalithic Europe. On the other side of the Atlantic, a different sort of development had taken place after the glaciers receded. As the weather warmed, the increasingly sunny skies be-

* Wine and . . . 1967.

gan to dry out the land. During the 5,000 or 6,000 years
before 6000 B.C., first the woolly mammoth, then the
sloths, the big-horned bison, the wild horses and the camels
died out from a combination of drought and hunting.
Gradually the Palaeo-Indians, their way of life destroyed
as their prey became extinct, adapted themselves to the
new conditions. Their descendants during succeeding millennia have been termed Archaic people, when different
tribes and societies made the best way they could from
whatever local conditions existed. Broadly, they split into
two groups: the Desert culture in the west, and the Eastern Archaic in the forests that stretched to the Atlantic.

It was from the Desert Indians that the farming breakthrough came. Richard MacNeish came to the end of an
extraordinarily persistent search in the Mexican highland
valley of Tehuacán when, he wrote, "I scrambled in and
out of 38 caves and finally struck pay dirt in the 39th . . .
On February 21, 1960, we dug up six corncobs, three of
which looked more primitive and older than any I had
seen before. Analysis in the carbon-14 laboratory in the
University of Michigan confirmed my guess by dating
these cobs as 5,600 years old—a good 500 years older
than any yet found in the New World."

With this discovery, and subsequent finds of an even
earlier form of maize in nearby caves, which pushed the
dates back to c. 5200 B.C., MacNeish not only established
conclusively that agriculture had indeed developed independently in the New World, but also that it was different
in kind and quality. "The principal difference lies in the
fact that the peoples of the Old World domesticated many
animals and comparatively few plants, whereas in the
New World the opposite was the case . . . [by the sixteenth
century A.D.] some of the civilizations from Mexico to
Peru possessed a larger variety of domesticated plants
than did their European conquerors and had made agricultural advances far beyond those of the Old World."

By 3500 B.C., about the time of the megalith building
in Europe, the people of middle America were settling in
small villages. They were growing, as well as maize, several varieties of squash, beans, chili peppers and avocados.
They were beginning to grind corn, and hollow out drinking vessels from stone. Pottery came later—about 2300
B.C.—and gradually the small settlements developed into
the high civilizations of the Mixtecs and the Aztecs.

But not every tribe took the path toward big-city life. In the southwest of northern America, the area roughly contained nowadays by Arizona and New Mexico, the Pueblo Indians developed much more slowly. In the first centuries A.D., they did not even have pottery, but instead made baskets of superb artistry, using them for cooking by lining them with resin to hold water, and dropping in red-hot stones until the water boiled. By the time the Spaniards arrived they seem to have developed a settled and secure life in quiet balance with their surroundings; there were no extremes of riches or poverty, their medicine men had an immense knowledge of plants and herbs, and how they could be used. The population was stable, their small town had stood for more than a thousand years. Their ceremonies were complex and profound. By any intellectual standard, they had achieved a civilization, and many people think that they must have unconsciously suppressed any urge to "progress" to use of the wheel or the plow. The British archaeologist Jacquetta Hawkes, after visiting the Hopi and the Navajo reservations, wrote in wonder that their self-limiting townships were "enormously important. Man appears as a creature with an innate urge to develop urban civilization, to build altars and temples and palaces. If I were an American archaeologist, I should think of nothing else but proving whether this is or is not the truth."

Similarly in northeastern America, during the time of the European megalith builders, local Indian tribes seem to have lived contentedly, without the impulse to change their life style. Peter Farb, who has made a long study of Indian history and has great respect for their early achievements, wrote in *Man's Rise to Civilization*:

> The Eastern Archaic emerges as an Arcadian time in the history of man in North America, during which he utilized his resources to the fullest, yet still lived in harmony with his environment . . . Their wide-ranging use of the environment was quite remarkable: by the time explorers reached the Great Lakes area, the descendants of this Archaic people were using 275 species of plants for medicine, 130 for food, 31 as magical charms, 27 for smoking, 25 as dyes, 18 in beverages and for flavoring, and 52 others for various purposes. No animal or any partic-

ular group of animals was singled out for exploitation; the Eastern Archaic peoples practiced what is today known as multiple-use conservation.

His comments are important as an insight on life in megalithic times, because although more nomadic than the early European farmers, the Archaic Indians he describes lived with roughly the same size of tribe, on approximately the same latitude, and in similarly forested countryside. When the megalith builders vanished so that only glimpses of their possible way of life can be seen and reconstructed, the traditions of the Archaic Indians lived on.

There is also the tantalizing possibility that, in spite of the fearsome barrier of the Atlantic, the two peoples once met.

OCEAN CROSSINGS?

One of the problems in reconstructing the distant past is that one of the principal materials used in its technology is now almost totally missing: wood. Peter Reynolds thinks that "Age of Timber" would be a more appropriate description of the prehistoric era even than Stone Age or Bronze Age. By collecting wooden forks, shovels and plows from peasant farmers in Europe, he has demonstrated the wide variety of ways in which timber must have been used by early man. But because it rots away, there are hardly any of the original tools and weapons left to examine, and nowhere is this lack more infuriating than in trying to discover what boats were made of in megalithic times.

Like the sickle, the flighted arrow, or the baking of pottery, the invention of the boat is one of those marvelous innovating concepts of which early man was capable. But nobody can say with confidence what the first ones were like, or where they appeared. Experimentally, boats have been built in the style of those shown in the rock art of Scandinavia, dating back to the Bronze Age of the second millennium B.C., which have been variously interpreted as skin boats, planked boats, dugouts and rafts. The most efficient turned out to be those made with a wooden framework, keeled, and covered with skin. They looked much like the Eskimo umiak still used in the Arctic, from which such fish as cod, plaice and dogfish were caught. Archaeologists think that it was probably in boats like these that the megalith builders crossed from Brittany to Britain and vice versa, with a combination of crew, passengers, animals and fodder going to and fro from about 5000 B.C. onward. The largest of the umiaks today, used by Eskimos for whaling, is thirty-two feet long, with eight paddlers or rowers and one man steering. On this can be carried a total weight of three tons—in megalithic times, for example, besides the crew, two dogs, two adult cows and two calves.

On the face of it, this seems a painfully laborious method of colonizing Britain and Ireland, and there must have been many other kinds of boats, larger and smaller, both here and in different parts of the world. The first Australians are known to have arrived on the continent as long ago as 30,000 B.C., and it is likely that even in those distant glacial times, they had to cross a barrier of water to get there. Thor Heyerdahl, first of all with his *Kon-Tiki* balsa raft from Peru to Polynesia, and then with his reed boat *Ra II* from Morocco to Barbados, amply demonstrated the practicality of both trans-Pacific and trans-Atlantic crossings without the use of metal boat-building tools. Other research has suggested that the smaller the boat, the more seaworthy it becomes; it is conceivable that rowing boats could have traveled across oceans, although there will probably never be satisfactory proof.

Nevertheless, as the pendulum of the old diffusion/independent evolution argument swings to and fro, archaeologists are currently very reluctant to admit the possibility of trans-oceanic contacts between early people. There have been plenty of proposals. The Austrian ethnologist-archaeologist Robert von Heine-Geldern is convinced of the importance of Chinese influence on civilizations of middle and south America, and notes the similarity of the Shang and Chao bronzes to the Chavin stone sculptures and ceramics of Peru. Cyrus Gordon quotes the many sculptures from Mayan and Mixtec civilizations which accurately portray the features of negroids who could only have come from Africa. One of the strongest legends of the Hopi Indians, who believe themselves to be the first inhabitants of America, is that they came across the ocean from the west, stopping at "stepping-

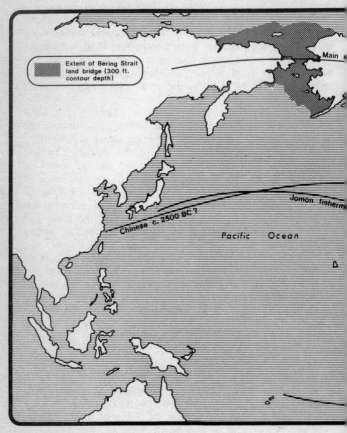

Legend on map:
Extent of Bering Strait land bridge (300 ft. contour depth)

Main

Jomon fisherm

Chinese c. 2500 BC ?

Pacific   Ocean

Suggested trans-Pacific crossings and contacts; date of earliest Americans still disputed.

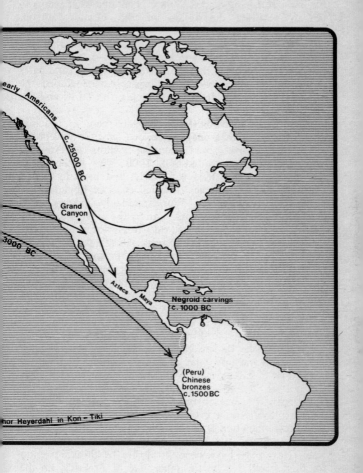

early Americans

c. 25000 BC

3000 BC

Grand
Canyon

Aztecs   Maya

Negroid carvings
c. 1000 BC

(Peru)
Chinese
bronzes
c. 1500 BC

hor Heyerdahl in Kon - Tiki

stones" (islands) on the way. The oldest Chinese classic, the *Shan Hai King* of *c.* 2250 B.C., contains what seems to be an accurate description of the Grand Canyon. Many Greek and Roman texts, including those of Plato and Diodorus, have been interpreted to mean that the great Phoenician seamen knew about, and regularly traded with, America in about 1000 B.C. Other candidates for prehistoric or early historic visits have included the Arabs, the Irish, the Jews, the Romans, the Turks and the Welsh.

However, archaeologists dismiss all these as speculations. They say that apart from one possible exception, the earliest proven pre-Columbian visitors to America were the Vikings, around A.D. 1000. This exception is fascinating, because it is very early, and hard to refute. Around 3000 B.C. on the Valdivian coast of Ecuador, the first pottery in the New World suddenly appears. It is decorated and incised, and—unlike the development of pottery elsewhere in the world—it is not preceded by plainer and simpler bowls and urns. Amazingly, its designs are identical to pottery from Jomon in southern Japan, which is dated at the same age. The coincidence has led its discoverers to the belief that, unlikely though it may seem, a Japanese fishing boat was caught in a storm, and subsequently drifted the 8,000 miles to Ecuador, a journey that lasted several months, during which the crew collected rainwater to drink and caught fish to eat. When they landed, the Indians agreed to let them stay. Among them was somebody who knew the complicated art of pottery (it is said, without real evidence, that women were the potters in early times), and who taught it to the Valdivians. It seems an unlikely sequence of events—but other explanations are even more tortuous.

If the explanation is true, it hinges on the premise that the two kinds of pottery were identical, and the Valdivians must have been incapable of thinking it up for themselves. Up on the other side of America, on the Atlantic coastline of New England, there is another extraordinary coincidence of an apparent "match" between cultures; and this one has not yet been seriously tested or even investigated by mainstream archaeology.

For here, as in no other part of the New World, is a collection of megaliths that immediately invite comparison with Europe.

MEGALITHIC AMERICA

Nobody knows how many unexplained stone structures there are in the area. Unlike the Ordnance Survey in Britain, the U. S. Geological Survey does not attempt to catalogue and map all ancient sites. But about 300 probable prehistoric megaliths have been listed by the New England Antiquities Research Association (NEARA), typified as chambered mounds, dolmens, rocking stones, standing stones, cairns, and stone circles. They are scattered through Rhode Island, New Hampshire, Maine, Massachusetts, Connecticut, New York State, and Vermont. In some areas—e.g. central Vermont—they are particularly profuse. They fit into no known Indian culture, yet it seems inconceivable that neolithic man from Europe could have spread his obsession with megalith building over so wide an area. It is in this apparently unanswerable conundrum that lies the reason for their neglect by most academics.

Megalithic America exists—but it doesn't fit. So, collectively, the tombs are held to be colonial root cellars, beehives, dog houses, or even pig pens. Glyn Daniel wrote to me: "I have only been shown one alleged megalithic site in America, i.e. Mystery Hill, and though this has large stones it is not a megalith in the sense that we use this word in relation to Western European archaeology. It is an 18th/19th century A.D. complex of buildings and follies."

In fact, the relationship between NEARA and the archaeological world typifies the misunderstandings and mistrust between fringe prehistorians and the professional archaeologists. On the one side is enthusiasm, an overeagerness to jump to conclusions, and the chance of a revolutionary breakthrough in our understanding of early man; on the other side caution, a proper academic respect for evidence and proof, and a reluctance to spend time on anything that seems outside the accepted framework of prehistory.

NEARA has nearly 200 members in three countries. The association was formed in 1964 with the aim of trying to locate as many of the stone structures as possible, and then to distinguish between those of colonial and precolonial origin. Among its members are trained archaeologists, but most are interested amateurs; the great majority believe wholeheartedly that most of the New England megalithic sites are unquestionably prehistoric, and that it is only a matter of time before enough evidence turns up to prove this to be so. They are sincerely worried about the number of sites that are being destroyed by building and road construction, and at the same time equally worried that if they publicize the exact locations of remaining sites, they will be disturbed by pot hunters and vandals.

MYSTERY HILL

This furtiveness about their discoveries has irritated archaeologists. "If we don't know where they are, how can we possibly investigate them?" asked one—to which NEARA replies that every site will be made known to anyone who promises to be discreet. Then, in the late 1960s, NEARA made a decision that still further alienated the professionals: to concentrate attention on Mystery Hill (then known as Mystery Hill Caves), in North Salem, New Hampshire. For the trouble with Mystery Hill is that it is either "potentially the most important place in the northern hemisphere . . . the oldest large stone structure in North or South America" (Dr. Edward J. Kealey, Professor of History at Holy Cross University, Worcester, Massachusetts), or it is (as Glyn Daniel pronounced after a half-hour guided tour) a totally unimportant eccentricity. Yet because the site has been so molested over the years, the truth of either point of view may never be established *in situ*.

In all, Mystery Hill covers about thirteen acres of typically wooded, hilly New England countryside, with sloping lanes bordered by stone walls made from the profusion of natural boulders lying on the surface. The interesting part is an acre of complex megaliths that form passageways, ramps, tunnels, small rooms, unexplained tomblike cavities just big enough for the human frame, a "speaking tube" from one level to another, evidence of a drainage system, the whole design irregular but undeniably the result of much labor—and with the same meticulous, jigsawlike construction of huge chunks of rocks that can be seen in ancient megalithic structures the world over. More or less in the center lies a so-called "sacrificial stone," a large, bell-shaped four-and-a-half-ton slab raised on four legs, incised with a groove that collects all liquid (rainwater? sacrificial blood?) and drains it into a gutter. The whole is like nothing else that anybody has ever seen (which is one reason an authentic antiquity is disputed), the "ruins of ruins" one writer has called it. As a mystery, it is fascinating; as archaeological evidence, it is a mess.

The first known owner of the site was Jonathan Pattee, who built a frame house adjoining it in 1823, using some of the stones as foundations. He then sold considerably more stone from the hill for reconstruction of the nearby city of Lawrence, Massachusetts. In 1855 the house burned down, and in 1860 yet more rocks were sold for building work. The site was abandoned, and the first written reference to it is not until 1907, when the local historian Edgar Gilbert dubbed it "Jonathan Pattee's Cave," and hinted that "the most weird and fantastic tale might be woven" about it. From 1937 onward, there was a second phase of destruction. William B. Goodwin, a wealthy and elderly insurance broker from Hartford, Connecticut, spotted the site while on vacation, bought it on impulse, and spent the rest of his life trying to demonstrate that Mystery Hill was built by Irish monks in the tenth century A.D., fleeing to America from the invading Scandinavians. In the course of not proving this, he recklessly excavated the bulk of the site, throwing away any evidence that happened not to fit in with his theory, and conducting vituperous arguments with archaeologists from Harvard and New York who happened to disagree with him. He died in 1950, after which the site came under the care of a foundation. The archaeologist Gary S. Vescelius conducted an excavation in 1955 which, from ten test pits, uncovered Jonathan Pattee's Jew's harp, harness buckles, pewter spoons, and buttons from the uniform of a colonial soldier. But there was nothing significantly ancient, and it has been on Vescelius's sixty-seven-page report tentatively suggesting that Pattee himself had built the complex, that majority archaeological opinion rests to this day.

But since then, the report has steadily come to be seen as inadequate. Frank Glynn, past president of the Connecticut Archaeological Society, discovered that the report did not mention the existence of the roots of a pine tree stump, growing into the stone structure in such a way that the seedling must have been planted after the stones were first put there. Various tests showed that the latest date the seedling could have been implanted was at least twenty-five years before Pattee was born. Subsequent radiocarbon dating on pine roots showed them to have grown at least a century and a half before Pattee. So whoever built Mystery Hill, it certainly wasn't he.

Since 1957 the site has been owned by Robert E. Stone, an engineer who lives locally, and is president of NEARA. He has opened the site to the public, together with a souvenir shop, and an honest display of excavated fragments. He bitterly resents suggestions that because it is now a commercial venture, he has a vested interest in proving it to be very old. "I could have sold the place many times for building plots at a huge profit," he says. "Any money the place makes goes into research." Some of this research is at last paying off. In 1968, the C-14 date from charcoal in a sump pit in one of the rock-cut drains was put at A.D. 1540, more than a century before the landing of the Pilgrims. The following year, charcoal excavated directly below one of the significant pine roots, and only two to four inches above bedrock, gave the earliest date yet: 1045 B.C.—at last, contemporary with the end of the European megalith building. Then in 1971, from an even lower level, came a piece of carbon dated at 1525 B.C., which gives a calibrated date of around 2000 B.C.—half a millennium before the final phase of Stonehenge.

CELTIC CARVINGS?

To the frustration of NEARA, these dates are still not accepted by the archaeological establishment. Professor Steven Williams, director of Harvard's Peabody Museum, is unhappy about the context in which the charcoal was found. "The carbon comes from a stratigraphic position that does not date the structures above it. I've been in the pit and been shown the location where the sample came from, and I think I know what I'm talking about," he told a newspaper reporter. He and his colleagues are even more scathing about the prehistoric sequence of events put together by some of NEARA's members in order to reconstruct the way in which the megalith builders reached America.

According to this version (to fit in with the early C-14 date), around the year 2000 B.C. the Beaker People from Iberia—now Portugal—who are known to have been adventurous travelers, sailed to America, as they did to the British Isles and northern Europe. It was they who were in Britain when the final version of Stonehenge was created, and whose familiar burial grounds can be seen in the round barrows that contain a distinctive bell-shaped pottery urn giving them their name—the Bell Beaker People. For more than 1,000 years after this, goes the theory, there was sporadic trade and contacts across the Atlantic until the invasion of the Iberian peninsula by Celts from central Europe around 800 B.C. These two cultures, the Beakers and the Celts, are then assumed to have quickly merged, after which there was a new wave of immigration to New England. This time the voyagers brought with them a form of primitive writing known as Ogam script, which they inscribed on stones and monuments widely over this part of America, and which Professor Barry Fell, of Harvard University, claims to have interpreted.

Again, mainstream archaeologists dismiss this not just as speculative, but as speculative nonsense; they demand the evidence they understand best—the excavated remains of man and his artifacts. As yet, there is no fragment of

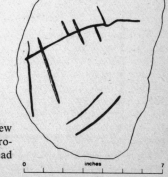

"Ogam" markings in New Hampshire: translated by Professor Barry Fell to read "Alas—Guy, son of H."

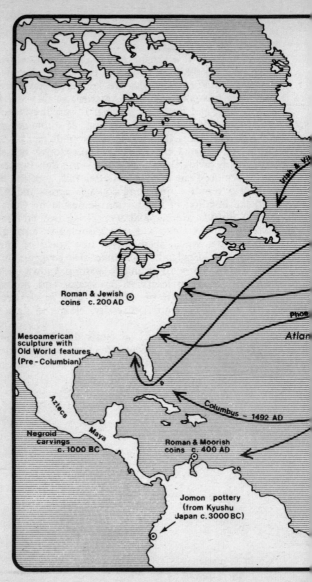

Roman & Jewish
coins c. 200 AD

Mesoamerican
sculpture with
Old World features
(Pre - Columbian)

Aztecs

Maya

Negroid
carvings
c. 1000 BC

Roman & Moorish
coins c. 400 AD

Jomon pottery
(from Kyushu
Japan c. 3000 BC)

Iran & Vi

phoe

Atlan

Columbus - 1492 AD

Suggested trans-Atlantic crossings and contacts.

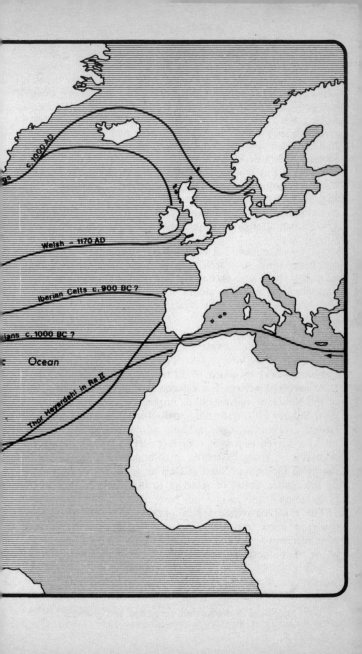

gs   c. 1000 AD

Welsh – 1170 AD

Iberian Celts c. 900 BC ?

ians c. 1000 BC ?

Ocean

Thor Heyerdahl in Ra II

a bell beaker—the equivalent proof of the Jomon pottery in Ecuador. There is scarcely anything made of bronze; certainly not as much as would be expected from many centuries of trading. In other ways, too, the theory does not provide a full or satisfactory explanation. The Beaker People were not the originators of megalithic tombs, for although they sometimes adapted them and used them for their own burials, the people whose megaliths were central to their religious belief came from an earlier time. Even more so is this true of the Celts, none of whose religious practices required the use of megaliths (although they sometimes put inscriptions on them).

Yet the New England megaliths are there, as, unquestionably, are markings that sometimes bear a relationship to Iberian Ogam, but just as often have a totally individual style. To an outsider, it seems extraordinary that more is not being done to search them out and record them. In quantity, there are probably more rock carvings on just one site in Vermont than in the whole of the neolithic Old World—yet there is scarcely anyone paying attention to them.

As for the evidence of man's habitation, it would probably emerge from excavations elsewhere than the ruins of Mystery Hill. But it may take a long time to find. Some of the earthworks in southern Britain must, by their scale, have involved a large labor force, just as the distribution of the New England megaliths implies a large, lost population. Silbury Hill, according to Richard Atkinson's calculations, represents the carefully directed work of 500 men for fifteen years (or whatever other permutation may be extracted from 18 million man-hours)—"a fraction of the gross national product at least as great as that devoted by the United States of America to the whole of its space programme."

The unsolved archaeological puzzle is not only where all this labor came from but where it lived and what happened to it afterward. On site after site, there is no evidence at all of the modest townships—or, at the least, labor camps —which would be expected to support and house the workers at Stonehenge, or the flint miners during their centuries of occupation of Grimes Graves mines in Norfolk. Nor have any large-scale graves or graveyards been found. The mystery leaves all investigators with the haunting impression of a ghost population that must have existed—but vanished without trace.

And was this labor voluntary? In other civilizations, it was usually not the case. The Egyptians used forced labor to build the Pyramids, and the laborers had little choice: they could work, or they could go into the desert and starve. When the great medieval cathedrals were built, workers lost their livelihood if they were uncooperative. But in megalithic times, the countryside was underpopulated. Anybody who did not care for the backbreaking labor of shifting tons of earth at Avebury or Silbury Hill could have taken himself and his family off into the forest with a goat and a cow, and created a new farmstead. So something, either in the social organization or in an overpowering communal motive, must have kept enough workers together long enough for the monuments to be built.

So it may have been with the New England megaliths, now it is becoming clear that a colonial explanation is not enough. It was always unlikely that Jonathan Pattee, a respected local citizen, could have built Mystery Hill without attracting some kind of written account of his eccentricity. Nor does it seem sensible to interpret many of the other stone chambers as root cellars, particularly when they are associated with other types of megaliths. Today's descendants of the original colonial farmers agree with one voice that it would have been completely out of character for early settlers to have wasted their time and energy on such elaborately built, carefully constructed chambers of huge blocks of stone; some have been so carefully chosen, and even perhaps hewn, that in regularity and bulk they stand comparison with the great tombs in Brittany. Nor would colonial farmers have needed to excavate menhirs as gateposts of stone two or three times as tall as was practically necessary. A much more likely interpretation is that the structures were there when they arrived, and they thankfully made use of them.

So just who put them there—if it wasn't the farmers, the Beaker People, the Celts, or any known Indian tribe? A research project at Norwich University, Northfield, Vermont, is at last beginning to approach the subject scientifically, using the modern tools of geographers—aerial photography checked by field work, soil analysis, and carbon dating. Ms. Noel Ring, Instructor of Geography, has identified from NASA U-2 photographs, taken at a height

Silbury Hill in Victorian times; the exaggeration in the engraving gives a much better idea of its size and prominence than modern photographs.

of 65,000 feet, a unique pattern of giant hexagons, laid out on the ground at some unknown time in the past, and identified today by stone walls and ditches. Many of them are independent of colonial and current field patterns, or overlap and cross them in such a way as to make it clear that they were there before the European farmers of the seventeenth and eighteenth centuries A.D. Within the hexagons, some a mile long, the soil shows up as a different color—an indication of earlier cultivation—and almost all the megaliths are also contained inside. "They include menhirs and dolmens, and I am pretty sure we have some henges as well," she says. She is convinced of their antiquity. "One known colonial deed mentions the prior presence of stone structures. I am confident that when we have assembled more data, we shall at least be able to suggest to archaeologists where to go and look."

Perhaps, when the New England megaliths are more carefully studied, there will turn out to be one other remarkable achievement to provide a link between what was going on in the Old World and the New. For in Europe, at the same time as the megalith builders were developing their skills as agricultural technologists, it now seems that they also created an organized and mathematically oriented society over huge distances. Their knowledge of astronomy and engineering was to become such that a nonarchaeologist, Professor Sir Fred Hoyle, feels there had to be another side to megalithic life, which went on simultaneously with a peasant farming existence: "The three essential requirements for high intellectual achievement are availability of food, leisure and social stability, and good communication. It must be possible for people in one district to know what is being done in other districts. Outstanding individuals must be able to get together. The young must be taught. Preferably the brightest youngsters should be brought into a 'university.' "

It could be that on both sides of the Atlantic, they were the world's first astronomers.

CHAPTER

4

UNWRITTEN SCIENCE

My opinion is that Stonehenge, and all such Stone temples, ever found in the most open and champaign countries, were the temples of the most lonely Heathen Sabaeans, who, having forgotten the one true God, did in their first lapse into idolatry, worship those greater luminaries, the Sun and the Moon, and subsequently took the minor planets, influenced as they doubtlessly were by their apparent powers of self-locomotion, into their scheme of religious worship.

—REVEREND E. DUKE, *Druidical Temples of the County of Wiltshire,* 1846

PROVIDING HE WAS NOT CONCERNED ABOUT GREAT PRE-
CISION or accuracy, a castaway on a desert island (or a
stranded spaceman from another planet) would not find
it very difficult to work out the approximate seasons of
the year here on earth, and mark them on the ground in
such a way that in the future he could anticipate the
coming of spring, summer, autumn and winter. From a
fixed point, he would note each day the position where
the sun set over the horizon. Daily, almost imperceptibly,
as the weather gradually became warmer, the sun would
move across to the right—if he was in the northern
hemisphere—for half a year, until it reached a point
where it would apparently set in the same place for about
a week: the midsummer solstice. Then it would begin its
slow progress leftward until six months later—in the case
of the planet Earth—it would again appear to wait at its
furthermost point for a week before turning back, and retrace its path to the right again: the midwinter solstice.

A Russian scientist, Dr. L. E. Maistrov, has described
villages in his country where, as recently as the beginning
of this century, it was the job of one man to observe
each day's sunset in just such a way. The village elders
would gather nightly beside the local church to discuss the
affairs of the community, and there was always a bench
which faced the mountains in the north. The mountain
peaks on the horizon formed a profile that was easy for
the observer, seated on the bench, to memorize, and thus
he identified the turning points of the year. In many villages, the observer would divide the distance between the
farthest setting points on the left and right roughly in half,
and these days, when the sun set over the particular peak,
were similarly noted: they were the equinoxes, when day
and night have the same number of hours. Other peaks on
the mountains served to split up the year into still smaller

105

units, and each time the sun set over them there was traditionally a holiday or rest day. This happened every eight days or so—about forty or fifty times a year—and so a convenient pattern of working "weeks" was established, without the necessity for a written astronomical calendar. The method also neatly overcame the awkward astronomical fact that the solar year is 365¼ days long, but at the same time there is a lunar cycle of four "weeks." The mountains, being fixed in relation to the firmament, provided a built-in correction.

The system worked adequately for these Russian peasant communities, and no doubt in other areas of the world, for thousands of years. Abiding by it, they knew when to plant and when to reap, when to collect stores of food and fuel for winter, when to shear the sheep—how, in fact, to keep the rhythm of an agricultural year in synchronization with the astronomical year. And one would suppose that some such system would have been equally appropriate for megalithic man, as he emerged from his days of nomadic hunting and began to settle down as a farmer with crops and livestock.

The extraordinary thing is that, although he may have started with solar and lunar observations as primitive yet workable as this, for some reason he was not satisfied with them. Before long, he felt compelled to develop a mathematical and astronomical understanding that in its finest details would not be matched, quite in this way, anywhere in the world for more than 3,000 years, until the time of the European astronomers of the Middle Ages. Even though his only basic materials to hand were wooden posts, heavy lumps of stone, and thongs of hide, he learned to make observations that were almost unbelievably precise. Quite soon, he was dissatisfied by the inaccuracies of measurement in recording sunset over a horizon: the breadth of the sun, the difficulty caused by refraction of light in determining the exact moment when it set, the apparent standstill in the setting position over a period of a week—all these created difficulties and imprecisions.

So he set about meeting these challenges. For his foresights—the mountains in the far distance behind which the sun would set—he chose slopes and notches through which the sun could be accurately observed as it gently slid away for the last few seconds of its rays. Then, daily at sunsets just before and after the solstice, he planted his backsight—usually a wooden post—at the exact point where he would have to stand to see the sun finally slipping below the horizon. As the sun moved across, his backsight posts did so similarly, until at the solstice they turned around and retraced their positions.

But he also worked out that if, at the same time as moving across and planting his stake, he moved a pace backward as well, the line made by the stakes in the ground became, at the time of the solstice, a gentle curve. The apex of that curve gave him the point of the solstice with an accuracy of about a third of one degree. Since every circle on a map is divided into 360 degrees, he achieved an accuracy of approximately one part in 1,000; as good as a modern theodolite, and better than the best of prismatic compasses. Having found his observation angle, he marked it with a monument—a standing stone, a stone built into a circle, a tomb, a cairn —of such weight and permanence that today, 5,000 or 6,000 years afterward, many of them are still accurate to within a few inches.

Whatever the motive for his determination to become so precise, he certainly felt it early in his development. The passage grave at Newgrange, carbon dated to the three centuries before 3000 B.C., is a good example, with its phenomenal "light box" above the entrance being so precisely aligned that the midwinter sunrise shines directly down the twenty-yard-long passage and into the tomb. The illumination lasts just a few minutes, and to achieve the effect, hundreds of stones weighing between two and fourteen tons were meticulously raised and balanced. Moreover, the burial mound is lined up with two other ruined grave sites to point the direction of the equinoxes, and may be part of an even larger astronomical layout.

Another example of vast heavy engineering in the cause—at least partly—of astronomical alignments has been found in the Dorset Cursus. Although still not fully interpreted, in its central section the midwinter sunset is aligned on a long barrow, a placing that gives it a date of *c.* 3000 B.C., and almost certainly not later than 2500 B.C.

This obsession for accuracy brought an unending list of complications in its wake. Nowadays, we are used to having two equal halves of the year between midsummer and midwinter. But this would only happen always if the

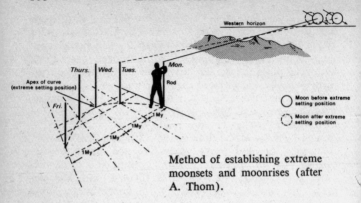

Method of establishing extreme
moonsets and moonrises (after
A. Thom).

earth moved in a perfect circle around the sun. In
fact it moves in a very slight ellipse, and the effect, *c.*
3000 B.C., was to make the second half of the year—between midsummer and midwinter—about five days shorter
than the first half. Among other effects, it means that, in
recording the equinoxes, the marker must be placed about
half a degree away from zero. In dozens of sites, it can be
shown that megalithic man knew precisely how to do this.

Next comes the problem of the length of the year—a
quarter of a day longer than a round figure, so that to
keep an accurate calendar going, the concept of a leap
year has to be invented. There is also the difficulty that at
365 days, the nearest round figure, the year is indivisible
into "months" or "weeks" of equal length. By the time
megalithic man built Newgrange, he had solved the first
puzzle—how to find four parts of the year as equal as possible in length. Could he now put down markers to divide it into eighths and then sixteenths, in such a way that
each marker served for a double date—first in the spring
half of the year and then in the autumn?

Again, dozens of sites suggest that he did. His sixteen
months consisted of four with 22 days, eleven with 23,
and one with 24. In order, they went like this: 23, 23, 24,
23, 23, 23, 23, 22, 22, 22, 22, 23, 23, 23, 23, 23. To establish these periods of time, he placed markers that
measured the mean observations of the rising or setting
sun at the crucial moments to the accuracy of 1/1000 of
a degree—a precision remarkable by any standards. Today, no matter how advanced mathematical and statistical

theory has become, we would find it impossible to come up with a better answer to the calendrical puzzle which megalithic man set himself, and solved by trial and error, during the course of hundreds of painstaking years. A distant echo of his achievement can still be found in the May/Lammas and Martinmas/Candlemas anniversaries in your diary. They still fall on those days in the year which were first defined more than 5,000 years ago.

THE ANTIQUARIAN SEARCH

In their attempts to reach back into the mind of early man, it is the precision of this calendar that has defied the imagination of prehistorians. They knew that a calendar was the first necessity of a farmer, and the sun itself an object of mystic awe, the bringer of warmth and life. So antiquarians from the earliest times have noted the obvious link between the sun and Stonehenge, although few —because of the almost universal assumption of the barbarian savagery of neolithic man—considered him capable of understanding astronomy. William Stukeley wrote in 1740 that Stonehenge was principally aligned "to the north-east, where abouts the sun rises, when the days are longest." Without attempting to understand how it could have been done, other writers soon came up with theories that Stonehenge was connected with the twelve signs of the zodiac, and even that it had once been capable of predicting eclipses. But it was not until the end of the nineteenth century that the frequency of northeast alignments throughout Stone Age monuments began to be systematically noted. During the 1890s, the archaeologist A. L. Lewis drew up tables which plotted the directions of "outlying stones, prominent hills, and other special objects," in relation to twenty-six stone circles surveyed from Cumberland to Cornwall. Imprecise though his observations were, compared to current standards, many of the alignments can now be seen to relate to the solar calendar.

But the most notable recruit to those who believed in ancient man's astronomical ability was the renowned British astronomer Sir Norman Lockyer, Fellow of the Royal Society and Director of the Solar Physics Laboratory at South Kensington. In 1901, having already established the solar orientation of the Pyramids, he looked at Stonehenge and made an attempt (unsuccessful, as we know now) at dating it by astronomical means. In 1906 he published *Stonehenge and Other British Stone Monuments*, and drew the conclusion that many of the country's stone circles, including those in Cornwall, on Dartmoor, at Stanton Drew in Somerset, and in Scotland, were aligned not just on the sun, but on many of the stars as well. His breakthrough was in using large-scale Ordnance Survey maps, and plotting alignments on them to prove to the skeptical that ancient monuments were placed not haphazardly but in a carefully organized pattern.

Unfortunately, he suffered from both enthusiasm and, occasionally, a surprisingly slipshod approach to his map making. The archaeological establishment was entitled to point out that he included so many possible stars in his calculations that he could draw an alignment almost anywhere, and it would point at some time to one of them. Nevertheless, his example set local archaeological societies on the hunt for more examples. Learned but amateur excursions took place, where on site after site stones were found to lean at exactly the right angle for the midsummer sunrise, or cast shadows around a circle so that they could been seen, even then, as sundials to tell the time of day. A report of four members of the North Staffordshire Field Club in 1910 noted with pleasure that the heel stone at Stonehenge was traditionally referred to as the Friar's Heel. The Celtic words for ascending sun were "freos Heol."

In the 1920s Admiral Boyle Somerville summarized the results of about ninety surveys that he had made of megalithic monuments. "In every instance . . . orientation of one kind or another has been found," he wrote in *Archaeologia*. As a naval man, he was not especially impressed with his neolithic ancestors' achievement in finding the solstitial points, "and the equinoctials were probably fixed by counting the days between the solstices and dividing by two." But Somerville should be credited as the first archaeologist who realized the detailed precision of the stone structures he was studying. He made a large-scale survey of three adjoining circles in the Clava group at Balnuarin in Scotland, each of which had a passage grave. When he superimposed them on top of each other, he found that they matched to within inches, with the summer solstitial sunset shining directly down the line of

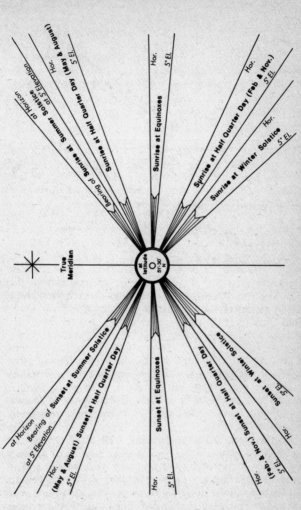

Boyle Somerville's template diagram of astronomical azimuths, southern Britain.

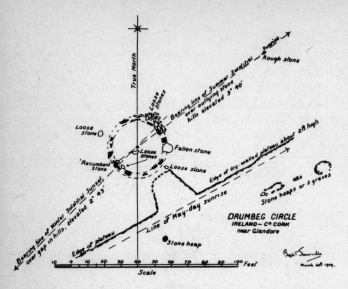

Boyle Somerville's discovery of alignments in Ireland. Research in New England suggests walls were similarly used there.

the passages to the central tombs. There were many other significant alignments, and the implications of the carefully planned geometry were so enormous, even revolutionary, that his findings might have changed the course of archaeology then and there. In fact, they were almost completely ignored.

For the next thirty years, until well after the Second World War, there was no detectable or published advance in this area of research, and knowing what we do now, it seems strange that so few people were able even to spot the clues, let alone decipher them. It was left to one man to start the search single-handed. For more than a quarter of a century he measured, mapped and calculated until he was able to describe with confidence what he had always suspected: a lost community of people, living from the Bay of Biscay to the Arctic Ocean, who found numbers more interesting than words.

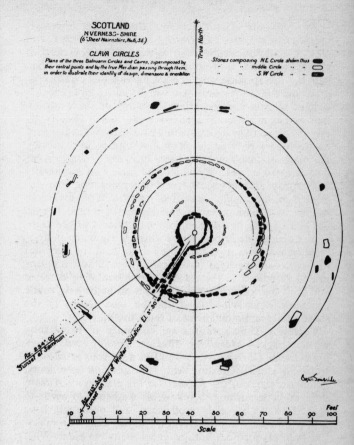

Boyle Somerville's plans of three Clava circles superimposed, showing identity of purpose and great accuracy of planning.

THE MEGALITHIC YARD

Dr. Alexander Thom, Emeritus Professor of Engineering Science at Oxford University from 1945 to 1961, and now an Emeritus Fellow of Brasenose College, Oxford, is a Scotsman born in 1894 who has dedicated more than half his life to surveying and evaluating the evidence at more than 600 megalithic sites in Britain and France. It is hard to overestimate either the effort or the contribution he has made to the study of those times. The discovery of radiocarbon dating, with its subsequent refinements, created one sort of archaeological revolution in redrawing the maps of man's development. Professor Thom, on his own, created another revolution: he forced on a generally unreceptive archaeological world the realization that ancient man had a mind as well as muscles. Without Thom, we would almost certainly still be unaware that toward the end of the third millennium B.C. there was the complex calendar described above; that a common unit of measurement was used from the far north of the Hebrides to France and perhaps farther; that tiny, almost immeasurable variations in the orbit of the moon were detected and built into observatories; and that an immensely subtle geometry is enshrined, and can be seen today, in the stone circles and monuments of those times.

Professor Thom's results are contained in two tightly written books—*Megalithic Sites in Britain** and *Megalithic Lunar Observatories†*—and in numerous articles for technical journals dealing with statistics and astronomy, notably a series in the *Journal for the History of Astronomy*. Anyone wishing to follow his mathematics needs to be at least "A" level in proficiency, and preferably have a good working knowledge of surveying and astronomy. But both his methods and his conclusions are plain. What shines through is his respect for the care with which the megaliths were originally put up:

The surveys must be made with the same accuracy as was used in the original setting out and it will be shown that some sites, for example, Avebury, were

* Oxford University Press, 1967.
† Oxford University Press, 1971.

set out with an accuracy approaching 1 in 1,000. Only an experienced surveyor with good equipment is likely to attain this sort of accuracy. The differences in tension applied to an ordinary measuring tape by different individuals can produce variations in length of this amount or even more. The necessity for this kind of accuracy has not in the past been appreciated and has in fact only become apparent as the work recorded here progressed.

For this reason Thom rejected almost all the work of previous historians and archaeologists as "crude," even when, as in the case of two nineteenth-century archaeologists, the Rev. W. C. Lukis and Sir Henry Dryden, they were working to the nearest inch or half-inch in their plans of the monuments and alignments. Instead, when on his own in the early stages of his research, he constructed a half-weight theodolite and carried it into the remote fields and hills of Scotland and Wales, where he meticulously plotted the sites to a minimum accuracy of one part in a hundred. More recently, joined in his work by his sons and grandsons, he has remeasured sites with surveying chains checked nightly against a steel tape kept at the base camp.

Hints of the labor involved occasionally creep through the dry statistics of his findings. At some sites "the inaccessibility and the long distance to be walked precluded the use of the theodolite." A stone is noted "so completely buried in ten-foot-deep gorse that it is unapproachable in ordinary clothes." Visiting Carnac for the first time, where he had agreed to carry out the first accurate survey of the 2,750-odd menhirs, his "first reaction was one of astonishment and indeed of dismay at the task we had undertaken." A stone circle in that area was "buried in whin and bramble so thick that even at Easter, when the leaves were off the trees, it was possible to approach a five-foot menhir within a few yards without seeing it. Because of this and the trees, surveying was difficult, but our experience had, by this time, convinced us of the extreme accuracy with which the more important works had been set out, and so we decided that we must make an effort to make an accurate survey."

The first glimmerings of interest in the subject that he remembers was as a teenager, noting the findings of Boyle

Somerville's survey of Callanish, the Scottish equivalent of Stonehenge but in a much better state of preservation. But it was some twenty years later, in 1934, that his search started seriously. It happened at the end of a long, tiring and difficult sail up the western coast of Scotland, and in a way combining insight and coincidence that seems so often to occur spontaneously in megalithic research. As he and a crew, which included his son, dropped anchor, the loch they chose happened to be alongside Callanish. The great stones stood blackly, silhouetted against the moon. On shore, his imagination fired by this image, a scene that had repeated itself endlessly since megalithic times, Thom noticed an oddity which had gone unremarked in recorded history: the circle was unmistakably aligned due north-south, the pole star twinkling above as visible proof.

"It fascinated me because I knew that in those times there was no pole star—its constellation hadn't reached today's position," he says. "What I wanted to find out was whether this had happened by accident, and whether it happened at other sites." So the long search started, at weekends and in vacations, sailing to remote moors in Scotland, hiking and camping on the hills and rocks wherever a prehistoric site was marked on a map. Gradually the evidence built up, not just of the knowledge of north and south, but of a far wider range of astronomical observations by megalithic man. No established archaeological magazine would publish his findings. Instead, they appeared in obscure journals, now long out of print and fetching a rarity value on the secondhand market.

In 1954, he was satisfied that solar observatories existed. In 1955, he detected the "megalithic fathom," measuring 5.44 feet, multiples of which made up the diameters of most stone circles. As more and more circles were surveyed, the evidence built up that the true unit was half this figure—2.72 feet, the "megalithic yard," which was used again and again in multiples of two, two and a half, three, three and a half, and so on. By the time he published his first book, in 1967, he had established its accuracy to ±.003 feet—an almost infinitesimally small maximum possible error of about one two-hundredth of an inch. He chose the word "yard" carefully: originally it meant a rod of wood or a stick, and its equivalent in Europe is the French *verge* and the Spanish *vara*. This led Thom to speculate that megalithic man's yard, having spread as far south as Iberia, may have become the *vara* still in use today in Spain, Texas, California, Mexico and Peru, with local values varying minutely from about 2.74 to 2.78 feet.

Speculation apart, his discovery of the megalithic yard, if it was accepted as factual and proven, had stunning implications for prehistory. His care in presentation, and the unquestioned scholarship of his work, made it hard to refute. But the idea of a numerate society, whose ability to measure and map meant that it had good communications and a continuing body of learning shared for centuries over a wide area, contradicted everything that any archaeologist had been trained to believe. Nor were most prehistorians, being scholars of the arts, intellectually equipped to follow the mathematical concepts involved— understandably, since a single calculation in this particular branch of statistical theory may cover a page or more. *Antiquity* called their dilemma "this whole vexed matter," and there is no doubt there were many who sat back and hoped that, at the end of the day, the megalithic yard would go away forever, together with the even more astonishing prehistoric geometric and astronomical discoveries that Thom was also publishing.

STATISTICAL EVIDENCE

Everything hinged on the existence of the megalithic yard. So far, Thom's best evidence had been obtained from Scotland, where most stone circles were more intact and less disturbed than those in England and Wales. In 1970, he found the means to survey the circles and alignments centered around Carnac in Brittany, an area that contains easily the largest concentration of megalithic remains anywhere in Europe. If, following his calculations in Scotland, it could be shown that the same unit of length was used in the construction and design of this huge, uncharted area of tombs, stones, and circles, this would be powerful additional proof of the megalithic yard.

And so indeed it turned out. The very first "circle" he surveyed, at Le Menec, turned out to have a geometric shape found commonly in Britain. It, and the alignments leading up to it, were based on the megalithic rod—a

unit precisely 2½ times the megalithic yard, and the
same unit used in most of the large British circles, including
Avebury and Stonehenge.

There was still one more test—it could almost be called
an ordeal—for Thom's theory to undergo. Such objections
as there still were to the megalithic yard centered around
two doubts. First, nearly all circles are incomplete, or
damaged by careless reerection, disturbance by tree roots,
and so on. This meant that Thom had to fill in big gaps
in his surveys by projecting a geometrical shape, and at
the same time had to "average" the effect caused by the
disturbance. On individual plans of stone circles, the disparity between Thom's elegant shapes and the position of
some of the stones is very marked. Taken as a whole over
hundreds of surveys, he would reply, the disparity is insignificant. Nevertheless even mathematicians, let alone
prehistorians, needed to be reassured on this point. Second, it was asked whether it was necessary for there to
have been an actual yardstick. Could the necessary designs have been achieved by the more simple methods of
pacing, and laid out on the ground with a post and a
rope? It was noted in passing that trained Guardsmen
today can maintain a pace of thirty inches on the parade
ground ±½ an inch. Even on rough ground, it was felt,
they ought to be able to keep the error to ±2 inches.

The test took place in 1972 in London, at an august
symposium organized jointly by the Royal Society and the
British Academy. Its subject was *The Place of Astron-
omy in the Ancient World,* and its list of speakers was
scholastically impressive. Besides Thom himself, Professor
Richard Atkinson spoke on neolithic technology; Professor
Gerald Hawkins, the American who had used a computer
some years before to deduce astronomical alignments in
Stonehenge, compared prehistoric astronomy in Britain,
Egypt and Peru; Professor H. H. Lamb described the
climatic and geographical conditions; Dr. E. W. McKie of
Glasgow University reported on a successful field experiment to check Thom's astronomical findings in Scotland;
and others of similar academic weight gave the gathering
a sense of drama and occasion. But in most people's
minds, the key paper would be that of Professor David
Kendall, head of the Statistical Laboratory at the University of Cambridge, and a mathematician of ferocious ability and renown. It was known that for some months

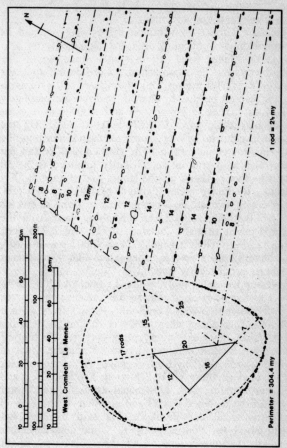

West Cromlech Le Menec

100 — 80m

Perimeter = 304.4 my

1 rod = 2½ my

N

17 rods

25

15

20

16

12

1

8
8
10
12my
12
12
14
14
14
10
8
0

Geometry of western alignment, Carnac (after A. Thom).

previously he had been subjecting Thom's findings, via a computer, to a long and complex series of theoretical tests, involving a new approach to their possible inadequacy. Few knew the outcome.

Professor Thom's contribution came early on, and he was unyielding. Confirming that the alignments in Brittany at Le Menec were set up with a quantum of 2½ megalithic yards, he summarized: "Considering that the rows are over 900 metres long the agreement is remarkable and cannot be due to chance. It disposes completely of the idea that pacing was used and it gives us a value for the megalithic yard of 2.271 ± 0.001 feet." On the Ring of Brogar in Orkney, some thousand miles to the north, he was equally firm. "The ring consists of tall flat stones forming a true circle obviously intended to be 50 rods in diameter. Using all the stones and stumps as they are today we find a mean diameter of 340.0 ± 0.6 feet, or neglecting two stones known to have been re-erected 340.7 ± 0.4 feet, so that the megalithic yard from the Brogar Ring is probably between 2.720 and 2.725 feet. For Britain as a whole I gave 2.720 ± 0.003 feet in 1967. The above values speak for themselves. They could not have been produced by pacing."

Professor Kendall's reply, when it came, was less forthright. He said he guessed that in the audience there were many on either side who would take Thom's theories as a whole, and then accept them as "overwhelmingly convincing" or reject them as "utterly preposterous." He himself had a more modest aim, which was to analyze them in just one aspect: the length of diameter of the true circles which had been surveyed by Thom in Scotland, England and Wales, totaling 169. This meant excluding the geometry of all the flattened circles and egg-shaped circles, and any astronomical considerations. He said his new approach, based on "Fourier analysis," could detect whether the greatly varying length of all these diameters might have occurred by chance, or whether there was a quantum such as the one Thom had suggested.

It was a long and inevitably difficult lecture, but at the end his conclusions were clear enough, and far from an anticlimax. Although he would have preferred more observations on the existing evidence there was only a one percent chance that the diameters of the stone circles could have occurred without the common, measured

length of Thom's megalithic yard. As for the argument
about whether they were set out by pacing or by a whalebone rod, he thought it was an irrelevance. "The primary
question is not how measurements were made, but
whether they were made." In bookmaking terms, it was
100 to 1 on that they were.

GEOMETRY

By excluding megalithic geometry from his calculations, Professor Kendall was ignoring perhaps the most
deeply mystifying and fascinating part of Thom's discoveries. Most people began to accept megalithic solar observations as a matter of fact; a solar calendar of some
sort as a matter of necessity; the megalithic yard as an
essential measurement; and even the extraordinary lunar
observations, in which all these were to culminate, as of
great mystical or navigational importance. But advanced
geometry is of a different order, and seems to prove
megalithic man's obsession with mathematics for its own
sake. Nobody has yet suggested a convincing function
for a stone circle that has been carefully flattened or
made egg-shaped; and in the absence of a practical purpose, it is worth looking at Professor Thom's evidence and
wondering whether they were designed and constructed as
a mixture of intellectual exercise and an enduring lesson
in mathematics in a time when textbooks did not exist.

To begin with, there is the constant use of a special sort
of right-angled triangle. Nowadays, the Pythagorean
theorem is perhaps the one that adults most readily recall
from their schooldays (the square on the hypotenuse of
a right-angled triangle is equal to the sum of the squares
on the other two sides), but in this case we are talking of
a time at least 2,000 years before the theorem was first
written down by Euclid. While the theorem is true of all
right-angled triangles, megalithic man was concerned almost solely with those special few that contain only whole
numbers, or integers, and are known as Pythagorean triangles. The simplest, and most frequently used, was the
3, 4, 5 triangle ($9 + 16 = 25$). But he also knew the 5,
12, 13 right-angled triangle, the 8, 15, 17, and the 12, 35,
37. He may also have known the 9, 40, 41, and—when it
suited him—chose others such as 8, 9, 12 which,

when laid out on the ground in stone, are almost indistinguishable from true Pythagorean triangles.

With this as his basis, he now seems to have attempted the impossible. He wanted to use these whole numbers for the straight lines within the "circle"—for the radius or the diameter, for example—but also to achieve a whole number for the perimeter. But here he came up against an unalterable mathematical fact, which is probably also the only other theorem that sticks in the mind: to find the circumference of a circle, you have to apply the formula $2\pi r$. But just as with his solar calendar megalithic man could not divide the year into months of equal length, here he found another awkward fraction. You can write π as $2\frac{2}{7}$, or as 3.141596 . . . but you cannot have a whole number. If megalithic man had achieved knowledge of π, and it looks as though he had, it was at least 3,000 years before it was first recorded in writing by the Hindu sage Arya-Bhata in the sixth century A.D. We can be certain that he was experimenting and searching toward an analysis of the two basic geometric figures, the right-angled triangle and the circle, and that some of his results were astonishing.

The egg-shaped ring at Woodhenge has five concentric "circles" whose perimeters measure exactly 40, 60, 80, 140 and 160 megalithic yards; the internal dimensions are based on the Pythagorean triangle 12, 35, 37.

The circle at Moel ty Ucha in Scotland is perfectly preserved except perhaps for slight movement caused by frosts. Thom reported: "The builders . . . started with a circle 14 megalithic yards in diameter and therefore $3\frac{1}{7}$ x 14 or 44 yards in circumference. But this was not enough: they wanted also to have a multiple of $2\frac{1}{2}$ yards in the perimeter. So they proceeded to invent a method of drawing flattened portions on the ring which, with a minimum of distortion, would reduce it to $42\frac{1}{2}$."

He found too at Avebury that "the basis of the design is a 3, 4, 5 triangle set out in units of exactly 25 MY so that all the resulting shapes come out in multiples of 5 or 10."

All this was discovered in Thom's earlier work, and nothing has altered except refinement and confirmation of his results. But it is in his massive survey of the alignments at Carnac that he has perhaps most graphically demonstrated the geometrical ability of megalithic man. Here

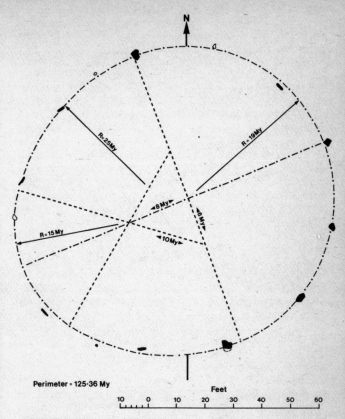

Experiments in pre-Pythagorean geometry and whole numbers in egg-shaped circle at Clava, Scotland (after A. Thom).

are nearly 3,000 menhirs, the most impressive of them twice the height of a man. When you stand and look at them today from the car park at the western end, they seem to stretch away endlessly, more or less in parallel rows, in an eastnortheasterly direction, until they are lost in the gorse-covered slopes.

Professor Thom and his colleagues, plotting them on a 1:500 scale that covers maps nearly ten feet long, have demonstrated that they are part of a vast geometrical design. One section has seven rows spaced exactly twelve

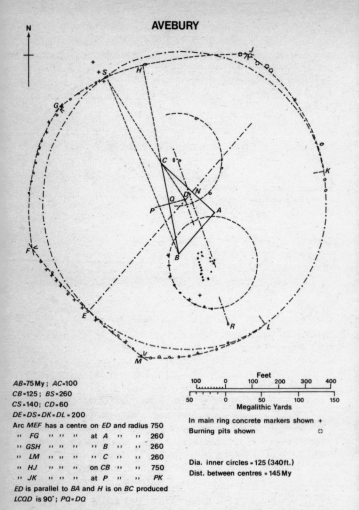

AVEBURY

AB=75My ; AC=100
CB=125 ; BS=260
CS=140; CD=60
DE=DS=DK=DL=200
Arc MEF has a centre on ED and radius 750
 " FG " " "   at A "   "   260
 " GSH " " "   " B "   "   260
 " LM " " "   " C "   "   260
 " HJ " " "   on CB "   "   750
 " JK " " "   at P "   "   PK
ED is parallel to BA and H is on BC produced
LCQD is 90°; PQ=DQ

Feet
100   0   100   200   300   400
50   0   50   100   150
Megalithic Yards

In main ring concrete markers shown +
Burning pits shown ○

Dia. inner circles = 125 (340ft.)
Dist. between centres = 145 My

Megalithic geometry of Avebury. Professor Thom has subsequently refined and confirmed this plan—but his work is
not yet considered respectable enough to be included in
Avebury Museum.

megalithic yards apart, placed on a hardly discernible curve whose radius is 2,500 megalithic yards (1,000 megalithic rods). Where this section joins another—to change direction slightly, or alter the number of rows—Pythagorean or near-Pythagorean triangles are incorporated in a manner so elegant that it could not be improved today.

LUNAR OBSERVATORIES

To the lay observer, perhaps the most striking implication of all these mathematics is not the almost incomprehensibly complex geometry, but the central organization that must have been needed to organize and coordinate these vast projects. If, as has been shown, measurement by rope would have been inadequate, then measuring rods, perhaps of oak or whalebone, must have been manufactured to within an accuracy of hundredths of an inch and then carried up and down the north Atlantic coast. Without a theodolite, some method of keeping the rods precisely vertical or horizontal must have been worked out. We may take Thom's word for it that the mathematical and engineering achievements at Avebury represented the summit of megalithic man's ability; but at the same time, to the average observer, two places stand out as having the most spectacular evidence that still remains—Carnac and Stonehenge.

Both sites, in their separate ways, are overwhelming in their immediate impact. Everybody's inclination on a first visit is to invest them with a religious or magical significance, and it is worth hanging on to that instinct, since mathematics alone cannot provide a total understanding of their place in the ancient world. However, we now know with certainty that one purpose for both monuments was to observe the movements of the moon. The difficulties of doing this are so enormous, and the time scale so long, that a form of religious or metaphysical motivation must surely have been there.

As with his solar observations, his calendar, and his geometry, what becomes clear is megalithic man's obsessive drive for measurable perfection. It is infinitely more difficult to study the orbit of the moon than of the earth around the sun; a comparison of, say, primary school sums

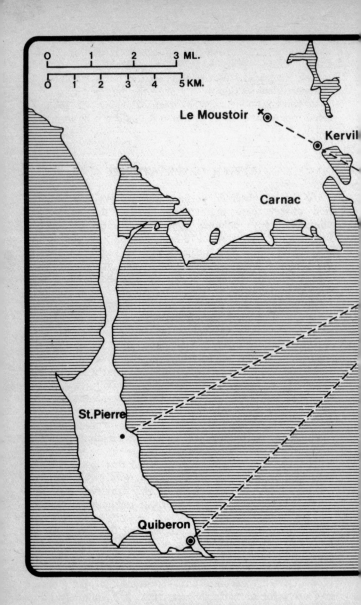

Le Moustoir ×⊙ ⋯⋯⋯ Kervil

Carnac

St.Pierre •

Quiberon ⊙

0　1　2　3 ML.
0　1　2　3　4　5 KM.

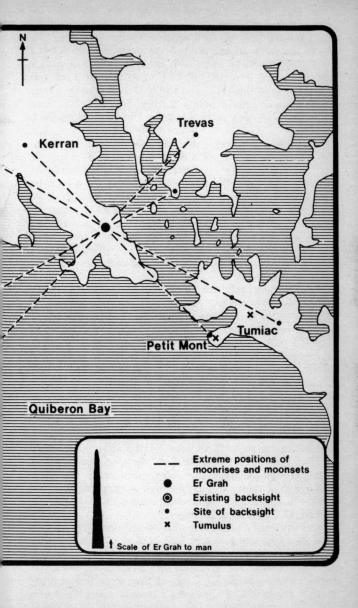

N

Trevas

Kerran

Tumiac

Petit Mont

Quiberon Bay

- - - Extreme positions of
moonrises and moonsets
● Er Grah
◉ Existing backsight
• Site of backsight
× Tumulus

▮ Scale of Er Grah to man

with university level mathematics. Unlike the sun, the
moon describes an arc around the earth that is not the
same from month to month—it is slightly tilted in such a
way that over a period of 18.6 years it first rises and
sets very far in the north and south, then gradually moves
its rising and setting points farther inward from these
extreme points, and after 9.3 years begins to move back
again.

This must have been extraordinarily difficult for megalithic man to have been able to work out. Few people
lived beyond the age of forty. If, say, someone started
seriously observing the moon in his teens, he would be
very unlikely to live long enough to follow through more
than one complete cycle, and thus establish a repeating
pattern. However, we know that somehow he managed to
do so, and by the evidence of more than two dozen sites,
Thom has shown that he established to within a degree
the eight declinations that marked the extreme points of
the moon's swing.

But this was only the beginning of megalithic man's
difficulties—the crudest of the observations he had to
make in order to understand the movements of the moon.
The extreme positions he had discovered, when the moon
each 9.3 years begins to turn around and retrace its steps
at moonrise and moonset, are known as the major and
minor standstills. And it is only for a few days on either
side of these standstills that it is possible to make an observation of another peculiarity of the moon's orbit—the
tiny wobble or perturbation that runs in a cycle of 173.3
days. This movement is so slight—less than one-third of a
degree in total—that until recently it was thought to have
lain undiscovered until the end of the sixteenth century
A.D. But it is crucial, because it is only when the perturbation is around its largest that eclipses can occur. We know
now, beyond reasonable doubt, that megalithic man was
able to measure the wobble; and because he could do this,
he had the means of predicting eclipses.

The whole of Carnac, together with Stonehenge, can be
seen as a vast experimental laboratory for testing and refining the procedures of lunar observation. Archaeologists
have speculated for years on the purpose of the huge
broken menhir called Er Grah, at fifty-seven feet approximately the height of Cleopatra's Needle, and at 340 tons
about 70 percent heavier. Why was it so tall? Why was it

erected just there? Once again it was Professor Thom who provided the answer. It was a mammoth foresight that was used to observe, from monuments and coastal points up to ten miles away, and to within a fraction of a degree, the major and minor standstills and the amount of perturbation.

As for the purpose of the thousands of menhirs which formed the alignments, Thom believes he has found in them ways in which megalithic man was able to improve yet further on the staking method which he had used to pinpoint the solstices, and the extreme points of the standstills.

STONEHENGE DECODED?

At Stonehenge, similar marvels could be achieved. In 1963, Gerald Hawkins, born English and naturalized American, Professor of Astronomy at Boston University, published an article in the scientific magazine *Nature* entitled "Stonehenge Decoded." He boldly suggested that most of the twelve major astronomical alignments—four solar, eight lunar—could be found in the geometry of the monument, and that a computer had checked his findings to show that this could not have happened by chance. He followed it a year later with a further article suggesting that the fifty-six "Aubrey holes" (the remains of an earlier form of Stonehenge laid out around the existing perimeter) were almost exactly three times the 18.61-year cycle of the moon, and were used in this connection to predict eclipses. In 1965 he published a book amplifying his findings.

It started a furious archaeological debate, and was widely criticized on several counts—it was archaeologically inaccurate, the plans from which the calculations were made were not precise, it was slipshod in its presentation. These failings were compounded by the ballyhoo that attended publication: a television film, headlines about an American detective/astronomer solving the riddle of Britain's most famous archaeological monument. Those prehistorians who cared to examine the astronomy further preferred the results of the Yorkshireman C. A. Newham, who independently, but privately, more accurately, and without publicity, had come up with much the same theoretical findings. Hawkins's strongest ally was another astronomer, Professor Sir Fred Hoyle, who felt that, given the technology available at the time, Stonehenge was the best eclipse predictor that could have been made. Certainly it demanded "a level of intellectual attainment orders of magnitude higher than the standard to be expected from a community of primitive farmers. A veritable Newton or Einstein must have been at work—but then why not?"

Today, more than ten years later, the consensus is that while the criticisms made of him at the time are still valid, Hawkins's theory had elements both right and wrong. A new, more accurate survey of the monument by Professor Thom shows it to have been set out, like all other circles, with geometric finesse and using the megalithic yard as the unit of measure. Stonehenge was indeed a lunar observatory but almost certainly not in the way Hawkins suggested. Rather like Er Grah, Thom has shown that Stonehenge seems to have been precisely positioned so that distant hills align astronomically with the great stone arches, thus achieving a standard of accuracy unobtainable by the methods suggested by Hawkins.

AMERICAN ECLIPTIC ARCHITECTURE

Thom's work is unique, both for its insight and its thoroughness. A number of studies in Britain have followed it up and confirmed his findings, and now a lone American has raised the possibility that, just as there is a resemblance between New and Old World megaliths, so there was a mutual ability to make complex astronomical observations in prehistoric times. Byron E. Dix is a young engineer living in Newport, Vermont, who before he was thirty had a wide number of inventions to his credit, mainly in the field of optics. This led to an interest in astronomy, and then to Thom's work; at the same time, he read of a claim by Robert Stone that Mystery Hill, like Stonehenge, had a winter solstice stone over which the setting midwinter sun could be observed from the "sacrificial table." He checked, and found that this was indeed so; it started a fascination with the megaliths of New England, which since then has occupied virtually the whole of his spare time.

Buying a motorcycle to give him greater mobility, he methodically visited all the NEARA sites in the state, searching for a place that would show that Thom's dis-

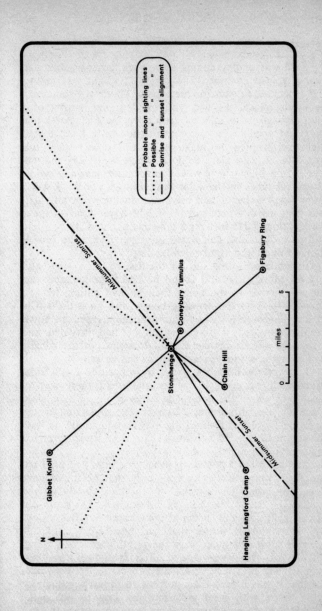

N

Gibbet Knoll

Hanging Langford Camp

Stonehenge

Midsummer Sunrise

Midsummer Sunset

Chain Hill

Coneybury Tumulus

Figabury Ring

Probable moon sighting lines
Possible "   "   "
Sunrise and sunset alignment

0   miles   5

coveries in Europe might have their parallel in the New
World. He found what he was looking for in February
1975. "I was photographing some rock carvings on a wall
near a ruined chamber," he says. "The light was fading,
and I decided to wait for the sunset. There was something
about the place, the way you stand at the bottom of a
natural bowl, with hills all around to the east, north and
west, but open to the sun toward the south. I felt that if
ever you wanted to make a natural observatory, this
would be an easy place to do it. There are peaks and valleys in the hills which would have made marking points
at critical times in the solar year. But, of course, I didn't
know yet whether it had been used in this way, nor, if it
had been used, where anyone might have stood to make
the sightings." He observed the sunset, noted its position,
and later, at home, calculated on paper where the sunsets
should fall on important calendar dates.

Dix returned to the site for the first of them—the equinox on March 21—and found he had miscalculated: the
sun set farther to the north than he had anticipated. So
he went back to the drawing board, and on a third trip,
to help discover a valid sighting position, used an equa-
torially mounted telescope which he had invented and
made. On site, it can be aligned to point out the sunrise
and sunset positions for any day of the year.

"I moved the telescope about from position to position,
using trial and error to try to establish if there was an
ideal spot where the natural features of the hills fell into
place. On the fifth attempt, I got it. The peaks and valleys
were ideally placed to mark the sunrise and sunset on both
the equinoxes and the solstices. There were obvious horizon
features for all eight."

Even so, there was still no proof that man had used the
site for astronomical purposes—only that he might have
done. But when Dix checked the hilltops closely on the
ground, he found that he was indeed right. On seven out
of the eight positions, often at the extreme limit of visibility, were marker stones that had once been artificially
erected. "Some of them were fallen, and one was leaning.
But the fact that I was able to discover stones in positions
which I had previously calculated theoretically, convinces
me that it was indeed their purpose to show the people of
those times, with great precision, just how to divide the
year into eight equal parts. The only position without a

stone now has a road running across it, so that any marker would have been moved or destroyed."

Byron Dix is sure that the people who used the site, besides having a knowledge of astronomy, also knew how to take compass bearings. The sighting position is aligned due south onto the facing wall of a stone chamber; due west with an artificial peak in the hills, created by a pile of stones; due north with a large standing stone set in a wall; and due east with the line of a ruined wall. Professor Barry Fell's interpretations of inscriptions on some of the stones, if he has translated correctly, confirm their use.

Over a longer period of time, Byron Dix studied an even more complex site, also in central Vermont. Here he found that one of the largest stone chambers in the state, the interior dimensions 6.4m X 3.2m, seemed to be built in such a way that, as with the light box at Newgrange, an observer inside could view the sunrise on the shortest day of the year, as it rose above a notch in the distant horizon. But, even more sophisticated, the size of the doorway entrance was such that, to the same observer, their limits marked the declination angles (18.5° and 28.5°) of the moon's major and minor standstills, thus providing a means, as for megalithic man in Europe, of predicting eclipses.

Dix says confidently: "I do not believe this could be coincidence. The more the site is investigated, the more complex it becomes. I have termed it ecliptic architecture. Related to the chamber is an observation platform from which important sunrise and sunset positions are marked by stones, or wall alignments pointing to the horizon. A lone standing stone, and a fallen one, marked true north-south from the platform. There are other indications that the site was used to observe the movement of stars, as well as the sun and moon. The whole place is incredibly rich—the knowledge of the people who put it there in the first place is mind-bending."

As with the other sites catalogued by NEARA, Byron Dix's work has not yet been checked by mainstream archaeologists, and so far he himself, from lack of time and equipment, has been unable to make measurements sufficiently precise and thorough for anyone to be convinced that he has all his answers right; nor that the megalithic yard was used in New England, which he thinks probable. Compared to the circles and standing stones whose mys-

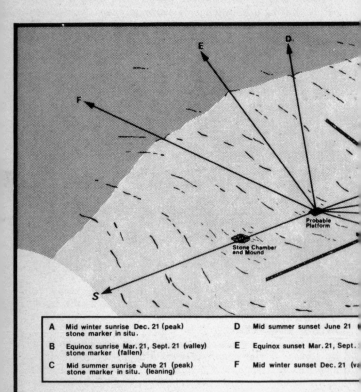

E

D

F

S

Probable
Platform

Stone Chamber
and Mound

A   Mid winter sunrise Dec. 21 (peak)
     stone marker in situ.

B   Equinox sunrise Mar. 21, Sept. 21 (valley)
     stone marker (fallen)

C   Mid summer sunrise June 21 (peak)
     stone marker in situ. (leaning)

D   Mid summer sunset June 21

E   Equinox sunset Mar. 21, Sept.

F   Mid winter sunset Dec. 21 (va

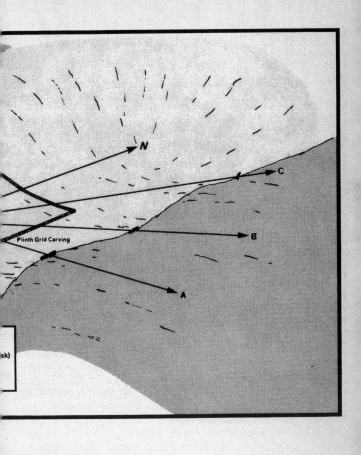

Plinth Grid Carving

N

C

B

A

ak)

Megalithic chamber in central Vermont, associated with standing stone and observation platform; its origins are disputed and no excavation has taken place.

tery Professor Thom has partially elucidated, there are a number of problems about interpreting the New England sites astronomically. For a start, the evidence is much less obvious: whereas a stone circle in, say, Scotland stands out plainly from the field in which it is set, the marker stones in Vermont often form part of a complex of walls or boulders that make them much less easily identifiable. An archaeologist looking at some of Dix's calendrical markers on his first site would say they are indistinguishable from other stones nearby.

Then, the complexity and sophistication of the sites are far beyond what has been found—or at least, demonstrated—in Europe. The multiple use of features on Dix's second site throws up so many results that, as with Sir Norman Lockyer's supposed stellar alignments for stone circles in Cornwall, skeptics are going to say that if you draw a lot of straight lines through a number of markers, some of them are bound to point at a significant astronomical event. There is also the difficulty of making proper observations in the New England countryside, now so heavily wooded that it is impossible in many cases to verify visually the accuracy of theoretical calculations. Finally, there is NEARA's ready acceptance of—even insistence on—an Iberian Celtic origin for the sites. A superficial comparison is drawn between some of the stone walls in northern Portugal, and the stone walls of New Hampshire and Vermont. But nobody has ever discovered, or even suggested, that the Portuguese stone walls were aligned astronomically; and there is no tradition anywhere of Celtic erection of megaliths.

Yet the sites are more than intriguing—they may be of fundamental importance in helping to find out about the development of early man. Dix's first site, particularly if excavation uncovers evidence of the sighting position, certainly passes the first stage of proof. As we shall see later, it also has mystical associations that truly and mystifyingly echo the sacred sites of Europe and its megalith builders. On one of the stones is a carefully hewn, portcullislike carving that Dix believes is a subtle geometrical calculus. "I'm sure I'm only scratching the surface. For instance, the two calendar sites I've discovered are fourteen miles apart, but they are on a true north-south alignment, accurate to within about 200 feet. I don't believe this is coincidence—but how on earth did they do it? And are there others stretched out in a great chain?"

UNANSWERED PROBLEMS

Indeed, astroarchaeologists are the first to admit that they can throw light only on part of what we dimly perceive of prehistoric life, and while their discoveries are undeniable, they create formidable difficulties for humanist imagination. For instance, how could megalithic man have overcome the twin problems of the length of time needed between significant lunar observations, and the need for good weather to make them? The climate was warmer then; but on the other hand, the periods when it was also drier were interrupted with long spells of damp Atlantic weather not unlike today's.

Douglas Heggie, of the Institute of Theoretical Astronomy at the University of Cambridge, is among those who are baffled. "Even when most of the sky is free from cloud, by a simple effect of perspective it is at the horizon

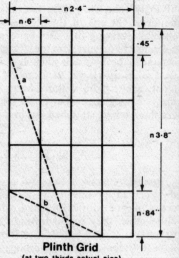

All interior rectangles are of a ratio 3:4:5

Exterior rectangle is of *Phi (φ)* ratio n 1·618 x 1

ⓐ Shadow angle for max. altitude of sun during mid day on the summer solstice.

ⓑ Shadow angle for max. altitude of the sun during mid day on the winter solstice.

Plinth Grid
(at two thirds actual size)

n 2·4″
n ·6″
·45″
n 3·8″
n ·84″

a
b

Geometric rock carving at Calendar Site One; interpretation by Byron S. Dix.

that the cloud appears to be thickest. Even when the sky is completely unobscured by cloud, there is often sufficient haze near the horizon that daylight moonrise is difficult to observe." Working on the generous assumption that the weather would let them observe two successive moonrises half the time (today it would be as few as once in ten); and that half the observations would be ruled out by daylight risings; and that you need at least two successive months to achieve results; and that you get a lunar standstill only twice in eighteen years—then, with these criteria, you can stake out a position only once in seventy years, or about four generations.

Which brings up the problem of passing the body of knowledge on from one generation to the next, without any form of written inheritance. As Richard Atkinson has suggested, it is like "supposing that the *Astronomical ephemeris* is not published, but is transmitted by word of mouth from its compilers to its users in the form of epic verse which must be strictly memorized and reproduced." Nor is it just a question of passing it from grandfather to father to son. Various forms of Stonehenge were in use for more than 1,000 years. Stonehenge I—the outer bank —has been carbon dated to around 2750 B.C., and contained in that is evidence that already ancient man was searching for the answers to the puzzle of the sun and moon. Stonehenge IIIc—the remains of which we see today—was probably completed about 1600 B.C., by which time men knew how to make simple soft bronze implements, and the small, light-boned people who had built the first monuments had largely been replaced by sturdier immigrants, the Beaker People. It may not have been until toward the end of this period that forest clearance had reached the stage where the lower slopes and plains had been cleared by felling and grazing, making possible finally the construction of hundreds of sites embodying similar astronomical and geometric principles.

Nor can astronomers or surveyors tell you why so many circles were felt to be necessary. Nor why the bluestone rocks were so laboriously carted and hauled from Prescelly to Stonehenge when local materials would have suited an observatory just as well. Nor why so many stones were needed for the alignments in Brittany. Nor the answers to dozens of similar questions.

In spite of all the years he has worked, tracking down

the achievements of megalithic man, Professor Thom has
resolutely refused to speculate. The furthest he will go
into guessing at motive is to say: "I'm an engineer. I'm
certain these people were too—and proud of it."

In fact, proving megalithic man's sophistication in astronomical observations is in many ways only the beginning of the story. For there is no reason why he should
have been exclusively concerned with the measurements
of the firmament, important to him though they evidently were—no reason, in other words, to suppose that
he worked out the orbit of the moon and decided that
enough was enough. Once you accept his ability to achieve
this degree of skill in engineering and surveying, you
open the door for a new look at a theory which has been
unfashionable and unacceptable (except to a very few
people) ever since it was first formulated.

Expressed simply, the theory is this: that the whole of
his civilization was locked together by a mysterious cob-
web of interlocking straight lines, the evidence for which
still exists on maps and in the scenery today.

5

LINES OF FORCE

As I was going to Widdecombe Fair,
All along, out along, down along lea . . .

—*Traditional Devonshire folk song,* ANON.

IN ORDER TO WATCH THE MOVEMENTS OF THE SUN AND moon accurately, Stonehenge has to be where it is. Not only has it been positioned locally with marvelous care, so that the natural humps and hollows and contours of the surrounding countryside fit into place, but its position on the face of the earth is also just right. One of the generally accepted points made by Gerald Hawkins was that if its site were moved by only a few miles north or south, the perfect rectangle of its outlying Station Stones would have been useless for the multiple observations that can be achieved. Indeed, a replica of Stonehenge has been built near Washington, D. C., and because its latitude is five degrees too far south, it cannot be used astronomically.

But many people believe Stonehenge was carefully placed for a larger purpose than just as an observatory. It is, according to this theory, a lasting example of ancient man's ability to choose the sites of his major monuments almost as if by magic, so that they can be seen to link with each other and with the natural features of the landscape in an overwhelmingly vast pattern. Sir Norman Lockyer was the first to point out, in 1909, that a line taken from the center of Stonehenge is precisely six miles long to the center of Old Sarum, the original site of Salisbury Cathedral until 1220, when it was pulled down and moved to its present position. The line for the midvinter setting sun at Stonehenge is aligned on Grovely Castle, which is also exactly six miles away. As Grovely Castle in turn is six miles from Old Sarum, these three points, when joined together by straight lines on a map, form a giant equilateral triangle. (It is only on a map that this becomes apparent: Old Sarum is out of sight behind the horizon.) Was megalithic man, once again, showing

his grandiose obsession with numbers and geometric
shapes?

But the Stonehenge–Old Sarum arm of the triangle
contains another, perhaps even larger, mystery. When the
site for the new cathedral was chosen—some 3,000 years
after Stonehenge was completed—it was placed on a dead
straight line continuing from Old Sarum, precisely two
miles farther on. And four and a quarter miles beyond
that, still in a straight line, is the edge of yet another important prehistoric monument, Clearbury Ring. Take the
line up in the opposite direction northward, and it leads
over the great medieval church at Cirencester. In neither
direction is this line astronomically important, but it is
evidently of a mystical or religious significance so powerful that its tradition was intact right up to the time of the
medieval church builders.

In a different way, the principal axis on which Stonehenge is aligned—the midsummer sunrise—is just as impressive. To the northeast, far beyond St. Peter's Mound
on the immediate horizon, a bearing goes past the edge
of Sidbury Hill fort, and on to Inkpen Beacon and Winterbourne prehistoric camp. Back the other way from the
center of Stonehenge, it stretches through to Dorset, over
the Cerne Abbas Giant cut into the chalk hillside, and
finishes on the south coast of Puncknowle Beacon 434
feet above sea level. As the crow flies—and a crow
would find it a lot easier than the men of the megalithic
times who tramped and surveyed the hills and marshes
to set up the line in the first place—the distance is about
seventy miles.

Like the Stonehenge—Salisbury alignment, its existence
only comes to light on a map, and it is perhaps because of
this that the validity of the line, and of thousands like it
all over the country, has been intensely questioned. Draw
a long enough line on a map between any two places, and
it is almost bound to pass over an ancient site here and
there. And if you draw enough of such lines, they join
and cross each other in a manic jumble of triangles and
geometric figures that defies comprehension. But nearly
everybody who has studied the subject for long enough
is convinced that at least some of the lines—"leys," as
they are known—were deliberately chosen, even though
their purposes are as yet obscure, and capable of many
speculative interpretations. They pass over far too many

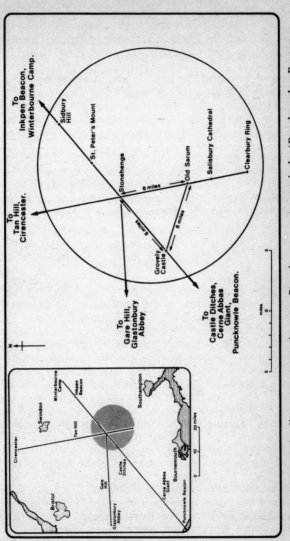

Some suggested alignments centering on Stonehenge: astronomical (Puncknowle Beacon—Winterbourne Camp); geometrical (six-mile isosceles triangle); ley line (Glastonbury Abbey).

sites for coincidence to explain them away, and the evidence of place-names and folklore supports them. On the other hand, the world of archaeology finds ley hunting a subject not even worth discussing; and if mentioned, to be dismissed.

One of the difficulties is that there is, as yet, no recognized person of the scholastic weight of Professor Thom to put together the mass of measurements and observations about ley lines into an unarguably proven thesis. Leys are studied by mathematicians, engineers, architects, geographers, philologers, and a few historians; they also attract dowsers, flying saucer investigators, mystics, astrologers and psychics. One man's proof of a ley line is another man's doubt. Theories of mathematical probability go hand in hand with a form of religiosity. "Our quest may be likened to that of the Holy Grail," wrote Paul Screeton, editor of the *Ley Hunter*.

ALFRED WATKINS

The discovery of leys is universally credited to Alfred Watkins, himself a blend of the two kinds of people drawn to the subject. Born in 1855, he often traveled the countryside of Herefordshire on horseback in his youth. Later, working for his father as a brewer's representative, he came to have a superb working knowledge of the scenery and its ancient remains, many of them by today plowed up or otherwise destroyed. At the same time he was an attentive and easy listener. From childhood, he built up in his mind a storehouse of legend and folklore passed on to him by the local countrymen. He grew up to become the sort of safe local dignitary of whom there are always a few dozen in any British country town. By his middle age an inventor and manufacturer of photographic equipment—notably an exposure meter which was widely used —he became senior partner in a flour milling business, a Justice of the Peace, a governor of local schools, a county councillor, a Fellow of the Royal Photographic Society, and a reliable supporter of worthy causes. Even mild eccentricities such as beekeeping, and his excellent conjuring tricks, were no more than affectionate oddities that lightened his otherwise conventional rural respectability.

His description of the discovery of ley lines, though it

outraged the archaeological world, was anything but sensational in its presentation. His first talk on the subject, when he was in his late sixties, was given to the Woolhope Naturalists Field Club, of which he had once been president, and whose members were mostly leisured or retired, typical of similar societies in counties all over England. Many of their meetings took the form of gentle picnics that led them through the byways and lanes of the Welsh border country, and Watkins's own photographs of this, now in Hereford Museum, give a superb picture of the shadows of Edwardian life in rural England in the 1920s.

Characteristically, he was aware from the beginning that proof was necessary. "What really matters is whether it is a humanly designed fact, an accidental coincidence, or a 'mare's nest,' that mounds, moats, beacons and mark stones fall into straight lines throughout Britain, with fragmentary evidence of trackways on the alignments." So, in a rough and ready way, he made a statistical test to judge the likelihood of straight lines occurring by chance—the most common objection to the theory of ley lines. Watkins took a representative area—the Ordnance Survey sheet 283 of the Andover district—and ringed the fifty-one churches on it. He found eight instances where four fell in a straight line, and one of five. Next he placed fifty-one crosses at random on a piece of paper the same size as the map. Only one straight line of four crosses emerged, and none of five. From then on he, and his followers who tramped the countryside with him, used these figures for their criteria: four to be acceptable, five to be sure. In any case, were further proof needed, there were many instances where they found alignments linking at least double the minimum numbers of sites.

All this time, Watkins kept a secret. He was psychic. He had realized this in childhood, when he carried out experiments in mind reading and prediction, but had repressed it for almost all the rest of his life, partly because he was frightened it would lead him too deeply into the occult, and partly for the hardheaded reason that being known to be psychic was socially and commercially unacceptable. Until late in his life, he gave even his family only an inkling of his gifts.

But on June 30, 1921, when he was sixty-six, they surged to the surface of his mind in an inspired flash of vision. Never before had he been interested in the geographical relationship between ancient monuments, although his knowledge and feel for the shape of the Herefordshire scenery was, by this time in his life, deeply sensitive. Now, as he sat in his motorcar outside the village of Blackwardine on a hot summer's afternoon, the map at which he was idly looking took on a new dimension. Rather as when aerial infrared photographs show up hidden earthworks not otherwise visible, the contours and symbols of the map transformed themselves while he looked.

In his mind's eye, he saw past the familiar landmarks that he knew so well, to a more ancient countryside that had been obscured for thousands of years. Revealed to him, as plainly as when they were still being used, was a web of veinlike lines that ran between hilltop and hilltop, church and castle, mound and moat, holy wells and crossroads—a prehistoric pattern laid down in a long-forgotten past, and lying there overgrown and unnoticed until this moment of rediscovery. His son, Allen Watkins, to whom he many years later described the experience, says that on that day in the car, when the lines emerged from the map, his father learned everything important that he ever felt he needed to know about ley lines "with the exception of beacons, which for some reason did not form part of the vision. They came later. But from that moment on it was just a question of proving the lines on the countryside."

Alfred Watkins, in his first account of his experience, carefully avoided the visionary aspect. He simply confirmed that the discovery of leys had happened on a single day, and that he had followed it up by checking maps. "I knew nothing on June 30th last of what I now communicate, and had no theories," he said. "I followed up the clue of sighting from hilltop, unhampered by other theories, and found it yielding astounding results in all districts, the straight lines to my amazement passing over and over again through the same class of objects, which I soon found to be (or to have been) practical sighting points."

Not until the publication of *The Old Straight Track* three years later does some of the bewitching wonder that he felt shine through:

Imagine a fairy chain, stretched from mountain peak to mountain peak, as far as the eye could reach, and paid out until it touched the "high places" of the earth at a number of ridges, banks, and knowls. Then visualise a mound, circular earthwork, or clump of trees, planted on these high points, and in low points in the valley other mounds ringed round with water to be seen from a distance. Then great standing stones brought to mark the way at intervals, and on a bank leading up to a mountain ridge or down to a ford the track cut deep so as to form a guiding notch on the skyline as you come up. In a bwlch or mountain pass the road cut deeply at the highest place straight through the ridge to show as a notch afar off. Here and there and at two ends of the way, a beacon fire used to lay out the track. With ponds dug on the line, or streams banked up into "flashes" to form reflecting points on the beacon track so that it might be checked when at least once a year the beacon was fired on the traditional day. All these works exactly on the sighting line. The wayfarer's instructions are still deeply rooted in the peasant mind today, when he tells you —quite wrongly now—"You just keep straight on."

LEY HUNTING

It was a discovery that, in his lifetime and after, led him to be both venerated and derided. His admirers formed a Straight Track Club to search out more examples of leys, which were promptly found in every part of Britain. The club lasted until after World War Two, and when it was revived under another name in the 1960s, it was the mystic potential of leys that attracted a new generation of researchers. Nowadays, he is looked on by some of his followers almost as a guru or prophet. "We revere Alfred Watkins, but do not worship him," wrote Paul Screeton in his guide to fringe theories about leys, *Quicksilver Heritage*.

The archaeological world, on the contrary, quickly made the opposite judgment, which it has never since altered: nonsense. The editor of *Antiquity* at the time was O. G. S. Crawford, who—ironically—had indirectly helped Watkins's researches a great deal in his principal job, running the ancient monuments section of the Ordnance Survey. It was by using the evidence of the maps under Crawford's control that Watkins was able to demonstrate the unwavering precision of straight lines linking the hills, mounds and monuments of ancient Britain. Nevertheless, Crawford found Watkins's work absolutely unacceptable, and refused to accept an advertisement for *The Old Straight Track* in *Antiquity*. His attitude prevails. At the end of the Royal Society/British Academy symposium at Oxford in 1972, Professor Stuart Piggott summarized: "Chambered tombs, stone circles, cairns and standing stones need have no relationship to one another, and if we are not careful, we will find alignments as meaningless as the 'old straight tracks' of Alfred Watkins."

But there is a sense in which remarks such as these have an air of defeat—as if certain kinds of potential archaeological evidence are best left uninvestigated, an echo of Daniel Defoe's sentiment about megaliths: "All that can be learn'd of them is, that *there they are.*" For while it is literally true that graves, circles, cairns and so on *need* have no relationship to one another, there is now overwhelming evidence that they probably do have; and while we may not know the meaning of alignments, nevertheless they still apparently exist. Given the findings of Thom, it is hard to understand why there is quite so much archaeological resistance to the hard core of fact in the theorizing of Watkins and his successors. It is not, after all, such a big step from accepting alignments that can be observed from a given site to investigating whether the alignments carry on over the hills and far away to other sites, whatever the reason for their doing so. But the current editor of *Antiquity*, Professor Glyn Daniel, has continued Crawford's tradition of refusing paid advertisements, lately for the bimonthly publication the *Ley Hunter*, a magazine which, while carrying a proportion of somewhat dotty (if harmless) articles, is still the forum of much serious and detailed research.

There is no doubt that, in their own way, ley lines are as difficult to demonstrate as the geometry of Professor Thom's circles. Do you start hunting for leys over a relatively short distance—say, around ten miles—or do you try to find them stretched across the length and breadth of the country? What constitutes a genuine ley "point," bearing in mind that many ancient sites are now obliterated or built over? Then there is the problem of deducing a ley from the imprecision of any map. Lines drawn on a one-inch-to-one-mile—or, nowadays, 1:50,000—map can

be misleading because of the graphic oversimplification
of the mapmaker's symbols. A line drawn by the sharpest
pencil point represents a band up to twenty-five yards
wide. Over very long distances, when sheets of maps have
to be joined and lines continued over them, the curvature
of the earth begins to have a small distorting effect.

Nevertheless, innumerable potential leys, of varying
degrees of probability, have been suggested, and the starting point for everybody interested in the subject is *The
Old Straight Track*. In it Watkins gave precise instructions and definitions. These were to have two drawing
boards and enough draughtsmen's equipment in the way
of T-squares and straight edges so as to be able to trans-
fer a ley line from one Ordnance Survey map to another.
Then, with a compass, make a ⅜-inch diameter circle
around each of the following named points:

(1) Ancient mounds, whether called tumulus, tump,
    barrow, cairn, or other name
(2) Ancient unworked stones—not those marked
    "boundary stone"
(3) Moats, and islands in ponds or lakelets
(4) Traditional or holy wells
(5) Beacon points
(6) Crossroads with place-names, and ancient way-
    side crosses
(7) Churches of ancient foundation, and hermitages
(8) Ancient castles, and old "castle" place-names

After that, it is simply a question of finding how many
of them fall in an apparently straight line, before going
into the field and checking the sight lines. Not only Watkins and his immediate followers, but many people since,
have found that even today, with all the damage to the
countryside that has been caused by heavy farm machin-
ery, it is often still possible to identify stones, mounds or
crosses not marked on the Ordnance Survey. Stumbling
across one of these in a field, according to Allen Watkins,
is "the greatest satisfaction of all—your own visible
proof."

Certainly, at its least demanding level, ley hunting is a
marvelous way of discovering the ancient countryside of
Britain, with its grassy paths, unexplained mounds, fords,
village churches and chapels. There is no doubt that

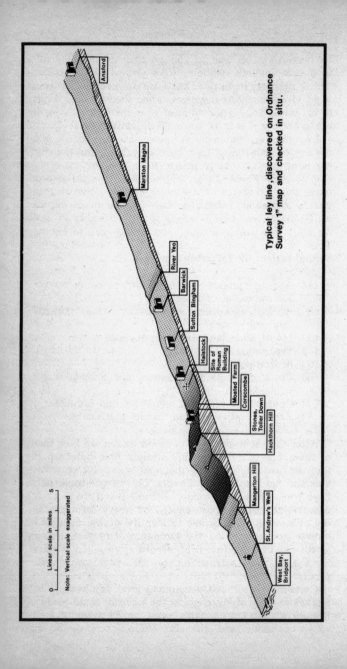

Typical ley line, discovered on Ordnance Survey 1" map and checked in situ.

Linear scale in miles
0   5

Note: Vertical scale exaggerated

Ansford

Marston Magna

River Yeo

Barwick

Sutton Bingham

Halstock

Site of Roman Building

Moated Farm

Corscombe

Stones, Toller Down

Hackthorn Hill

Mangerton Hill

St. Andrew's Well

West Bay, Bridport

many thousands of people, though they have read Watkins, prefer to take his findings as no more than an added way of enjoying fresh country air. It is a mostly private enthusiasm, yet when the *Sunday Times* carried a short article on the subject on its leisure page early in 1974, it attracted more correspondence than any before or since. In it the writer, Brian Jackman, described one of the leys that he himself had found, incorporating many of the landmarks suggested by Watkins.

Starting from Ansford Church alongside the prehistoric fort of Castle Cary in Somerset, it ends up on the south coast at West Bay, Bridport. Staying true to a compass bearing of 21° west of south, it goes through the moat and old church at Marston Magna; over the river at an ancient site in Yeovil five miles away; then, at approximately two-mile intervals, come the churches of Barwick, Sutton Bingham and Halstock; over the site of a Roman building; another two miles, and then in quick succession through a moated farm, the site of an old abbey, and Corscombe church; next a group of standing stones on Toller Down (not marked on the Ordnance Survey); over the summits of Hackthorn Hill and Mangerton Hill to the ancient holy well of St. Andrews in Bridport; and on to the lookout post over the harbor. In a distance of about thirty miles, it passes directly over fifteen acceptable ley points.

STRAIGHT TRACKS

Watkins himself remained faithful to his first concept that what he had discovered was nothing more than indications of a long-lost network of paths and trackways laid down long before the Romans arrived, and his book leans heavily on supplementary evidence from place-names. The word *ley* itself was chosen by him as one of the spellings of the Anglo-Saxon word otherwise written as *lay, lee, lea,* or *leigh.* The *Oxford English Dictionary* gives a number of variations of its most common usage as land "laid down for pasture, grass land": as uncultivated land, as a scythe, an ancient measure of yarn, and as an adjective meaning "fallow" or "unploughed." It also notes in passing its frequent use in place-names, and it was this that encouraged Watkins to believe that it came down from prehistoric times to mean the trackways he was describing. He found "leys" everywhere—on word endings, on moors and mountains, on ponds and lochs, even out to sea, as Ley Rock off Tintagel in Cornwall. Through a very large proportion of them, a ley line could be traced.

He also imagined that he had found the motive for the people who built the roads:

> Presume a primitive people, with few or no enclosures, wanting a few necessities (as salt, flint flakes, and, later on, metals) only to be had from a distance. The shortest way to such a distant point was a straight line, the human way of attaining a straight line is by sighting, and accordingly all these early trackways were straight, and laid out in much the same way that a marksman gets his back and fore sights of his rifle in line with the target.

From the frequency with which *Cole* (or cold), *Dod* (or tot) and *Black* occurred in place names on leys, he built up the theory that these words referred to the Colemen, Dodmen and Blackmen who were the prehistoric surveyors, laying down the leys with their two sighting rods. Distant memories of their work could still be found in dictionary definitions for a "cole-prophet," a wizard, sorcerer or diviner; and in "dod," a stalk, staff, or club, and—in country lore—also a snail whose two horns stick up like staves. "Black," he suggested somewhat more hesitantly and improbably, came from the blackened faces that the surveyors would get when lighting their beacon fires.

Place-names provided him with other clues for his theory of the origin of trackways, including:

BELL: Perhaps related to the Babylonian sun god Bel or Baal. Often found contained in the names of beacon hills, notifying the sites where within living memory balefires were ceremonially lit at certain times of the year.
BROAD: Referring to a much-used track, and frequently found in leys.
BURY (Burg, Borough, etc.): Settlements, now towns

or cities, originally based on the burial mounds or barrows of neolithic man.

WHITE and WICK: Referring to tracks along which loads of salt were carried, the wick deriving from salt marshes such as Nantwich and Middlewich.

These names are, of course, so common that once again the question of probability arises, and on statistical grounds alone most archaeologists would reject Watkins out of hand. But, in fact, a number of mathematical formulae have been suggested to test the chance factor in ley hunting, of which probably the most convincing is the one prepared by Peter Furness for the *Ley Hunter* and reproduced in the Appendix to this book. Unlike some others, it takes account of the varying density of ley points on a map, and in summary, its main conclusions from a sample map are these: a line of four points is more likely than not to happen by chance, in which case supplementary evidence in the form of place-names, or a common starting point or crossing point with other leys, is needed. Similarly, even a five-point ley could be one of the two that, statistically, occurred by chance on his sample map. But there is only a 1 in 200 chance of a six-point ley, and 1 in 1,000 for a seven-point ley.

Since we know that, using Watkins's criteria, there are many leys containing this number of points and more, it is almost a statistical certainty that some ley lines, at least, exist. The ley points to note have been brought up to date by Paul Screeton, to take into account both the changes in modern map descriptions, and further research work by himself and others. On maps, rings should be drawn around: stone circles, standing and symbol stones, camps, tumuli, cairns, dolmens, moats and mounds; pre-Reformation churches, cathedrals, priories, chapels, monasteries; castles; and ancient and holy wells. When checking ley lines *in situ,* look for: mark stones such as mileposts and ancient crosses, tree clumps, skyline notches, fords, ponds, springs, false hills, and mountain peaks.

Looking at this list, it is not difficult to appreciate the other main archaeological criticism of Watkins: that his mark points include sites covering thousands of years of history and prehistory, so that it is absurd to suggest that they mark ancient trackways. Ley hunters have a number of replies to this. First, they will point to the statistical evidence: if all these disparate places are falling on a dead straight line more often than chance would predict, then *something* made it happen like this. Second, they suggest that the sites were in continuous use from neolithic times onward, which careful excavation would probably reveal. Third, they broaden the interpretation of ley lines in a way described more fully later in this book. For just as Thom's astronomical alignments do not, in themselves alone, hint at the motives of megalithic man, similarly few people now think that Watkins's theory of trackways is the whole answer. Excavated fragments have revealed parts of ancient trackways along ley lines, and these were sometimes used by the Romans as the foundation for their major roads. But judged just as paths, many leys are highly improbable. Frequently, they climb the steepest side of a hill, go through bogs when there is dry land on either side, or cross rivers where they are deep and not shallow.

PRIMARY LEYS

Academically, the most conclusive inquiry into the existence of leys can be found in a field survey by John Michell, one of Britain's best-known proponents of original and unorthodox interpretations of prehistory, who has, through his writings, developed and expanded the pioneering work of Watkins. In 1973, he studied forty-four sites and described them in his book *The Old Stones of Land's End*. To avoid any criticism that he was including points that were of later origin, such as churches, he measured only menhirs, stone circles, and dolmens, all of them at least 4,000 years old. The area, on the western tip of Cornwall, contains in its few square miles more evidence of these monuments than any other place of comparable size. In every case he used an Ordnance Survey map of six inches to one mile, measured with a steel ruler, and checked by prismatic compass in the field.

In many places, he was treading in the footsteps of Sir Norman Lockyer, and found again what had been found at Stonehenge and elsewhere—that supposedly astronomical lines to mark points on the horizon often led on to other stones or sites. He discovered that almost every one of the ancient centers he visited was in perfect alignment with two or more others, "often placed at the extreme limit of visibility so that only its tip showed above the horizon." He concluded that:

> Some of the alignments could have occurred by chance, but not all. As an example, one of Lockyer's astronomical lines, when extended eastwards, revealed three other stones, two standing, one recumbent, and none previously recorded, on the same alignment. The occurrence of these three stones, together with the circle and outlying stone on an alignment of established astronomical significance, is surely proof of design.

Other researchers, their findings derived from ley-hunting activity in Britain, France and America, have individually contributed hundreds of alignments of up to a dozen ley points, drawn partly from a map, and partly by the discovery of other evidence such as small marker stones, or notches in distant hills, that could only be noticed during field work. The difficulty in evaluating them lies mainly in the sheer number and variety. Here, a hill— Cley Hill near Warminster, Wiltshire is an example— seems to be the focal point for a large number of leys; there an unmistakable alignment of churches and ancient sites peters out at either end into nothing; some of Watkins's own lines are convincing as tracks over part of the ley, yet stretch credulity when they are extended over the whole distance. Taken together, there is far too much positive evidence of alignments for it to be ignored; but nobody has yet carried out the daunting research of sorting out the convincing leys from the unconvincing ones.

It may be that the first thing to do, in the light of Professor Thom's discoveries, is to establish what standards of accuracy have to be applied to ley lines. At the moment, a fair assessment of the evidence for megalithic alignments might be that over short distances, particularly where they can be observed from horizon to horizon, a very rigid standard of straightness can be applied. But over long distances—the so-called "primary leys"—the case for alignments is unproven, or can only be judged by more flexible rules.

For instance, John Michell was much struck by the way the major ancient holy sites were carefully placed so

that they were apparently linked by unerringly straight
lines. He noted three remarkable examples: first, the
Glastonbury–Avebury axis that formed the central part of
an astonishing alignment beginning in the farthest western
outpost of Britain at St. Michael's Mount in the bay near
Lands End, and finishing in the North Sea after passing
through another great medieval religious center at Bury
St. Edmunds—thus marking in the course of some 380
miles the longest unbroken stretch of land in southern
Britain; second, the Salisbury Cathedral–Stonehenge link
that had been found earlier by both Lockyer and Watkins,
which continued over Tan Hill, Cirencester Church,
Cleeve Hill, Bredon Hill, and up into the Lake District, a
distance of nearly 300 miles; third, the connection
between Glastonbury and Stonehenge approximately
forty miles away, where the track starts off from the Abbey along a Dod Lane, passes over a prominent ley center
at Gare Hill, and finishes at Stonehenge.

Now each of these lines suffers in different ways from
lack of what archaeologists or surveyors would regard as
definite proof. In the first one, the evidence for the Glastonbury–Avebury length, and the area immediately surrounding, is powerful: churches, hills shaped artificially,
remnants of tracks, a holy well—all these mark the way.
But when it is stretched the full length it misses its objective at either end: by half a mile at Bury St. Edmunds,
and by two miles at St. Michael's Mount—perhaps still an
impressive achievement, but not up to the highest
megalithic standards, and not enough to convince that it
was ever intended or laid out in quite this way.

The second line suffers similarly. Salisbury–Stonehenge
can be taken as undoubted. But the rest of the mark
points are so infrequent (and also fractionally off a dead
straight course) that coincidence cannot be ruled out.
Again with Glastonbury–Stonehenge: Dod Lane at the
beginning may be significant, but in the whole of the remaining forty miles it is only one hill and one ruined abbey that still remain to show where the trackway might
have been. Nor is the case for ley lines improved when
other researchers, less meticulous than Michell, impose
extensions to the lines that are demonstrably untrue, as in
the case of those who have tried to continue Glastonbury–
Stonehenge to Canterbury Cathedral in Kent.

Philip Heselton, another ley hunter, now regrets his

premature announcement of a "Great Isosceles Triangle" marked out on the face of England. Its apex was put at the Arbor Low stone circle in Derbyshire (from which between 50 and 150 leys are said to emanate), its left-hand point at St. Michael's church, Othery (by chance or not, almost exactly on Michell's Avebury line), and the right-hand point at West Mersea, Essex. Heselton now says: "It has the same problem as many leys. The countryside has been so defaced, and so small a proportion of megalithic remains can be found, that all you get are tantalizing glimpses of the lines that were once there. I still think there was a triangle like the one I described. But only little bits can be traced, and there isn't really enough to stand up to a serious scientific investigation. I think it would probably be better if we ley-hunters concentrated more on the areas which we know, and can prove to be true."

Certainly, ley hunters have no chance of their research being accepted by the academic world while so much of it is loosely presented; and in any case, judging by the archaeologists' cautious record in accepting the validity of Professor Thom's findings, it will be a long time before even the proven leys are absorbed into archaeological theory. The gulf between the two sides was encapsulated in a brief exchange of letters between Professor Richard Atkinson and a solicitor from Abergavenny, John Williams, who has made a lifetime study of stone monuments, and has an alternative theory of straight lines. His researches—and he is a careful and thorough man who has personally visited, mapped and annotated more than 3,000 sites—had led him to suggest a link between standing stones and underground water, and also a frequently occurring angle of 23½° (or its multiple) in the relationship of lines between ancient sites.

Atkinson wrote back enclosing a map of railway stations, a number of them linked in a straight line, and explained that this was his standard reply to those misguided enough to believe in the existence of prehistoric straight lines. Aha, replied Williams, you have proved my point—like railways, they were put there with an organized scientific motive. To which Atkinson responded that he felt there was no purpose in prolonging the correspondence.

To quote Stuart Piggott again, writing about henge

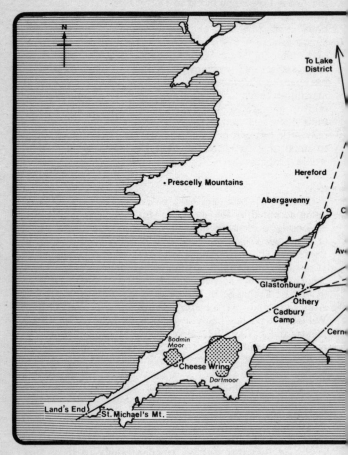

Some suggested primary leys in Britain, and other locations of megalithic significance.

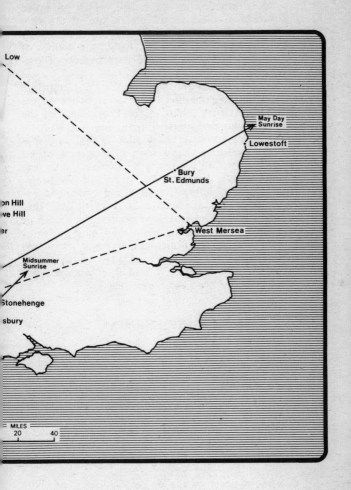

Low

May Day
Sunrise

Lowestoft

Bury
St. Edmunds

on Hill
ve Hill

er

West Mersea

Midsummer
Sunrise

Stonehenge

sbury

MILES
20   40

circles: "Since we are dealing with non-literate societies, we have no information on the beliefs which prompted the construction of these sacred places, nor of the rites performed within them: the nature of purely archaeological evidence is such that it cannot, within the bounds of permissible inference, inform us of such aspects of prehistoric peoples."

Dr. John Coles, a lecturer in archaeology at Cambridge University, who has published two popular books on the subject as well as being editor of the Proceedings of the rigorously thorough Prehistoric Society, and who is openminded enough to embrace unorthodox as well as orthodox help in excavations, expresses the uneasiness of his colleagues like this: "In a country so abundant with prehistoric monuments, barrows and cairns, stone circles and standing stones, impressive forts and embanked enclosures, there has accumulated a body of opinion that concerns itself with alignments and positions of stones or trackways or field boundaries, themselves entirely legitimate areas for research; sometimes, however, these are considered as evidence for extraordinary, almost supernatural, events . . . completely and utterly unrecorded by any scientifically observable evidence."

MEGALITHIC ENIGMAS

Yet the enigmas of megalithic times, unsolved by archaeological methods, sometimes seem to be precisely what Coles complains of—"extraordinary, almost supernatural." Why the obsession with mathematics and geometry? Why the importance of all that stone? Why the straight lines to the limits of the horizon and beyond to the heavens? Why the effort to build such mammoth earthworks? How on earth did megalithic man organize science without writing—or did he have help from elsewhere?

Or take the mystery of the single standing stone. Nobody who has stood by one, touched one, and thought about one for a few moments, can fail to be engrossed and baffled by the kind of society that put it there. Its sheer age—5,000 years? 7,000 years? 9,000 years?—makes it hauntingly remote. In the whole world, it is perhaps the most ancient of man's monuments. If you push one over, you will usually find nothing beneath it but earth. Yet somebody, once, put it there in its exact position, deliberately, having dragged its dead weight a distance that may have been a few hundred yards or many miles.

In trying to guess at its purpose, an archaeologist would measure it and map it, analyze it and compare it with other stones, bring beams and ropes, lift it from the ground, and see what was underneath. If he found cremation ashes (of which there is sometimes a small amount) he would perhaps conclude that it may have marked the burial place of an important person of those times, and additionally served a ritual or totemic purpose for the community. On the other hand, an astronomer would look at its place in relation to the countryside and perhaps find that it aligned significantly with a point on the horizon that coincided with an important cosmic event. A ley hunter would join it on a map with other ancient sites, and—if he was a purist follower of Watkins—conclude that it marked part of an ancient trackway. Somebody from "the lunatic fringe or dotty archaeology" (as John Coles puts it) might say that the stone gave off a supernatural power, which was harnessed by people in those times. At which point (John Coles again) "amateurs and professionals tend to part company abruptly."

Yet all four could be right—the archaeologist the most comprehensively so, and the dotty archaeologist the most compellingly. Just because the suggestions of the latter are unlikely and unorthodox does not necessarily mean that they are valueless. Sometimes, using the same sort of scientific instrumentation that accompanies any modern excavation, it is even possible to prove them, at least partially. It was a Welsh water diviner, Bill Lewis, who prompted me to arrange for measurements and tests to be made around a twelve-foot-high standing stone near Crickhowell in South Wales. Lewis made several claims about the power of the stone, the basic one being that the stone contained or emitted a force that he could sense, and which periodically waxed and waned, and which he wanted to find out if this could be scientifically demonstrated.

John Taylor, professor of mathematics at King's College, London, who has done a great deal of research into people with so-called psychic or paranormal abilities, thought that, rare though the phenomenon was, Lewis might be recognizing subtle changes in the magnetic field of the

earth; there was a certain amount of French research that
seemed to show that water diviners were sensitive to electromagnetism. So Taylor provided a gaussmeter, which
measures static magnetic field strength, and a young
Argentinian physicist from Imperial College in London,
Dr. Eduardo Balanovski, went with me to check if there
was anything odd or anomalous about the stone or the
site.

This particular stone, half-covered by hawthorn in a
hedge standing midway up a hill above the river Usk, is
typically baffling and sparse of evidence. It is big—perhaps one of the dozen or so biggest in Wales. It is in an
area where there are many other signs of megalithic life
—cairns, stones, burial chambers, and so on—which the
scattered farmsteads have left relatively undisturbed. It
has never been excavated, nor even properly surveyed. It
does not seem to have any astronomical bearing. It does
not mark any obvious natural feature such as a hilltop.
It does not appear to lie on a clear or significant ley or
other alignment.

But, said Lewis, it contains power.

Before visiting the site, Balanovski put on record some
of the things that were known about the subject. Minor
anomalies in electromagnetic fields were caused by the
presence of particles of iron in the stone, or by the
composition of the stone being slightly different from the
ground nearby. These were not usually great. The unit of
measurement of magnetic field strength is called a gauss,
and it was thought that good water diviners could distinguish the difference between levels of intensity of a few
thousandths of a gauss. In general, the magnetic field
strength of the earth is remarkably stable, averaging 0.47
of a gauss in Britain, increasing to 0.70 of a gauss near the
poles, and decreasing to 0.30 of a gauss in some parts of
equatorial regions. In a given area—an acre of countryside,
say—he would expect the anomalies to be counted in a
few hundredths, and as an indication of how minute these
changes are, the gaussmeter could detect differences of
one-thousandth of a gauss.

What Balanovski found surprised him very much indeed.

After checking the background levels and setting the
meter at zero, he pointed the measuring probe at the stone.
The needle on the dial shot up, showing an anomaly far
greater than the few thousandths or hundredths of a gauss

that would have been normal. Just how much greater, it was too early to tell—he needed more sophisticated equipment under controlled conditions. But the indications were that it might even be of the order of half a gauss, the maximum capacity of the meter.

That first day's observations were sufficiently surprising to start a longer and more detailed research project, in which John Taylor tested some of Bill Lewis's even more startling suggestions about the power and purpose of standing stones. But as these tests are associated with the speculations of fringe prehistorians and are still incomplete, they are looked at along with other "soft" evidence in the second part of this book.

Balanovski has no doubt that the basic anomaly—that there is indeed power in and around a standing stone—is significant: "The point is that a water-diviner told us about it, and then we went there and found something measurable. It may be that the stone contains, geologically, the reason for the anomaly. Or it may be caused by something that we don't yet understand. But I do not personally believe that the stone was accidentally chosen or accidentally placed. The people who put it there knew about its power, even if they didn't know about electromagnetism."

It is not decrying the scholarship of archaeology to say that its disciplines inhibit the way archaeologists think. Toward the end of the academic furor over the findings of Professor Thom, Richard Atkinson expressed a *cri de cœur* that struck a chord among many of his fellows:

It is important that non-archaeologists should understand how disturbing to archaeologists are the implications of Thom's work, because they do not fit the conceptual model of the prehistory of Europe which has been current during the whole of the present century, and even now is only beginning to crumble at the edges. . . . In terms of this model, it is almost inconceivable that mere barbarians on the remote north-west fringes of the continent should display a knowledge of mathematics and its applications hardly inferior, if at all, to that of Egypt at about the same date, or that of Mesopotamia considerably later.

It is hardly surprising, therefore, that many prehistorians either ignore the implications of Thom's work, because they do not understand them, or resist them because it is more comfortable to do so. I have myself gone through the latter process; but I have come to the conclusion that to reject Thom's thesis because it does not conform to the model of prehistory on which I was brought up involves also the acceptance of improbabilities of an even higher order. I am prepared, in other words, to believe that my model of European prehistory is wrong, rather than that the results presented by Thom are due to nothing but chance.

Thom, sponsored by Atkinson, is now a Fellow of the Society of Antiquaries, an olympian body with a superb library next to the Royal Academy in Burlington House, which has sat for two centuries in judgment on archaeological innovations, and has a splendid tradition of blackballing upstarts and their like. Thus, poacher turned gamekeeper, after upsetting the established textbooks of prehistory he himself becomes one of the guardians of 100 years of painstaking scholarship. Such people teach how to interpret the past through the careful examination of statistics, measurements and excavations. They usually prefer to record what can be seen now, than to speculate on the nature of life in the distant past that brought it about.

By using their approach, by digging, analyzing, cataloguing and comparing, we can find out much of what was going on, when it happened, who did it, and where. But not why, and not altogether how. We know, for instance, that megalithic man thought it essential to make astronomical observations and to predict exactly the right time of year—but not why. We know the probable way he dragged the bluestones from Prescelly to Stonehenge—but not his purpose for doing so. We know that he reshaped and marked the landscape—but not his motive.

So if we hope to find something of the working of man's mind in megalithic times, we must look for other clues and shreds of evidence. Some of them may be intangible and unorthodox, but (like the power sensed by Bill Lewis) still worth pursuing for a fuller picture of what was going on: legend and folklore, the instinct of diviners and psychics, the distant echoes of pre-Christian worship.

So strangely great were the achievements of man in the

lost world of 5,000 years ago that the ambitions of its
people must have been fired by forces totally different from
our own, and perhaps almost imcomprehensible to most
of us today. That these forces were mysterious, primitive
and powerful, there is little doubt. To begin to understand
them we must open our minds and learn to expect the unlikely and the extraordinary; perhaps even the supernatural.

For in Professor Thom's words: "We must no longer
assert that these people could not possibly have known
this or done that."

PART

II

CHAPTER

6

DIVINING THE PAST

*In treating of the superstition and ROCK-MONU-
MENTS of the Druids, I may seem too conjec-
tural to those who will make no allowances for
the deficiencies of history, nor be satisfy'd with
any thing but evident truths; but where there is
no Certainty to be obtain'd Probabilities must.
Conjectures are no faults, but when they are either
advanc'd as real truths, or too copiously pursued,
or peremptorily insisted upon as decisive. In sub-
jects of such distant ages, where history will so
often withdraw her taper, Conjecture may sometimes strike a new light, and the truths of Antiquity be more effectually pursu'd, than where
people will make no guess at all. One Conjecture
may move the veil, another partly remove it, and
a third happier still, borrowing light and strength
from what went before, may wholly disclose what
we want to know.*

—Dr. William Borlase, *Antiquities of
the County of Cornwall,* 1754

WATCHING A GOOD DOWSER AT WORK IS A DRAMATIC EX-perience, if only because of the element of surprise. With-out warning, his divining rod will spring upward with such force that it will strike him firmly in the chest. Or his pendulum, stationary or gently swinging, will suddenly re-volve fiercely as he walks over a certain point. Nor does it seem to matter where the dowser is—the same reaction happens if he is in an airplane, in a car, or on horseback. To any onlooker, it is at first deeply baffling—an uncanny and even (for the skeptical) doubtful spectacle. But famil-iarity nearly always brings acceptance and before long it appears no more disconcerting than other highly developed but mysterious gifts of man that are part learned, part instinctive, like a painter's eye for form and color, or a conductor's ability to convey his musical perception to an orchestra.

In its most common form, water divining, dowsing is so widely known and used that it is accepted even without being scientifically understood. It would be hard to find a Water Department anywhere in the world that has not employed a dowser, often on a regular basis. Government departments and ministries, bodies such as the National Trust, telephone companies, and other large firms, form one end of the list of occasional employers; at the other end are all the farmers, estate agents, golf clubs and land-owners who have had it proved to their own satisfaction that a dowser can not only find water and other sub-stances beneath the earth, but specify in what quantity and at what depth. There are countless authenticated examples of this—thousands would not be an exaggeration—and the kinds of people who have been helped include archaeolo-gists. John Coles gives an example in his book *Field Archaeology in Britain:*

Dowsers appear to be able to detect the presence of metals, and differences in superficial geological deposits. There is no doubt that buried ditches can be discovered by this method, the explanation for which has yet to be discovered. . . . At Pitnacree in Perthshire, dowsing suggested that a barrow was not encircled by a ditch, and that the barrow had been placed upon a low gravel bank in the otherwise sandy terrace of the Tay; the edges of the gravel were detected by dowsing. Both suggestions were confirmed by excavation.

The kinds of people who have successfully dowsed cover as wide a spectrum as the people they have helped. A member of the British Society of Dowsers (there are similar societies in many countries), which has approximately 650 members, said at a meeting in 1974 that he could produce an alphabetical list of their occupations that would cover "architects, bus-drivers, chartered accountants, dustmen, university professors, ventriloquists, watchmakers, xylophonists, yachtsmen and zoologists."

If he was exaggerating, it was only to emphasize the point that all dowsers feel is the most important of all: that dowsing is an absolutely natural activity which has been with man since the earliest times, which has been lost through inactivity or suppression, but which can usually be regained with practice by most people. They believe that while some people are supremely gifted dowsers, and others apparently unable to dowse at all, this is spread through the population in much the same way as intelligence, with a very small percentage of geniuses matched by an equally small percentage who are severely subnormal, and the great majority in the middle capable of improvement through experience. To a practiced dowser, the sensation of dowsing is unmistakable even if inexplicable. It is at least as real and unavoidable as the feelings experienced through the other five senses of sight, sound, touch, taste and smell. For this reason, most dowsers do not understand why it seems more difficult for outsiders to accept dowsing than for the color-blind to accept the existence of colors, or the tone-deaf to believe in music. Nor do they believe dowsing is necessarily more obscure than the sense of smell, which is readily ex-

perienced by nearly all people, but is equally incapable of
detailed scientific analysis.

All that is needed, they say, is an uncluttered and
open mind. This was understood well enough by the
seventeenth-century writer William Cookworthy, of Plym-
outh, who reported:

> The rod must be held with indifference, for if the
> mind is occupied by doubts, reasoning, or other op-
> eration that engages the animal spirits, it will divert
> their powers from being exerted in this process, in
> which their instrumentality is absolutely necessary:
> from whence it is that the rod constantly answers in
> the hands of peasants, women and children, who
> hold it simply without puzzling their minds with
> doubts and reasonings. Whatever may be thought of
> this observation it is a very just one, and of great
> consequence in the practice of the rod.

Another view, which dowsers hold unanimously, is that
the sensation of successful dowsing, while unmistakable,
is entirely personal. As one has explained: "We all say we
know what it is, even if we don't know its source and
mechanism. But really we mean we know *what it is for us,*
and I suspect that this is different for every single one of
us." This individualism is reflected in the multitude of contraptions of metal and wood used and demonstrated by
different dowsers. Basically, there are three distinct types:
L-shaped angle rods, held one in each hand so that the
long arms of the rods, horizontal to the ground and pointing forward, swing this way and that as the dowser works;
a pendulum, which can be stationary, oscillate (swing),
or gyrate (revolve) either clockwise or anticlockwise; and
the traditional divining rod held by the hands in a state of
tense equilibrium so that it may move suddenly upward or
downward.

Within these categories the variations are limitless. The
rods are sometimes of copper or brass, fitted with collars
to enable them to swing freely, and of all weights and
lengths. Pendulums, too, are of all shapes and sizes, although the most common one is like a small plumb bob
as used in bricklaying. A noted French dowser, M.
Fourcart, had a collection of more than 1,000, which he
used for different kinds of dowsing. They included such

oddities as a monocle, a brazil nut, and a variety of glass beads. For the divining rod, a pair of whalebones bound together at one end, or the traditional hazel, are most often used. But so is copper wire, or willow, rowan, apple, privet, whitethorn, rhododendron and other trees. Any dowsing conference will also have a number of homemade, Heath Robinson contraptions, which are claimed by their owners to be especially sensitive; and so no doubt they are, for their owners personally. A few good dowsers need nothing at all—a tingling of the fingertips, or a feeling of resistance as they move their hands, is enough. Many dowsers believe that there is far too much mystique about the instrument, which is important only insofar as it helps the dowser to recognize a reaction. Anyone can make a pair of workable angle rods out of a metal coat hanger, a pendulum from roughly carving a small lump of wood and jamming a length of cotton in it, or a divining rod out of two plastic knitting needles with the points shoved into a cork.

EXPERIMENTS AND THEORIES

Most dowsers were introduced to the art by watching another dowser at work and then having a try themselves, and simple experiments for newcomers have been devised. Tom Lethbridge, the archaeologist who was able to date Stonehenge correctly, used to suggest holding a short pendulum, about three inches long, between thumb and finger, and letting it swing between two coins placed a few inches apart on a table. If the coins are the same metal and value—say, two 10-penny pieces—a natural rhythm will set up in the pendulum, keeping it swinging in a straight line between them. If someone then replaces one of the coins with a different kind of coin—say, a 2-penny piece—the pendulum will swing out of line and probably begin to gyrate. Switch the coins back again, and the pendulum will return to its swing.

Major-General James Scott Elliot, a president of the British Society of Dowsers for some years, thinks it is easier to imagine the pendulum as simply an instrument to find out the answer "yes" or "no" to a question. If you switch on an electric light, hold a pendulum over the cord, and ask the question (in your mind): "Is this cord live or not?" the chances are that the pendulum, instead of staying stationary or oscillating, will begin to gyrate clockwise or anticlockwise. If you try the experiment again, this time with the light switched off, and ask the same question, the pendulum will probably gyrate in the opposite direction. The purpose of the exercise is to establish for yourself which way the pendulum gyrates when you want to find the answer "yes" or "no." Afterward, it is just a question of practice, using common household objects to experiment with. Those suggested often include:

Put four similar coins and one different, under a cloth; seek the different one. (The question you ask must be precise, such as "Is the different coin here?" The pendulum's "yes" or "no" gyration will tell you.)

Take half a dozen or so black playing cards and one red; shuffle and lay face downward on the table: seek the red one.

Get someone to hide a note or an object in the shelf of a bookcase. Work along the bookcase with a pendulum and locate it.

Take half a dozen cups of water. Ask someone to dissolve a little salt in one. Find the cup with salt water.

How successful anybody is at these tests, beginners or not, may depend on a number of unmeasurable factors: how good an innate dowser the person is, his or her state of mind, the influence of outsiders—almost anything including, some dowsers would say, the phase of the moon. For the truth is that although expert dowsers would regard the exercises as very basic, none of them would guarantee to get the answers right all the time, and on unresponsive days no better than chance would predict. The very best water dowsers, of whom there are only a handful in the whole of Great Britain, can claim and prove a success rate of at least 90 percent, but they of all people know that dowsing is a tantalizing, personal and irrational gift, and that because of its unpredictability, it is extremely difficult to produce enough of the repeated and repeatable experiments demanded for scientific proof.

"When we try for these kind of tests, they so often go wrong," says one such dowser. "Expecting or hoping for a specific result, anxiety that we'll fail, distraction caused by other people on the site, self-consciousness—any of these things can lead to a misleading result."

In speculating about the origin and nature of dowsing,

the view of the majority is probably the same as it has been for at least the last 200 years: that there is some unknown wave or emanation, so far undetectable by scientific methods, which sensitive people are able to pick up. According to this theory, every single thing in the world, now and in the past, has given out an individual wave pattern, and dowsers act like superb radio receivers, able to tune in to what they are looking for. The "human wireless set" is an analogy much used by this school of thought, and there is, of course, no doubt that the human body is capable of acting as a receiver of waves, as holding a radio aerial and thus amplifying the sound will show. W. H. Trinder, in his classic book *Dowsing,* published in 1939, summarized: "Just as artists are responsive to the vibrations of colours, and musicians to the vibrations of notes, so is the dowser responsive to the dowsing ray."

Most research in dowsing has therefore been devoted to the search for the nature of these supposed rays, and to identify and classify how the wavelengths differ between one object and another. Tom Lethbridge, like many other dowsers, and following in the footsteps of some French research, found that his pendulum reacted at different lengths to different things. Held over a piece of ash wood, for instance, it would gyrate only if the length of cotton suspending it was six inches long. For a piece of carbon it had to be twelve inches, for aluminum twenty-five inches, iron thirty-two inches, and so on. Through a long series of tests he found that, in his hands, the pendulum would gyrate at a specific length for each and every object, and he began a system of classification which he hoped could apply universally. Of course, as he discovered the length or "rate" for more and more substances, he found that many of them overlapped: thirty-two inches worked for aspirin, and for the wild flower violet, as well as for iron.

But he was sure that from each substance came an invisible ray, unaffected by distance, and his belief in this theory led to some astonishing results, particularly in finding hidden objects and unknown archaeological sites. His method was to "tune" his pendulum to the length which, he knew from past experiments, reacted to substances in the object he was looking for. Then, pointing his left hand toward the mid-distance and slowly scanning from left to right, he would wait for the pendulum to react by gyrating.

That would pinpoint one direction. By taking sight lines from other directions and closing in on the point that was indicated, he could identify to within an inch or so the object he was seeking. He wrote in his book *ESP—Beyond Time and Distance:*

Perhaps I should say that I have done this act of finding buried objects on many occasions and in front of many witnesses. The only complete failure was due to a curious chance. A woman guest ran out into the court and returned triumphantly to say that she had buried a halfpenny, and I couldn't find it. No more could I find it, for the simple reason that I tuned in the pendulum for copper (30.5 inches) without realising that copper coins are made of some alloy which had a rate of 32.5 inches. The perpetrator of this offence went off with a knowing smile thinking that she had exposed the pendulum as being bogus. But she was the only loser. We found a brass pin, a cobalt glass bead and a silver-plated copper spoon with the plating peeling off the copper, under the turf near where she was supposed to have planted the spurious coin. There were also several nodules of a copper compound lawn dressing.

Though the theory of rays undoubtedly worked for Lethbridge, as an all-encompassing explanation the approach has many shortcomings. For instance, it is impossible to conceive the infinite size of the encyclopedic catalogue that would be needed to record and categorize the different types of ray and wavelength for each object. Nor could such an approach ever be "scientific"—the differing and variable results from one dowser to another would see to that, with pendulum lengths varying from one person to another, with this man's rod springing up where the other's sprang down, and this woman's pendulum gyrating clockwise where another's went anticlockwise. It may, after all, be literally impossible to write down in words something that is beyond the five senses.

So a simpler and more universal theory has been proposed. It relies on identifying a basic and natural instinct that, dowsers believe, has been with man since his ancient beginnings and can still be seen in, for instance, the apparently supernatural ability of the Australian aborigine to "know" when something has happened many miles away. According to this theory, the rod or pendulum becomes simply an indicator of what a dowser's mind is able to perceive when he switches off all the normal ways in which the brain works. By obliterating, perhaps only briefly, all his acquired learning and experience, and by ignoring the five conscious senses, he is able to let an unconscious and natural sensitivity function; and when he has found what he is looking for, this is displayed in a movement of the instrument he is handling. The movement and the instrument may react differently for different people. But it will be consistent for each individual, and providing he knows how to interpret the code he has established (as by letting the pendulum tell him "yes" or "no"), his results will be unambiguous.

Although vaguer and more mystical than science would like, this theory goes a long way to explaining the almost trancelike concentration that some dowsers find necessary if they are to be successful. In trying to describe how they feel when dowsing, many of them use phrases such as "you have to shut off your day-to-day senses," or "you empty your brain and use something else," or "you've got to keep your brain out of it." One says:

> When I start working with my tools, I shut the brain out and simply rely on the mind. The nearest way I can describe it visually is to say that the mind works in the dark like a cat's whiskers, or a blind man seeking in front of him with his fingers. My tools work like his fingers, they tell me when I've got there, when I've found it. I can't tell you how the mind knows—nobody can. People talk about universal knowledge which we tap into; some Indians call it higher sensitivity.

Being a mental rather than a physical explanation, the theory remains valid when it is applied to perhaps the most puzzling and extraordinary of all the proved results of dowsing: the ability of dowsers to pinpoint what they are looking for, completely accurately, simply by using a pendulum over a map of the area concerned.

DISTANT DOWSING

D. M. Lewis, a British scientist who can himself map dowse, told a meeting in 1974 that it "strains one's imagination to believe that a paper clip on the end of a cotton thread can tell us the location of underground streams in the Australian outback." He was not, however, questioning the fact that spectacularly successful mineral- and water-finding dowsing has been achieved in this way—only that it was absurd to imagine the paper clip doing the job rather than the mind of the dowser. In order to map dowse, the operator opens a map, holds his pendulum over it, and uses his other hand to point or mark. Then he silently asks the question whose answer he is seeking—such as "Is the water here?" "Is the person here?" "Is there a tunnel here?" Then he searches his way over the map with his pendulum until he is satisfied with the result.

So normal and matter-of-fact (to them) is this procedure that many dowsers much prefer to do their work first of all in private on a map before going out into the field and proving their results by site dowsing and then excavation. It is, they point out, much more convenient and less tiring than walking about muddy fields not knowing where to look, and for many of them the lack of distraction is another advantage. They might add that, for those who are skeptical about dowsing, map dowsing allows no ambiguity. If you work on a map and plot out that something hidden is in such-and-such a place, either it is or it isn't. Of the many authenticated examples in the archives of the British Society of Dowsers, about a dozen refer to the finding of missing people or bodies for the police. Typical of these would be the work carried out by an Irish dowser, Thomas Trench, who was contacted after an inquiry by the Belgian police. They wanted to trace the body of one of their officers killed in the Brussels riots of February 1966, and taken away in a car by the murderers. Trench, with a photograph of the man in front of him, first of all worked on a small-scale map of Belgium, and found his pendulum reacted to a spot near Blankenberge. He asked for a large-scale map of the area, and with this—working from 500 miles away on a map of a forty-mile coastline he had never visited—identified the position of the body to within about fifty yards.

In the same mystifying manner, map dowsing can also be used to discover the date of a site or an object marked on the map, with an equally astonishing rate of success. The methods vary slightly, but the intention and the effect are always the same. Tom Lethbridge, in his dating of Stonehenge, used a pendulum thirty inches long, which for him was the right "rate" for the job of finding how old something was. In the way he worked, each gyration of the pendulum counted ten years, and when the pendulum stopped gyrating, he had found the date of Stonehenge. He used the same method on many megaliths, nearly always coming up with dates for stone circles that were earlier than the accepted archaeological dates at that time, but which have now, through calibrated radiocarbon dating, been proved right.

Although his method worked, it was extremely time-consuming: to get back to 2000 B.C., he had to count nearly 400 gyrations. Dr. J. H. Fidler, another dowser with an interest in history, worked out a different method, still using a thirty-inch pendulum. He made up a pack of cards with a number in the binary system written on each—1, 2, 4, 8, 16, and so on up to 8,192—fourteen cards in all. The right combination of these can give any number up to 16,383 years. With the pendulum in his right hand, he would suspend it over the place on the map, or the object, which he was trying to date, and place his left forefinger over each of the cards in turn. Using the pendulum as a yes/no indicator (gyrations for "yes," oscillations for "no"), he put all the "yes" cards into a pile and simply added them up to find the age in years. Major-General Scott Elliot's system is even simpler: he first asks if the site is B.C. or A.D., gets a "yes" or a "no" from his pendulum, then counts aloud in thousands, and successively in hundeds, tens and units, and lets the pendulum show him when to stop. In this way, it takes him less than half a minute to date a stone circle or a neolithic rock carving to, say, 2720 B.C.

Scott Elliot's speciality is map dowsing to find undiscovered historical and prehistocial sites (or to complete on a map the missing parts of sites already known), and dating them. Apart from his work in simplifying the theory of dowsing, perhaps his biggest contribution is that, because of his background and the standards of proof he demands before publication of his results, he manages to make a method that produces apparently magical results look both respectable and natural. He left the army in 1954 after a distinguished career, and straight away began to study both practical dowsing and archaeology—the former after reading a book on the subject, the latter by joining the local archaeological society. His method is invariable: to map dowse; to dowse on the site to check for accuracy; and then to excavate for proof.

After some ten years, his experience of field archaeology was so wide that he was made president of the Scottish Society of Antiquaries. Over recent years, he has found that he is nearly always right with his archaeological map dowsing—not quite so often as the very best water dowsers, but close to them. "If we are professionals we must deliver the goods. Gone are the days when we feel we have been lucky when we find water, or minerals, or an archaeological site. We must expect to do so, accurately, and be upset if things go wrong. When they do, we must want to know why, and how the mistake happened," he told the American Society of Dowsers in 1974.

Most of Scott Elliot's work has been concerned with Roman or Iron Age sites, but a glance at the few stone circles and megalithic sites which he has map dowsed shows the immense range of applications that a dowsing talent can bring to archaeology. On three of Alexander Thom's surveys of circles, he has mapped a ditch in which the stones were placed, and marked the positions of holes in which missing stones once stood. Interestingly, the outline of the ditch seems to correspond much more closely to Thom's geometric shapes than the likely position of the stones.

Scott Elliot, while resolutely refusing to speculate on the function of stone circles, has found evidence, through dowsing, of avenues of stones leading to all of those he has investigated. If this were proved to be universally true, it would be a genuine archaeological advance, because although the larger monuments such as Avebury and Stonehenge are known to have avenues, nobody has so far suspected that this was at one time an essential feature of all circles. Again, while he has never published

his findings because they have not yet been proved by
excavation, he suspects that all or nearly all stone circles
have an area of force within them that is probably related to an underground geological fault, usually between
twenty and thirty feet below the surface.

But the most far-reaching aspect of his views on the late
Stone Age and early Bronze Age is his conviction, shared
by many others, that megalithic man had a natural ability to dowse, and used it as a matter of course in his
everyday life. Exactly what ancient man used it for is,
once more, a speculation which he is not prepared to
make. Perhaps, as with some of today's dowsers, it was
to diagnose illness and find suitable remedies from herbs
and potions. Or perhaps it was to let the mind communicate or "know" over long distances without the need to
read and write.

"If there was an area of force caused by an underground fault, or if there was a spring or an underground
stream beneath the stone circles, they would certainly
have known about it," he says. And, in an echo of Thom's
words about the limitless potential capabilities of megalithic man, he says: "I believe there is very little that
cannot be found (or found out) by dowsing means."

Others have suggested that the intimate connection between megaliths and mysterious underground forces is
related to hidden water. Reginald Allender Smith was,
until his death in 1941, one of Britain's most distinguished
archaeologists. He had been Keeper of the British and
Roman Antiquities Department of the British Museum,
and Director of the Society of Antiquaries. Rather like
Alfred Watkins before him, he kept to himself his one
unconventional ability, which was to dowse. In 1939, he
read a paper to the British Society of Dowsers expressing
his belief that beneath every "prehistoric temple"—his
definition of the larger stone circles—there was what
some water diviners describe as a "blind spring." This
is where water rises vertically as in a natural pipe,
and then, failing to break surface, radiates outward hori-
zontally in one or more underground streams. Nearly
a quarter of a century later another paper posthumously
emphasized his conclusion: there was "constant presence
of underground water at the exact centre of earthworks
and circles." He believed that every prehistoric monument had therefore been chosen on this basis, in order

to make some use of the hidden forces beneath the ground.

Another researcher in this field was Guy Underwood, who, before his death in 1964 at the age of eighty-one, spent more than twenty years dowsing at such sites as Stonehenge, the White Horse at Uffington in Berkshire, the Cerne Abbas Giant, and Stanton Drew. He believed he had identified a universally powerful "earth force," known instinctively to animals and plants, and used from megalithic times onward by priesthoods to locate the communities' sacred centers, and, later, churches and cathedrals. Like others, he felt that the migration of birds and fish was achieved by their unconscious sense of hidden lines of this earth force, and took photographs of trees and rushes leaning toward blind springs that he had located. He also found that field tracks made by cattle and sheep, and ancient pathways, followed the wandering lines of underground water.

Instances from all over the world back up his findings. At the first Vermont calendar site identified by Byron Dix, a long grass-covered mound backs on to the remains of the stone chamber, reminiscent of a Wiltshire long barrow. In the center of it is an area on which the grass lies permanently flat, through spring, summer, and fall, because of deer which choose to lie by night just there— and only there. Underneath, dowsers have traced water patterns leading to a spring nearby; and it is noteworthy that a local dowser, Mrs. Betty Sincerbeaux, accurately traced out the location of Dix's sighting position independently of him, entirely by dowsing methods.

Nowadays, the most informed researcher in this area is Bill Lewis, whose report of electromagnetic power in standing stones so much surprised Professor John Taylor and Eduardo Balanovski. Lewis, a retired electrical engineer who lives in Abergavenny, South Wales, would certainly be regarded by his fellows as among the handful of most gifted dowsers in Britain. He has been employed successfully as a water diviner by numerous official bodies. He uses without difficulty all the techniques of dowsing—for instance, he has map dowsed a water well in Australia; traced, on a map, the whereabouts of stolen goods, which were found by police and returned to the owners; found, on a map and then on site, a fault in a buried electric cable which had been baffling the

electricity authorities for several weeks; and he has a high
reputation as a healer.

With his friend and near neighbor John Williams (the
solicitor whom Richard Atkinson politely brushed aside),
he has used dowsing methods, via many dozen maps and
in the field, to find out information about megalithic
sites. Both men are convinced that there is an inseparable
connection between these sites and underground water
—indeed, Lewis believes that whole series of sites were
placed and constructed so that they were linked by
labyrinthine underground watercourses. He has found that
stone circles were built in such a way that underground
streams radiate outward from the center directly beneath
the gaps between the stones, and that precisely below
standing stones there was always the crossing point of
two or more streams, many of which are still flowing
today and can be readily identified with the pendulum.

Both men also date dowse, using the method of silently
counting backward in millennia or centuries until the
pendulum gives a reaction telling them to go no further,
and then refining the date until it reaches the standard
of accuracy needed. Much of the time, of course, their
dating is not capable of independent confirmation. But in
general they have found that, as with Tom Lethbridge,
radiocarbon dating has tended to support the earlier dates
which they were recording long before the new chronology came to be accepted. Once, to check their findings,
they dated a number of Roman and Celtic objects—beads,
pieces of pottery and so on—which they had found on
their travels locally. Then they sent the objects to Cardiff
museum for archaeological comment and dates. "There
was a remarkable agreement between the museum and
ourselves," says Williams.

A question-and-answer session with Bill Lewis gives a
vivid idea of how he uses dowsing. The subject was the
standing stone near Crickhowell on which Eduardo
Balanovski had measured the remarkable field-strength
anomaly. Before the session, Lewis had satisfied himself
(by map dowsing) that the stone came originally from
the river bed of the Usk, a few hundred yards away from
where it was erected, up a steeply sloping hill. For the
numerical questions, the answers took him up to a minute to work out with his pendulum; for the later yes/
no questions the answers were almost immediate.

What year was the stone taken from the river? *5636 B.C.*
What month of the year? *August.*
How many tons weight is the stone? *Twelve.*
How many people were used to transport it? *Thirty-one.*
How many were men and how many were women? *Twenty-three men and eight women.*
What ages were the oldest and youngest men, and the oldest and youngest women? *Men—thirty-three and twenty-four. Women—thirty-three and fourteen.*
How many days did it take to transport the stone? *Six.*
How many days did it take to erect the stone? *Two.*
How far into the ground does the stone extend? *Six feet.*
Are there human cremation ashes underneath it? *No.*
Was the stone used by the tribe daily? *No.*
Was the stone used on tribal ceremonial occasions? *Yes.*
How many times a year did these ceremonies take place? *Eight.*
Did they take place on the same days in every year? *No.*
Did the phase of the moon influence which day the ceremonies were held? *Yes.*

And so on, with the pendulum indicating "yes" or "no" to questions that had to be precisely framed. Most of the answers above are, of course, unprovable, or could be arrived at by experienced guesswork, or both; what weight should be put on the information depends entirely on whether you believe that Bill Lewis, on his record in other areas of dowsing, has gifts that allow him access to the correct answers.

When shown a photograph of the large stone chamber at the second of Byron Dix's calendar sites in Vermont (illustration page 136), he dowsed the information that the site had been reconstructed many times. The first burials had taken place there in 5945 B.C., the last in 58 B.C., and human bones could still be found six feet under the ground in front of the entrance. "It was never used as a root cellar. I found that in A.D. 176 the mound was interfered with, and the shelter it provides was used for storing game, furs and so on. I think the shelter has been rebuilt five times, the last time being A.D. 1442."

In fact, Lewis believes that this sort of detailed, largely unverifiable information matters less than his overall views on the nature of power in standing stones. This particular stone, which Lewis had never visited before, had for him the same extraordinary characteristics as many others which he and John Williams had studied; and it was his description of these characteristics that attracted the attention of Professor John Taylor. For if Lewis was right, he was announcing a discovery that was highly important in three areas. It would throw light on the nature of dowsing. He was suggesting the appearance of electro-magnetic force in an area that had never been explored. And if what he was saying applied generally to mega-liths, and could be statistically corroborated, it would con-tribute a signficant and disturbing new element to archae-ological understanding of life in those times.

What was more, it ought to be possible to find out sci-entifically if Bill Lewis was talking nonsense.

The starting point of his findings is the theory (which he supports) that there is a crossing of underground streams beneath each "active" standing stone. Lewis, through his work as an electrical engineer, says there is experimental evidence which shows that the movement of water through a tunnel of earth, particularly in clay, creates a small static electric field. The crossing of streams, albeit in different strata, makes the field stronger. He be-lieves the stone, placed immediately above this, acts in some way as an amplifier, although there is no known theory of physics that can explain how. Thus the mag-netic field strength anomaly noted by Eduardo Balanov-ski.

Now this alone is an original and unlikely suggestion. But Bill Lewis went much further. He said that the power, when it emerged from the ground and up the stone, came out in the form of a spiral. Each undamaged standing stone had a spiral ascending around it in seven coils, the lowest two beneath ground. But the force was not stable. According to various influences—lunar, solar, polar, planetary and others—it waxed and waned. What made the force even more complicated and incompre-hensible was that it changed polarity every month. After a period of waning, the force would die away and become disoriented for a period of anything from a few hours to a few days; when it reemerged, the spiral was in the opposite direction, and stayed in that direction, cyclically increasing and decreasing, until the end of the lunar phase.

This could all be dismissed as lunatic theorizing were it not for one thing: the initial measurements on the gaussmeter showed that Bill Lewis might well be at least partially right.

First, there were Balanovski's results to show that there was certainly a remarkably strong field around the stone; also, it seemed to fall in bands. Second, when Balanovski returned with the author and Professor John Taylor a week later to continue the measurements, Taylor asked Bill Lewis to chalk on the stone where he felt (with the palm of his hand) the spiral band was running. For the record, he was filmed making the marks. Then, at ten-centimeter intervals from the top of the stone to the bottom, Taylor recorded gaussmeter measurements of the magnetic field strength.

It was these measurements that again provided a positive indication. On some of the bands which Bill Lewis had marked, the recorded strength was about double the strength elsewhere on the stone.

"These early results must be treated with great caution," Taylor warned. "If they are confirmed, they are very remarkable indeed. It is a phenomenon that should certainly be investigated with great thoroughness over a long period, preferably on several stones."

Tentative and incomplete though the measurements may have been at that stage, they nevertheless may mark a breakthrough. Electromagnetism is probably not the complete answer to dowsing—as Lewis points out, he does not see how it can explain his ability to dowse through ten feet of concrete, or from a moving car, or on a map. It may be of more help in explaining water divining. But the main point is that in folklore, symbolism, and personal subjective experiences surrounding megaliths, belief in an unexplained power and the concept of a spiral force occur again and again. And the first time a sensitive magnetometer was used to check these beliefs, there were positive, if enigmatic, results.

For although a gaussmeter had not previously been used on the face of a stone, physical sensations when touching megaliths have been felt spontaneously by many people. Another researcher, Andrew Davidson, found that

the upright stones at Stonehenge had seven power centers
that he could identify. Gloucestershire has stones that are
locally named, from long ago, the Tingle Stone and the
Twizzle Stone. Other reports tell of faintness, dizziness, or
chest pains, tending to support the many dowsers who
feel that the power in megalithic sites is not necessarily
benevolent or harmless.

The effect of an active stone on John Williams is physically remarkable. If he leans on one, the palms of his
hands flat on a part of the spiral band at eye level, he
quickly finds an unbalancing force building up inside
him, which makes it impossible for him to continue holding the stone, and he is spun off to the right or to the
left. At the top of the stone, he finds there is another
band of power, which he believes has something to do
with the frequency of ultraviolet light. Whatever the
cause, he receives a physical sensation that can range
from a slight prickling of the fingertips to a jerk as vio-
lent as a shock from a twelve-volt car battery.

Many dowsers are worried about the unpredictability
of whatever force there is in the stones. "If I feel it building up in my body, I back away very quickly," says Bill
Lewis. "It can upset your metabolism as well as your
equilibrium." Sir William Barrett and Theodore Bester-
man, in their monumental work on dowsing, *The Divining Rod*, quote the case of the great French dowser
Barthelemy Bleton, when he was a child in about 1750:

Bleton, when seven years of age, had carried din-
ner to some workmen; he sat down on a stone, when
a fever of faintness seized him; the workmen having
brought him to their side, the faintness ceased, but
each time he returned to the stone, he suffered again.
This was told to the Prior of the Chartreuse, who
wished to see it for himself. Being thus convinced
of the fact, he had the ground under the stone dug
up; where they found a spring, which at the time of
writing was still in use to turn a mill.

The general concept of megalithic sites holding a supernatural force is supported by an extraordinary wealth
of folklore. If archaeological evidence about standing
stones, dolmens, and circles is inevitably sparse, myth
and legend are correspondingly profuse and widespread,

whether recorded in local books or passed on, even today, in storytelling by villagers. Almost everywhere the stones are to be found, variations of the same legends are told in the same districts—the connection between megaliths and giants or fairies, with power, treasure, healing or sanctity. There is no need, of course, to take these stories literally. Their importance is that at some period in history they were believed to be true, or to contain a hidden truth.

Most of the early legends have been dated by experts in folklore to a time close to the period when megaliths were still in use (a second crop of legends grew up when northwestern Europe was Christianized, and the stones were absorbed and resanctified by the Church). Time and again, in myths handed down independently in places hundreds of miles apart, the stone circles and other sites are said to have a power or force within them—often connected with water, which gives them a magical life and independence. They are alive in the way felt by dowsers and others. Folklore supports the view, too, that burial was a relatively unimportant function for the monuments. The vast majority of legends indicate that megaliths generate life, rather than commemorate death.

STONES THAT MOVE

The commonest of all legends is of stones that move, often at some important moment such as midnight, daybreak or noon, and also because they need water. The Rollright Stones in Oxfordshire go down the hill to drink from a spring in a spinney—according to some accounts when the clock strikes twelve, according to others on certain Saints' Days. The stones at Carnac go to drink on Christmas Eve. The Whittlestone in Gloucestershire goes to the Lady Well at the foot of the hill to drink at midnight. The Minchinhampton Long Stone in the Cotswolds runs around the field at the same hour. French stones are frequently known as Pierres de Chantecocq, Pierres Tournantes, and Pierres de Minuit. In Ireland, the White Boulder of Cronebane goes every May Day morning to wash at the Meeting of the Waters.

Another prolific legend about the power and life in stones is that, because of some innate property, they can-

View of the Temple of Rowldrich from the South.

A. the King Stone as called. B. the Archdruids barrow. C.C. round barrows. or King barrows.

Rollright Stones in Oxfordshire, source of many legends and still the center of witchcraft ceremonies today.

not be measured or counted—or if they are, a tragedy will follow. At Kit's Coty, a long barrow in Kent, a baker tried to count the stones by putting a loaf on each one and seeing how many were left; but he was foiled by the Devil who came around behind him eating some loaves and leaving others. Similar stories come from the Rollright Stones, from the Hurlers in Cornwall, from Stonehenge, and from Stanton Drew.

Other stories tell of cattle or crops dying if megaliths are interfered with or removed. A Scottish farmer in the eighteenth century, who took two stones of a circle to make gateposts, found that his horses refused to go through them, so he took them back. In the same area, a megalith was made into the lintel over a doorway in a cattle shed. The door then refused to stay closed, and once again the farmer had to return the stone. In other legends, the stones themselves often helped the return journey. At Rollright, the local landowner was supposed to have tried to use the capstone of the Whispering Knights, a dolmen to the east of the stone circle, to make a bridge across the brook at the bottom of the hill. According to various accounts, a large number of horses—at least six, maybe forty—were needed to drag it down the hill. The stone was still so difficult to move that the harness broke, and some horses were killed in the struggle. Finally, it was put in place—only for the villagers to discover that each night it removed itself from the brook and turned over backward in the grass. They gave up the unequal battle —and only one horse was needed to take the stone back up the hill to its proper resting place. At Zennor Quoit in Cornwall, the stones were said to be immovable—or alternatively, if moved, would go back to where they came from by dawn the next day.

DANCING STONES

This widespread belief in life and movement in the stones is confirmed everywhere by their association with dancing. Geoffrey of Monmouth, in 1135, called Stonehenge the *Chorea Gigantum* or "Giant's Dance," and one of the Cornish collective names for stones has been, since earliest times, *Dons Meyn,* or dance of stones. Most of the folklore is ambiguous about whether it was the stones themselves that danced, or whether dancing took place around them. At Rollright, the stones danced at midnight (they seem to have been an especially active circle, with their simultaneous drinking activities) and the Belstone "Nine Stones" danced at noon. At the Merry Maidens stone circle in Cornwall, post-Christian myth says that the stones are foolish girls turned to stone for dancing on a Sunday, and this same story can be found in at least seven other circles in Cornwall as well as in Shropshire, Ireland and Britanny. Alternatively, as at Stanton Drew, and at many megaliths in France, it is a wedding party that has been turned to stone for being disrespectful to the Church.

Whether dances or weddings, music was always involved. The outlying stones from the circles are said to be the petrified piper or fiddler. Both Aubrey and Stukeley found the same legend at Stanton Drew, where an impious wedding party swore that it would carry on dancing "if the Devil himself had to play"—which he promptly did. At some round barrows, such as that near St. Just in Cornwall, fairies danced at nighttime, and an aura of lights could be seen and their music heard.

BURIED TREASURE

Another persistent legend to have become muddled and adapted with the passage of time concerns the existence of buried treasure beneath the megaliths. During the eighteenth and nineteenth centuries the search for gold or metal grave goods was one of the main purposes of the excavation. But there was little success. Time and again, men dug into the chambers and barrows and were astonished to come up with little or nothing—a few broken pieces of pottery, occasionally some scattered bones. A very few round barrows, constructed in the early Bronze Age by Beaker invaders, revealed a priceless work of craftsmanship such as the gold breastplate for a pony discovered at the Bryn er Ellylon (Hill of the Fairies) in Flintshire. At Borrie's Laq in Fifeshire a large number of silver goods were found. But discoveries such as these are not enough to account for the almost universal myth that treasure existed beneath the monuments. The treasure is much more likely to have represented symbolically a power that was hidden within or beneath them.

Villagers at Marnoch in Aberdeenshire tried to remove a block of quartz known as White Cow in order to reach the treasure, but were unable to finish their excavation within the day. By next morning the stones, as in other places and on other occasions, had put themselves back in position, and the villagers decided not to go on. There are many similar stories—that it is impossible for anyone to get the "treasure" by moving the stone—and a number of them say that if anyone tries to do so while the stone is on one of its occasional perambulations, it will immediately come back and crush the thief to death.

In myth, this treasure/force/power is mysterious, unpredictable, and not necessarily benevolent in its workings. Dr. William Borlase, in his travels through Cornwall in the late eighteenth century, recorded the stories of hurricanes and thunderstorms that followed interference with megaliths, notably the storm off the Scilly Islands that followed the opening of the Giant's Grave barrow there. A villager in Challacombe, Devon, died of fright after being chased by ghosts and horses galloping behind him when he had opened a barrow. A clergyman at Widecombe-in-the-Moor who broke open a small stone cist had his house destroyed by explosion the following night. All of which, certainly, can be explained away as coincidence. But the important thing is not so much the events themselves, nor their improbability, but the fact that they have passed into folklore as examples and evidence of the hidden power which for at least 5,000 years has been part of an inherited feeling about megaliths.

STONES THAT HEAL

But folklore also gives evidence of the force as being one which heals, and there are at least as many legends about this as there are about the violence which is its other side. The Holed Stone known as Men-an-Tol in Cornwall (also called the Crick Stone) was used to cure children of rickets and whooping cough, and adults of rheumatism and lumbago. The cure took place if they climbed through the hole, and the same or similar stories

Men-an-Tol, where the healing ritual involved clambering nine times through the holed stone "against the sun."

are attached to the many other holed stones that still remain from megalithic times. Women in Brittany used to embrace their local standing stone in order to tap its hidden force; they felt, perhaps, the energy of the spiral flow into them as they wished for a husband or for children.

A report in the *Proceedings* of the Society of Antiquaries of Scotland in 1888 tells of cup-marked stones near Aberfeldy in Perthshire: "The grooves and cavities are always, even in the driest weather, more or less full of water, presenting a glistening appearance in the distance when the sun is shining upon them; and that people of the locality are still in the habit every year of going to them on the first day of May, to wash their faces with the contained liquid, to which they impute special properties of healing and blessing—a custom which is probably a survival of a pagan one." In 1700, the Reverend J. Brome said people visited Stonehenge because they knew of its healing powers: "If the stones be rubbed, or scraped, and water thrown upon the scrapings, they will (say some) heal any green wound, or old sore."

The fairies connected with megaliths, too, are generally reputed in legend to be more helpful than not, and numerous stories from widely different sites give an impression of travelers and others who can be refreshed by drawing on the power that could be found in the monuments. At a Gloucestershire long barrow, hunters could call out "I thirst," and a fairy would appear bearing a gold, gem-encrusted cup full of delicious-tasting drink. The Cheesewring on Bodmin Moor, where the top stone of the extraordinarily eroded rock is supposed to turn around three times at dawn, was also the home of an astronomer-priest with an inexhaustible cup of gold. At other monuments, fairies would shoe horses or leave food for the hungry. In turn they expected to receive offerings of food and drink, and until very recent times this practice has been common in Brittany, and occasionally found in Britain where standing stones in the Scottish Highlands were anointed with oil or milk to propitiate the fairies, or honey-cakes placed on the dolmen called Arthur's Stone on the Gower Coast of Wales.

But above all, the legends indicate that it was best to be wary of the power. In many places, to drink from the cup of gold meant being ensnared by the fairies and the force that they represented, and there are stories of hunters who cheated by stealing the cup without drinking from it. At the Cheesewring, the hunter threw the drink in the face of the priest, and galloped away with the cup. But he could not escape—his horse plunged over the rocks and was killed. (Coincidence or not, a gold cup was found in the early nineteenth century hidden in a cairn at the Cheesewring.) The chronicler William of Newbridge, writing in the thirteenth century, tells of the Yorkshire long barrow called Willy Howe:

> One night a man was riding home from the village of North Burton, when he heard, as he drew near, sounds of merriment coming from the Howe. He saw a door open in the side of the mound and, riding close to it, he looked in and beheld a great feast. One of the cup-bearers approached and offered him a drink. He took the cup, threw out the contents, and galloped off. The fairy banqueters gave chase, but he succeeded in distancing them and reaching home with his prize in safety.

Clearly, from the very earliest times, the mounds and monuments built by megalithic man have been thought to exert a magical power on people who used them or tried to destroy them, and certain calendrical moments were important too. Their capacity to produce supernatural sensations and visions is another of their persistent, extraordinary qualities; and here, as well as the misty evidence of myth, one can look at the experience of people alive today.

CHAPTER

7

SUPERNATURAL, SPIRITUAL

The stones are great
And magic power they have.
Men that are sick
Fare to that stone;
And they wash that stone
And bathe away their evil.

—THE TWELFTH-CENTURY CHRONICLER LAYAMON,
WRITING OF STONEHENGE IN HIS BALLAD *Brut*

For whatever reason, megalithic sites attract more than their fair share of people who might variously be described as psychic, gifted, sensitive, or just plain cranky. The British Government's Department of the Environment, which controls many of the monuments including Stonehenge, keeps a file of the letters they write, growing in total each year by a few dozen. In it, people complain of dizziness and faintness; of an irresistible attraction to certain stones and places; of experiencing visions of the past (often lurid and bloodstained ceremonies). All the letters are politely acknowledged, and there is, of course, no easy way of telling which of the writers show genuine insight, and which have been suffering from sunstroke.

But it remains a fact that the weight of such letters concerns ancient sites—not, for instance, stately homes or medieval castles or even cathedrals. Perhaps this is because megaliths have their quality of total difference; looking at them, it is impossible not to realize that the people who built them lived a life different in scale and concept, subject to different motives and different priorities, from anything today. So perhaps letter writers feel compelled to imagine an explanation for this strangeness, and induce in themselves fantasies about the ancient past and its powers. Perhaps, too, the traditions of folklore are stronger than one imagines in an educated modern society, and the writers are simply reviving and reshaping personally the ancient legends about megalithic sites.

But personal investigation does not confirm this. Invariably, people who have had an unusual experience on a megalithic site have found it spontaneous and inexplicable, and not necessarily something they would like to repeat. The letter writers, too, represent only a pocketful of ex-

201

periences; for every person who feels it necessary to write
and explain what has happened, there are many more
who shrug it off and ignore it—or, surprisingly often, find
it somehow shameful and frightening. For a scientist or
archaeologist to admit to such subjective occurrences is
doubly difficult. Tom Lethbridge was ridiculed by his
former colleagues when he wrote in *Legend of the Sons of
God* about his experiences dowsing with a pendulum at the
Merry Maidens stone circle in Cornwall in 1964:

> As soon as the pendulum started to swing, a strange
> thing happened. The hand resting on the stone re-
> ceived a strong tingling sensation like a mild electric
> shock and the pendulum itself shot out until it was
> circling nearly horizontally to the ground. The stone
> itself, which must have weighed over a ton, felt as if it
> were rocking and almost dancing about. . . . The
> next day I sent my wife up along to see what hap-
> pened to her. She had the same experience. It has
> happened nowhere else. The Pipers were mute and so
> were many crosses and other monuments which I
> tried. But most circular monuments are now incom-
> plete and perhaps something has gone from them.

His wife, Mina, confirmed in 1975 that the incidents
were completely unprompted. "For me, it felt as though
the stones were moving and dancing about somehow in a
circular direction. The pendulum was whizzing round,
stuck out sideways, and it hasn't done that anywhere else
again. I myself felt like dancing round the stones. I got a
very strong impression this was how they must have been
charged originally—by people moving and dancing round
them. Perhaps when Tom and I dowsed there, we removed whatever charge was left."

Other dowsers, independently, have had similar feelings.
Rosemary Gundry, who was employed with her husband
by the Admiralty during the 1939–45 war to map dowse
enemy harbors to discover whether there were ships in
there worth bombing ("You were right a bit more than
75 percent of the time," they were told afterward), lives
in Devon but until recently has taken no particular interest
in archaeology. In the summer of 1975, however, she was
curious to try her pendulum on the Witch Stone that stands
on a crossroads outside the Hare and Hounds inn near

Honiton, a stone with the familiar legend that on midsummer's eve it goes at midnight to drink at a stream at the bottom of the hill, embellished locally by the story that the purpose for this is to wash off the blood of victims who had been ceremonially slaughtered on it. As she approached the stone she felt a sudden giddiness, and when this stopped she began to pass her left hand over the surface of the stone, waiting for a reaction from the pendulum.

Little happened except in one small area, not much larger than the palm of her hand, when the pendulum suddenly swung violently to life. "I put the pendulum away and tried resting both hands near the spot. I had an extraordinary sensation. It was as if the stone was rocking from side to side. Obviously it wasn't, because other people were watching and couldn't see it move. But it was an unmistakable feeling, absolutely uncontrollable. There was some kind of force being extracted, and I couldn't tell whether it was coming out of me or out of the stone. Perhaps it was both, going from one to the other and back again, and that was why it felt like rocking. It wasn't like anything I have felt before, and I can't say whether it was good or bad for me. When I let go of the stone, things were back to normal within a few seconds. I didn't feel any different, at least not consciously. But I knew I had undergone something very powerful indeed."

The point of force that she found was perhaps on the spiral waveband that John Williams and Bill Lewis describe, and other people there who tried feeling the power in the stone after Mrs. Gundry were also able to recognize the physically unbalancing effect that it causes. A Midlands dowser, Mrs. Enid Smithett, underwent an even more startling experience at the Rollright Stones. She had been dowsing in the circle for some hours: "Too long, I think. I began to get dizzy and the sun had gone down. There is a definite change in the feeling of a stone circle after dusk. I don't like them after dark. The power seems quite different."

As she came out of the circle, she says she felt extremely light-headed, and because of this, lost her grip on the pendulum, which slipped into the long grass. "It was in the height of summer, and the grass was as high as my waist. I didn't think I would have a chance of finding it, because it was only a small piece of plastic with a thread attached. But I ran my fingers through the grass, just in case, and my arm came up against what felt like a particularly tough blade of grass. It was difficult to bend over. I felt for it with my fingers and found it was the thread of the pendulum, sticking straight up in the air like an Indian rope trick."

To an observer, the difficulty with evaluating all such experiences is that they may be imagined or self-induced; so personal that they are valueless as objective evidence. To which one reply is that proficient dowsers are very precise in the questions to which they are seeking the answer—is there water here? how old is this object? has this stone been moved? When something paranormal happens, such as a pendulum defying the laws of gravity, or a rock-solid stone apparently moving from side to side, it always seems to be a secondary effect, which comes in addition to the answer to the question. It is as unexpected to the dowser as to the observer. Another reply might be that as we are looking at a force or effect that has until recently defied mechanical or scientific measurement, the only way of examining it is through personal testimony. Certainly, dowsers do not have a monopoly of these experiences, even though the nature of their gifts makes them more receptive to the arcane than some people; it seems more likely that the power of the ancient sites and the paths that link them sometimes emerges without warning through the subconscious of everybody, whether they wish it or not.

One of the most unusual, yet convincing, examples happened to a middle-aged housewife who had lived all her life in the modest suburbs of Weston-super-Mare, Somerset. Apart from a couple of vacations in Cornwall, and an occasional bus trip, she had visited nowhere outside her local area. In 1974, shortly after the family bought a car, she made a 120-mile journey with her husband to Oxford to visit a sick friend in the hospital. The roads they traveled on, avoiding the main highways because traffic went too quickly for their comfort, were completely unknown to her. "I was a bit nervous," she says. "Oxford seemed such a long way."

Since childhood, she had experienced dreams of an extraordinarily compelling nature. They fell into a pattern; she would dream, vividly and in detail, of a number of places. She could see them as realistically as if she were there—recognize the trees, hedges and plants, picture a village street, see water and woodlands. There were only a limited number of dreams, and like jump-cut sequences in a film, some of them seemed to be connected without necessarily joining directly to the previous one. The dreams happened at unpredictable intervals; sometimes two or three times in a week, sometimes not for two or three months. They were so powerful that she always woke after dreaming, and over the years she made notes, maps and sketches of what she had seen. Her overpowering urge was to find and visit the places: "I knew them so well it was as if I had to go back and find them again. It was as if I'd been there before, and I wouldn't properly be my-self unless I went back there."

On the day she drove with her husband to Oxford through the leafy back lanes on the borders of Somerset and Wiltshire, it had been about a week since she had last dreamed of one of the recurring places—a village street that went on up a lane and past a large open space on the left. She recollected it with total clarity. "As we were driving along my mind was suddenly filled with a picture of this place. I was looking out of the car windows and could see the hills all around. I told my husband that I was sure the place I dreamed about was just the other side of them. I felt I knew exactly where the place was. I couldn't see altogether which hill it was behind, because of the hedges, but I could feel the direction. I was drawn —sort of pulled—first of all towards the left-hand side and then, after the car had gone a mile or two farther, towards the right. But my husband said we couldn't stop because we would be late, and a bit further on I knew we were past it."

However, when they made the same journey the next week, she was more insistent. She persuaded her husband to make a detour about a mile up a steep narrow lane, and stop in the village street at the top. It was, as she had felt, identical to her dream. She recognized the churches, and some centuries-old cottages. As she went up the cul-de-sac at the end of the village, she saw the open space, the lane, the hedges, a gate and a hawthorn tree precisely as she had perceived them. Her feelings were "shocked and amazed, both together, but mostly relieved and happy. I couldn't speak, I was so full of joy to have found the place. But I was frightened too, not knowing how I'd found it."

The village she landed up in is called Bradenstoke, and the significance of the way she discovered it is that, because of the way she felt drawn first to one side and then to the other, she seems to have unconsciously detected a power still existing in a ley that runs through the village from Wootton Bassett church to Solsbury Hill Camp northwest of Bath. On its length of twenty-one miles it passes precisely through at least eleven mark points, including a flattened hilltop (described as a castle), a strangely positioned church, a kink in a road, earthworks, springs, and the site of an ancient building called Conduit House. Bradenstoke itself has Clack Mount (an artificial hill), an ancient holy well, and the remains of an Augustinian Abbey. Except for standing stones and circles, which in the immediate area are not common, it is as well defined a ley as anyone is likely to find. When Eunice Black and her husband were driving near there, the places where she "felt drawn" to the left and right correspond exactly to the road in relation to the ley. Where she made her husband stop the car was within ten yards of the point where the road crosses the ley. The lane that she followed is on the ley to the holy well.

The incident has been worth looking at in detail because Eunice Black knew nothing of leys at the time, but was nevertheless unconsciously drawn toward an alignment which any ley hunter would identify as containing some kind of power. It was a year later when she first knew of leys, when a researcher in prehistory who had heard of the incident discussed it with her. She explained that what she had found was only the first part of that particular dream, and drew the second part on some sheets of paper which she dated and sent by registered mail to establish their authenticity. Map dowsing indicated that the area she had dreamed and drawn was again on the same ley between Bradenstoke and Wootton Bassett, by some woods and a stream, and this was subsequently confirmed by photographs. Some of the features had altered through growth or replanting, but the basic elements of water, tummocks of grass, and trees, were all there in their right relationship. This time, however, Mrs. Black had no urge to visit the site—the opposite, in fact. "It may have been the same place as my dream, but this time it felt evil. I couldn't bring myself to go there. It would have been wrong."

If the strange power in the stones may nowadays be

weaker, and experienced only occasionally, it is perhaps astonishing that it exists at all. It has lingered there, inexplicably, in spite of the vast majority of stones having been moved or destroyed, in spite of their disuse for more than 1,000 years, and in spite of the most determined efforts during centuries by the Christian church to neutralize their magic. Nobody knows exactly when Christianity first came to the northwest of Europe. Legend has it that Christ himself came to Britain, and in particular to the little village of Priddy in Somerset; this is historically possible—there was tin trade between the two countries at this time—although unprovable on currently known facts. An even stronger tradition says that Christ's uncle, Joseph of Arimathea, who ministered to the body of Christ after his death, arrived in Glastonbury in A.D. 64 bearing the Cup of the Last Supper, which he buried on Chalice Hill. Certainly, during the first centuries A.D, there were isolated communities of Christians among the Celts in Ireland and on the Atlantic fringe.

But there is equally no doubt that for the majority of Celts, and for their conquerors the Anglo-Saxons in Britain and Europe, the megaliths were still very important to their metaphysical beliefs and ceremonies. By this time, many of the monuments were several thousand years old, and most prehistorians agree that many, perhaps most of them had been continuously in some sort of use during all that time, and were still the most important sacred places of worship and ritual. Pope Gregory the Great (A.D. 590–604) wrote to Eulogius, Bishop of Alexandria: "The English Nation, placed in an obscure corner of the world, has hitherto been wholly taken up with the adoration of wood and stones." The chief objects of Anglo-Saxon worship, according to the laws of Knut, were: "The sun and the moon, fire and water, springs, stones and trees." It was believers in these natural forces and places whom the Christian church decided to convert.

St. Patrick arrived on his principal mission to Ireland in A.D. 432, and within 100 years his Christian followers were in turn sending missionaries across the Irish Sea to Wales and Scotland. St. Augustine was dispatched from Rome to England by Gregory in A.D. 596, and Sussex, the last area to resist the Cross, was converted in A.D. 681. By historical standards this is a remarkably short space of time—less than a century for each country to accept, at

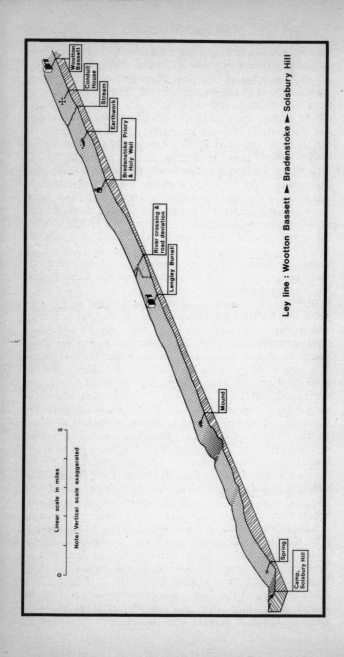

Linear scale in miles

0   5

Note: Vertical scale exaggerated

Wootton Bassett

Conduit House

Stream

Earthwork

Bradenstoke Priory & Holy Well

River crossing & road deviation

Langley Burrell

Mound

Spring

Camp, Solsbury Hill

Ley line : Wootton Bassett ▲ Bradenstoke ▲ Solsbury Hill

least outwardly, a new faith. That it was so quick lay
largely in the methods adopted by the two leading missionaries. St. Patrick, having been born locally with the
native name of Succath or Sucat (meaning warlike) before
his own conversion had, according to *Lives of the Saints,*
"too intimate a knowledge . . . to make unnecessary and
tactless difficulties. His policy was that of compromise."
Pope Gregory, in his time, wrote: "It is not well to make
people of an obstinate turn grow better by leaps, but
rather by slow steps."

Just how obstinate and how slow can be seen in the
many edicts issued by the Church between A.D. 500 and
1100. They show that, however apparently quick and
successful was the Christianization, in reality it was a long
and far from triumphant struggle. These edicts, issued by
the most weighty and distinguished leaders of the Church,
have another importance: as well as showing the continuing power which the megaliths and their pagan rituals
exerted over people, they are among our first written clues
as to just what that power was. Theodore's *Penitential,*
an early book on Church doctrine and ceremony, is one
of the many which list magical practices that worried the
Christians, and in which we can see glimmerings of what
was happening on the ancient sites. He banned:

1. Idolatry and worship of demons
2. Cult of the dead
3. Worship of nature (trees, wells, stones, fire, etc.)
4. Pagan calendar customs and festivals
5. Witchcraft and sorcery
6. Augury and divination
7. Astrology

"No one," he added, "shall go to trees, or wells, or
stones, or enclosures (circles) or anywhere else except to
God's church, and there make vows or release himself
from them." A sermon by St. Eligius, Bishop of Noyon,
in about A.D. 640, adds a few details: "Let no Christian
place lights at the temples, or the stones, or at fountains,
or at trees, or enclosures, or at places where three ways
meet . . . let no one presume to make lustrations, or to
enchant herbs, or to make flocks pass through a hollow
tree or an aperture in the earth; for by doing so he seems
to consecrate them to the devil."

The practices were extraordinarily persistent. More than 300 years later, in the reign of King Edgar, the clergy were told they must "totally extinguish every heathenism; and forbid well-worshipping and necromancies, and divinations . . . with various trees and stones." A *Penitential* of Egbert says that "any woman who would cure her infant by any sorcery, or shall have it drawn through the earth at the crossroads, is to fast for three years; for this is great paganism." King Knut, in A.D. 1035, forbade the barbarous "worship of stones, trees, fountains and the heavenly bodies."

Thus there is no doubt that the Church found the lingering power of the old religion, expressed through the stones and other sacred pagan sites, extremely difficult to nullify. At first, the practice of missionaries was to attack and destroy these centers of worship, but when this was evidently unsuccessful, they adopted a complete change of strategy. Instead of meeting the challenge head on, they concentrated instead on absorbing and rededicating the two main symbols of pagan worship—their ancient sacred sites, and their gods. A famous letter, which Pope Gregory bade the Abbé Melitus take to St. Augustine, contains the instruction that for centuries afterward dominated the attitude of the Christian church to the old religions: Augustine was told "by no means to destroy the temples of the idols belonging to the English, but only the idols which are found in them; let holy water be sprinkled over them, let altars be constructed, and relics placed in them, inasmuch as these temples are well constructed it is necessary that they should be converted from the dowership of demons to the true God."

Thus it was that in countless churches, not just in Britain but all over Europe, the power of the ancient megaliths was assimilated and consecrated by the Christian missionaries. The sites chosen—circles, dolmens, holy trees, wells—had stood untouched for thousands of years, the continuing centers of ceremonies, which probably changed only slightly with each generation, retaining through the years some of their original power and force. (This unbroken tradition of worship helps answer one of the principal archaeological objections to Alfred Watkins's definition of points that can be counted in a ley line: that it covers sites of widely differing eras—Stone Age, Bronze Age, Iron Age, Roman and Anglo-Saxon.) All the evidence is that the centers were not, as they have so often been interpreted, merely isolated burial chambers or casually placed memorial stones, but a network so constructed that each monument could be used as the focal center of local custom and magic. Dr. William Borlase, in *Dolmens of Ireland*, said they were "not mere sepulchres of the dead, but places set apart for the sacrificia mortiorum (ritual sacrifice), for pilgrimages, for the periodical assembling of the tribe or tribes for religious or social purposes, for the holding of fairs, for the contracting of marriages, and for unrestricted feasting and revel."

A closer look at the original sites of churches, bearing in mind Pope Gregory's description of them as pagan "temples," shows that every type of megalith, whether barrow, dolmen, menhir or circle, was used in this way. Churches at Taplow (Berkshire), Fimber (Yorkshire), and Ludlow (Shropshire) are built over long barrows. There is a celebrated standing stone, more than twenty-five feet high, in the churchyard of Rudston (Yorkshire). The ruins of Knowlton Church, Dorset, lie within the great circle of an ancient earthwork. The ruins of Maplescombe church, Kent, revealed menhirs within the fabric. As recently as 1906, the Longstone near St. Mabyn's church in Cornwall was broken up and carried away "to brave ridiculous legends and superstitions." W. Johnson's *Byways in Archaeology*, published in 1912, a standard work on the subject, has more than 100 pages listing similar sites, and points out that there would certainly be more examples but for the fact that archaeological excavations seldom take place in consecrated churches or churchyards.

In this way, the sites of Paganism and Christianity passed one into the other, a mystifying blend that could still be found in this century in the Gaelic phrase commonly in use: "Am bheil thu dol d'on clachan?" It can be translated with equal precision as "Are you going to the stones?" or "Are you going to church?" There is an old Welsh saying : "Da yw'r maen gyda 'r Efengyl"—" 'Tis a good enough stone provided it be Christian." In Ireland, within living memory, there was a widespread custom called "tura," which consisted of a local pilgrimage at certain important dates around all the stones and megaliths in the area.

But not less important, the Christians absorbed the an-

The Chapelle des Sept-Saints,
Brittany, has been built around
the foundation of a large dolmen.

cient gods—and the elemental forces that they were believed to control—by changing their names and beatifying
them. Ma and Matrona became Mary, and Sinclair, the
Sacred Light, became St. Clare. Again, in some of the
instances of canonization, clues to the nature of the old
pagan beliefs and rituals can be found; for example, the
importance of fire to the workings of the monuments and
their hidden power. Alfred Watkins noted how *tan*—the
modern Welsh for fire, and used in Celtic times to denote
a beacon fire on a hilltop—became corrupted into St.
Anne's. Santan was the ancient Holy Fire God, and in his
new form he can be found as a dedication on hundreds
of hills as well as early churches. The Salisbury Cathedral–
Stonehenge ley goes through St. Anne's Hill to the northwest, at 958 feet the highest point on the Wiltshire Downs.

Another very early reference to the importance of fire,
and the associated god or goddess, comes from St. Patrick
himself. On his way to Tara he lit a sacred and blessed
Easter fire, as was customary. But Easter, on this occasion, coincided with May Day, which since the most ancient times had been the moment when Beltane fires were
lit from hilltop to hilltop to celebrate the coming of the
new year. In this area of Ireland, it was the custom of
the Druid priests to order all fires to be formally extin-
guished, so that they could be rekindled from a ritual
flame lit by the Arch Druid. Seeing St. Patrick's fire alight,

the priests dispatched their king—Leoghaire—to find and punish him. But (presumably influenced by their own occult experiences in similar circumstances) they warned the king not to go inside the magic circle formed by St. Patrick's fires, because of the powerful influences there that might overcome him.

Later the fire-goddess herself, Brigit, was beatified by the Christian church and made the favorite companion of St. Patrick. She was discovered in a sacred grove near Kildare, where with her nineteen priestesses a sacred fire was kept eternally burning. Christianity took over her site as a hermitage, but did not dare quench the fire, which kept burning until the days of the Reformation some 1,000 years later.

HEALING WELLS AND HIGH PLACES

Of all the sites and ceremonies taken over and adapted by the early Christians, the two mysterious forces which seem most to have preoccupied them—and therefore, presumably, to have been the most powerful forces existing in the old religion—were those connected with underground water and with high places. The first of these has, again, an association with dowsing that can help us understand its nature. Water-finding is the best-known part of dowsing, and is the easiest of any hidden force for an inexperienced dowser to recognize; finding beneficial or healing water is regarded by many dowsers as an even more important part of their work.

Some scientists have noted the connection between underground water, and sickness or health. One of them, the Yorkshireman Dr. Arthur Bailey, who is a well-established dowser, wrote: "One thing is quite certain, and that is that people can be affected by living on top of streams or earth rays—the influence is called by many names. There are many instances of cows, horses and other animals definitely suffering as a result of being kept over these noxious influences, and you cannot accuse an animal of autosuggestion." The contrary side of these findings is that there is some water that works the other way: it can cure.

Well-worship is universal among early people. The Indians, Egyptians, Persians and Greeks all had deities of

Harold's Stones, Trelech, Monmouthshire, Wales: their angle of lean, and mass, have been well captured by the artist, but in reality they stand much farther apart.

fountains and streams; in one of the oldest fragments of Hebrew poetry, the fountain is addressed as a living being, and in all these countries there are places—the Ganges, for example—where the waters are sacred, and will cleanse or purify those who bathe in them. What seems to distinguish the European wells is the huge number of them that appear to have contained the same practical magic which the early Christians found in the stone monuments: they were widely supposed, like today's spring at Notre Dame de Lourdes, to have supernatural qualities which would cure or regenerate those who used them. As with holed stones, they would heal rickets or infertility or skin diseases.

The Church adopted toward them its familiar technique of absorbing their ancient powers. In France, there are known to be formerly pagan-worshipped springs under the cathedrals of Chartres, Nîmes and Sangres; in Britain at York Minster, Carlisle cathedral, Glastonbury and elsewhere; in Ireland, St. Patrick chose sacred wells as well as other pagan sites for his churches, and once preached at a fountain "which the Druids worshipped as a God." In due course, the Church began to take the credit for such

healing powers as the wells contained. At Llandeilo
Llwydarth in West Wales, the water cured whooping
cough—providing it was drunk from a skull reputed to
be that of St. Teilo. At St. Agnes Well near Whitestaunton
church in Somerset, the water was always warm, and had
curative properties only if it was drunk from a consecrated
vessel. But many non-Christian practices persisted, and
they are interesting because they must echo, however
faintly, the original pagan rituals which were used to in-
voke the magical healing powers.

As late as 1934, villagers at Bradstone in Devon could
recite a piece of doggerel about their local healing well,
covered with small flat stones:

> If you would rise before the sun
> And out to Broadstones well would run,
> Wash your eyes three times and then
> Leave a gift and go again,
> Nor grieve for what you leave behind—
> A perfect cure you will find;
> A threefold journey you must take,
> Before you will that cure make.

Often, rituals involved certain days on which the signs
were held to be propitious. At Tissington, Derbyshire, the
most celebrated holy well in Britain at the beginning of this
century, it was Ascension Day; every year a kind of
floral mosaic, designed on a framework, was placed
over the fountain. Other ceremonies involved movement
by people in a certain formalized way around the well,
usually spoken of in connection with the movement of the
sun, and perhaps requiring the help of a magic number.
In the nineteenth century, in the Perthshire town of Til-
lie Beltane, there was a hill surmounted by a stone circle
dedicated to the sun-god Baal. On May Day, the feast of
Beltane, local people would drink from the well and
walk around it nine times in a clockwise direction; then
they went to the circle and did the same thing there. In
the first part of this century, devotees of the well of Tub-
berpatrick in County Derry, Ireland, said prayers, washed
themselves in the waters, and hung up rags as offerings
on a nearby bush. Next they entered the church to per-
form a similar ceremony, finally returning in procession
to the upright stone—the whole ritual being an excep-

tionally vivid example of pagan/Christian ceremonial confusion.

Just how many of the wells achieved their reportedly miraculous results before, and how many after, the arrival of the Christians cannot be discovered. But since modern science has shown what man has always known, that there are curative properties in some mineral waters, it is easy enough to accept both that megalithic man found them generally beneficial, and that the Church found it necessary to incorporate their healing magic. What is much less simple to unravel is megalithic man's preoccupation with the highest and farthest places, the hills and extremities of his lands. The story of how the Christian church used its most important saint, St. Michael, to assimilate the natural forces of these sites is potentially the most illuminating of all the sanctifications; but also the most elusive and intangible.

All over Europe, in improbably remote and inaccesible places quite unattached to parishes or villages, tiny churches or chapels dedicated to St. Michael cling to hilltops, standing there in mute remembrance of some earlier veneration. They stretch the length and breadth of the continent. James Fergusson described two in Spain:

> At Cangas de Onis, in the Asturias, is a small church built into a mound which contains in it a dolmen. The church was built in the tenth or eleventh century, to which this dolmen served as a crypt. . . . It would seem as if the Christians had built the church when the dolmen was still a sacred edifice. A still more remarkable instance of this kind is to be found at a place called Arrichinaga, about twenty-five miles from Bilbao. In the hermitage of St. Michael, at this place, a dolmen of very considerable dimensions is enclosed within the walls of a modern church. It may, however, be the successor of one more ancient, but the fact of these great stones being adopted by the Christians shows that they must have been considered sacred, and objects of worship by the natives at the time when the Christians enclosed them in this edifice.

Both these churches are on high ground, and other St. Michael churches are built so high as to be incomprehen-

Megaliths in the church of Arrichinaga, Spain.

sible except in terms of a very powerful earlier sacredness. At the village of St. Michel-en-Grêve in Brittany, the church is a good hour's walk to the top of the nearby hill; next to it is an immense lichen-covered menhir. Mont St. Michel, on the summit of which early Christians built a chapel, is a huge man-made mound on the edge of the Atlantic, linked to the stone alignments at Carnac. It is matched off northern France by the precipitous Mont St. Michel off the coast of Normandy, and in Britain by St. Michael's Mount in the bay at Lands End, the farthermost tip of Britain pointing westward over the ocean. Here, once, was the Priory of St. Michael, built on a pagan circle. It is the starting point of the ancient 200-mile route that led to Glastonbury, Avebury and beyond, and along its remaining fragments are some of the most evocative examples of the subtle landscaping and artificial topography that took place during several thousand years before the work was inherited by the early Christian church, and sanctified in the name of St. Michael and others.

From many points along the route you can see the strange, flat-topped hills often marked on the maps as hill forts or castles, but nowadays more often called cause-

wayed camps because the archaeological evidence for any
defensive purpose is thin. There is seldom much evidence
in the way of early flint axheads or sling stones—or indeed, of any substantial or sustained human occupation.
They have therefore been interpreted as part of a vast
network of megalithic sites created by ancient man and
used as part of an overall geophysical scheme whose purpose has since been lost and forgotten. Often, so carefully
have the contours been altered, the hills seem interchangeable: Burrowbridge Mound and Montacute Hill, one with
a ruined St. Michael's church on its summit, the other with
the remnants of an ancient circular earthwork, are examples. The familiar shape occurs again at Glastonbury Tor,
where the volcanic oddity that forced it from the flat and
marshy landscape around has been so shaped and sculp-
tured with intricate patterns that, from a distance, the hill
looks as man-made as Silbury. Other natural prominences
like Brent Tor on the edge of Dartmoor, or Rough Tor
on Bodmin Moor, have been crowned by a tiny ancient
church or great stones, indefinably but indisputably part
of some larger pattern that was understood by megalithic
man.

In order to explain to their parishioners why their
churches had been built in such unlikely and inconvenient
places, medieval parsons used to tell legends about how
the stones making up the fabric of the building were taken
there by divine power or guidance, or by some other
superhuman agency. St. Michael himself has been seen by
some theologians as the saint nearest to God on high, the
equivalent of the classical god Apollo who came from
the sun, and this is why he was placed on the pagan hills.

However, others think that, if he is a successor to any
pagan god it may have been the Anglo-Saxon deity Wotan,
the warlike queller of dragons. St. Michael, the recognized Christian leader of the spiritual forces contending
for the Church against the powers of darkness, is described
in the Book of Revelation as head of the band of angels
that went to war with the dragon and his cohorts: "And
the great dragon was cast down, the old serpent, he that
is called the Devil and Satan, the deceiver of the whole
world." St. Michael and St. George, his fellow saint, can
be found in the art of hundreds of their churches, shown
killing the dragon or standing triumphant over one, and it
was John Michell in *A View Over Atlantis* who first

spotted that the Christian church might have been using this dragon symbol to represent the ancient power contained in ley lines and megalithic monuments. As evidence, he noted the abnormal number of St. Michael or St. George churches spaced along the Lands End–Glastonbury–Avebury–Bury St. Edmunds ley, which he dubbed a "dragon path."

It is instructive to examine this line in some detail, because along its length it demonstrates both the weaknesses of an overrigid interpretation of leys, and at the same time much evidence that there was once indeed something strange and irresistible, which can be seen today in legend, symbol, and ruined monuments. On the first count, it fails the most important test of purist ley hunters because it isn't dead straight. If you take a compass bearing from St. Michael's Mount through any significant ley point, whether you choose the tiny village called Ley, or the megalithic sites of the Hurlers or the Cheesewring on Bodmin Moor, or the St. Michael's church on Brent Tor, you miss Glastonbury by some miles, and Avebury by even more. Yet the profusion of stone circles and other monuments close to the line leaves little doubt that it was a busy and well-populated route. From the clusters of circles on the heights of both Dartmoor and Bodmin Moor, on clear days, you can see right back to Lands End, and carefully placed cairns on the highest points are still used by walkers today to mark their way ahead. It is interesting, too, in view of megalithic man's fascination with significant calendar dates, that the average orientation along the line, at 62° W. of North, is the approximate direction of the May Day sunrise.

Much the most densely marked part of the path is the section on either side of Glastonbury, and here, although the line is again not exactly straight, the profusion of dragonlore makes it easy to believe that you are following the footsteps of countless travelers 5,000 years or more ago, who had identified a mystic force that was concentrated in their sacred centers, and at the same time linked them. A clearly defined southwest starting point is the tiny St. Michael's church nestling in the wooded valley of Cadbury, Devonshire (not the Cadbury of Arthurian legend). Beside it is an ancient wayside cross, and some 250 feet above is one of those causewayed camps so commonly found, and immediately recognizable. A great earthwork

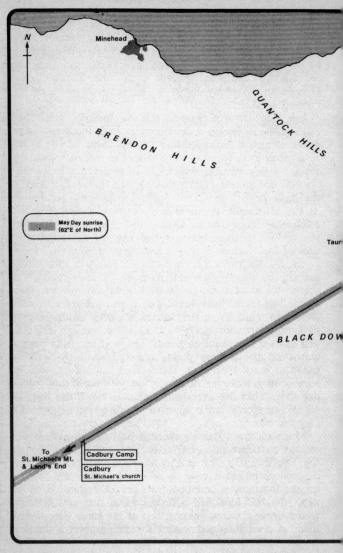

Dragon path, Cadbury-Avebury: A ley line distorted like a strand of a spider's web?

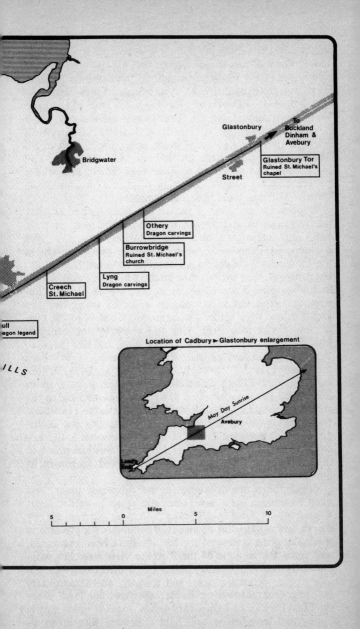

Bridgwater

Glastonbury

To
Buckland
Dinham &
Avebury

Street

Glastonbury Tor
Ruined St. Michael's
chapel

Othery
Dragon carvings

Burrowbridge
Ruined St. Michael's
church

Lyng
Dragon carvings

Creech
St. Michael

ull
agon legend

ILLS

Location of Cadbury ► Glastonbury enlargement

May Day Sunrise

Avebury

Miles

5   0   5   10

surrounds the artificially flattened top, and it dominates
the landscape for three-quarters of the horizon to the
north, west and south. Excavations have shown its constant use from neolithic to Anglo-Saxon times, and Ris-
bury's *Survey of Devon* of 1626 has the legend of a dragon
that flies from its summit. Twenty-two miles away, on a
bearing of 60½° W. of North, you arrive via Leylands
Farm at the next significant mark point, the church of St.
Michael in Trull, where on the nearby Castleman's Hill
the dragon was supposed to have been killed, and whose
church has a window depicting all three dragon-killing
saints—Michael, George and Margaret.

Depending on your view of ley lines—whether they
are very narrow and precise over short distances, or wide
and only approximate over long distances—you now have
a choice. A bearing of 60½° will take you precisely to
the St. Michael chapel on the summit of Glastonbury Tor;
but you will miss every other landmark on the way by up
to half a mile. Since these landmarks are of obvious importance, it is easier to imagine a ley as being like the
radial thread on a spider's web, leading directly to the center, but distorted a little here and there by the contrary
pull of connecting threads. A bearing of 62° goes to
Creech St. Michael church, five miles away. From here
the bearing is 58° through the church at Lyng, whose
earlier dragon-killing associations can clearly be seen in
the carved pews and stained glass windows, and on to the
ruined St. Michael church on top of the largely artificial
Burrowbridge mount. From this hill you can see in the
distance Glastonbury Tor, and midway between is the key
church of Othery St. Michael (also the western point of
the Great Isosceles Triangle), with a carved dragon in its
porchway.

Glastonbury stands alone in the Somerset plain, and
must have been even more dramatic when in earlier times
—perhaps as late as 1000 B.C.—it was surrounded by
marsh and isolated lake villages. Remnants of a prehistoric
track along the course of the ley line have been excavated,
and from the summit of the Tor the view stretches mag-
nificently for fifty or sixty miles in all directions—an obvious place of ancient awe and wonder, an extraordinary
volcanic rock thrown up in an otherwise flat land. Here
on May Day in contemporary times, local people, mostly
young and long-haired, still light a Beltane Fire in an at-

tempt to recapture some of the ancient magic as the sun rises exactly on line with Avebury some forty miles away.

The way to Avebury is marked by the church at Buckland Dinham, sited carefully on much the most prominent hill before reaching the Wiltshire Downs, dedicated at one time to St. Michael, and the center of other leys. Sixteen miles farther on, precisely on line, is Mother Anthony's Well, an ancient holy spring subsequently built on by the Romans and now nothing more than a boggy patch at the bottom of a wild and ivy-filled thicket. No doubt it refreshed and invigorated ancient travelers before they went the last few miles past Oliver's Fort, eminent as a sighting mark for many miles, but useless as a defense. The last mile to Avebury goes along the ancient road used by the Romans and their successors right up to today, and past the southern edge of the great circle. In Avebury church is a famous carving on the font of a bishop killing a dragon, and the final mark point in the immediate area is another dragon church at Ogbourne St. George.

Such a powerful collection of dragon images concentrated in a significant alignment on the largest prehistoric site, and the oldest Christian site, in Britain, demands investigation. For if, when the early Christian missionaries took over the pagan places of worship, healing and ceremony, they found something there which was symbolized by the power of the dragon, then the nature of this power must be revealing about the knowledge of megalithic man, and the forces that shaped his world.

8

HEAVENS ON EARTH?

Thus is astrologie and astronomie carefullie and exactly married and measured in a scientific reconstruction of the heavens which shows that the ancients understode all which today the lerned know to be factes.

—ATTRIBUTED TO DR. JOHN DEE, PHYSICIAN
TO QUEEN ELIZABETH I OF ENGLAND

WHERE 10,000 YEARS OR SO EARLIER PALAEOLITHIC MAN
had developed representational art of high beauty in his
cave paintings of life around him, megalithic man was
interested only in symbolism. Zigzags, circles, triangles,
diamonds, spirals—they can be found all over the world at
a certain stage of man's development, with an uncanny
resemblance between them. Of these, perhaps the most
fascinating and fundamental is the spiral. Professor
Flinders Petrie, one of the great Victorian archaeologists,
called it "the main feature of primitive decoration, often
elaborately involved." Sir Arthur Evans found it on scar-
abs in Crete. The Rev. H. J. Dukinfield Astley, writing
in the *Archaeological Journal* in 1901, said he had found
spirals and similar serpentine markings in Scandinavia,
Asia Minor, China, New Zealand, Australia, India, North
and South America, and the Pacific Islands. It appears on
the two most abundantly decorated megalithic monuments
in northwest Europe—at Gavr Innis in Brittany and at
Newgrange in Ireland. In the little church of Llanbedr in
north Wales there is a single small granite standing stone,
rescued from the hills above and placed there for protection, on which a spiral has been painstakingly pounded
out.

It is so basic a symbol that each person looking into it
seems to be able to discover a new significance. Alexander
Thom has found there further evidence of mathematics,
in the way that it can be used to decipher the secrets of
the megalithic yard; certainly, it is a unique geometrical
figure in the way that it reaches toward an infinity of
smallness at one end, and an infinity of greatness at the
other. The dowser John Williams, in the double spirals at
Newgrange, feels the representation of a positive and negative force; if he makes a connection between the two he
receives a shock as if by electricity. In three dimensions,

Mort et Convai du Serpent piqué

Temple

Spiral life-force still attaches to corpse of Natchez Indian
(end seventeenth century) as he is carried to burial mound
in background.

Spiral markings on megalithic tombs at Newgrange and Cloverhill, Ireland.

inches

as a whirlpool or vortex, the forms and implications of a spiral multiply. Astronomers and physicists now believe that it is a spiral force which creates the universe itself. Galaxies such as our own Milky Way are shaped in a spirally rotating wave pattern from which new stars are born; at the opposite end of the scale, the DNA molecule that shapes all life is made up of twin spirals.

For the young Irish archaeologist Michael Morris, writing in the *Irish Archaeological Research Forum* in 1974, megalithic art on passage graves and elsewhere, is far more than a mere embellishment. "We are dealing with an integral part of total ritual symbolism which the monument expresses. The spiral and the concentric circle are doubtlessly the dominant motifs . . . at its most abstract level of meanings, the spiral may have expressed the concept of life-energy . . . of cosmic energy and life rhythms with which early man was concerned."

If the spiral is the most widespread prehistoric symbol, perhaps the most universal legend is that of the power of the serpent dragon, which in its different forms can be traced back to early times almost everywhere. It is notable that in the whole world, it is only in the areas which have been converted by the Christian church that both the serpent and the dragon have jointly come to signify evil. Everywhere else (including the Old Testament) they are either beneficial, or embody in their powers both good and evil, or potentially are capable of either.

The serpent who tempted Eve in the the Garden of Eden contained all wisdom. In India, the serpent is the giver of fertility. In Roman mythology, the serpent entwined around the staff of the god Asclepius became the symbol of healing and the physician, which is still used by the medical profession today. The Greeks and Romans conceived *drakontes* as life-enhancing forces, sharp-eyed dwellers in the inner body of the earth. In ancient Egyptian myth, the dragon represented the beneficent powers of water, and the serpent the harmful—the god Apepi was the great serpent of the world of darkness. In China and Japan, the dragon is almost entirely beneficent and powerful—the embodiment of water and other life-giving powers. Their emperors took the symbol of the dragon and placed it foremost on their standards and their royal vestments. The protection and guidance of the dragon brought good luck, the rejuvenation of mankind, and the possibility of immortality.

That he was endowed with these capacities, drawn from the magic power of water, was believed also by the Algonquin and Iroquois Indians in America. A flying dragon depicted on the rocks at Piasa, Illinois, is identical to those found in the Far East, and the great serpent mound of Ohio, dated at about the first century B.C., indicates the reverence in which the serpent dragon was held. Sir Grafton Elliot Smith, who traveled the world in the 1920s looking for the significance of dragon legends that he found in North and South America, Japan, China, Indonesia, India and through the Middle East, thought that the power of the dragon was invariably connected with its command over the forces of water, both for good and bad: "It controls the rivers or seas, dwells in pools or wells, or in the clouds on the tops of mountains, regulates the tides, the flow of streams, or the rainfall, and is associated with thunder and lightning," he wrote. Its home is sometimes "a mansion at the bottom of the sea, where it guards vast treasures, usually pearls, but also gold and precious stones. In other instances, the dwelling is on the top of a high mountain."

Another facet of the dragon myths in China is the way they are invoked in the ancient art of geomancy, or *feng-shui*. The geomancers in that country, men with special sensitivity and long training in astrology and the meaning of the calendar, were employed right up until this century to show people where to place and orientate their cities, palaces and tombs so that the subtle magnetic currents of the earth would act most favorably for them. These currents were detected by dowsing as well as by the use of a magnetic compass, and were of two kinds, negative (*yin*) and positive (*yang*). *Yang,* represented by the male dragon, comprised mostly the high rocks and sharp peaks in which water and rain were generated, and the dragon paths on which he traveled were known as *lung-mei*. So similar are the apparent forces of ley lines and the Chinese *lung-mei* that many followers of John Mitchell think that we see today in Watkins's old straight tracks the remnants of a worldwide prehistoric system of geomancy. Michell wrote in *A View Over Atlantis:*

We have no means of expressing, other than in aesthetic terms, what is it that makes one part of the
country seem different to another. We speak vaguely
of a certain spot being picturesque, powerful and
stimulating or peaceful and soothing. Yet the Chinese
geomancers had . a definite standard by which the
quality of a place could be measured and judged.
They reckoned every site in terms of a flow of current
they called the dragon force and, from what we know
of the characteristics they attributed this current, it
seems they could only have been referring to the
mysterious stream of terrestrial magnetism about
which we now know so little.

In the most favored places of all, burial grounds for
emperors and princes were built in the shape of artificial
mounds that bear a marked resemblance to Silbury Hill
—or to the Pyramids of the Pharaohs. The future success
of families or dynasties was supposed to rest on the ability
of the geomancer to choose the most rewarding and beneficial spot for burial.

In art the world over, the early serpent dragons are
represented symbolically in two ways: as a spiral, the one
symbol that looks like a coiled sleeping serpent; and in the
form of a zigzag, the lines going up and down like a serpent in motion, or waves on water. Over the years, as the
serpent itself became a dragon, succeeding generations
added wings, horns or crests to turn him ino a fire-
breathing, flying beast. The two basic, primitive symbols
are, of course, precisely the ones most commonly found
on megalithic sites. The zigzag form persisted for many
centuries. It is usually in this form that he is seen in early
church iconography, St. Michael and St. George standing
above him having conquered his power.

So it seems likely that megalithic man, like pre-
Christian people almost everywhere, came to identify as a
dragon the unseen forces that he instinctively felt were
shaping and affecting his life. Whether he felt these forces
were good or bad, helpful or harmful, or—like most other
people in the world—an ambiguous and unpredictable
mixture of the two, there is not enough evidence to be
sure. But early Christian practice again gives an indication
of how strong a hold these forces had over the imagina-

Mound near Locust Grove, Ohio, is the largest portrayal of serpent power yet discovered; it can only be seen properly from the air.

tion of a pagan people. The dragon became fixed in Christian verse and myth as greedy and possessive.

Early Christian heroes from St. George to Beowulf, Arthur and Sir Lancelot fight a dragon as their crowning achievement. Legends were created that vilified and transformed the nature of dragon power until it became dangerous and frightening. Any remnants of beneficence were expunged so that by the eighth century A.D., Anglo-Saxon poetry telling the tale of Beowulf described the dragon that eventually killed him as "a bright and horrible monster," "grisly bright and scorched with flame," the "smooth malicious dragon that seeks out mounds all afire, and flies by night wrapped in flame; he is feared by the land-dwellers."

Dragon and other megalithic sites not used for churches were dubbed as places belonging to the devil. Wansdyke, a vast earthwork in the west of England named after the Anglo-Saxon god Wotan, was also known as the Devil's Ditch. Long barrows became the Devil's Bed and Bolster or the Devil's Den, round barrows and circles became the Devil's Hump or the Devil's Ring. Beowulf's dragon guarded a long barrow: "It is his lot to seek out the hoard in the earth; ancient in years, he mounts guard over the heathen gold, yet he is not one whit the better for it."

Those familiarly shaped hills of megalithic man, with their artificially flattened tops and coils of serpentlike earthworks leading up to their summits, became known as dragon hills. One such is the Dragon Hill below the White Horse of Uffington in Oxfordshire. On top of this hill is a patch of ground where, it is said, the grass will never grow. On the hill facing it, aerial photographs indicate the position of an earlier white horse that stood there triumphantly in Christian legend as the portrait of the steed of King George (or St. George), who slew the dragon and destroyed his power. Over the years soil erosion, washing away the outline of the horse at the top and piling up the soil and grass at the base, has moved the figure steadily up the hill until it has reached its present position, and is now difficult to see clearly from anywhere on the ground locally. For those interested in uncanny coincidences, this natural process of erosion has subtly changed the character of the figure so that, from the air, it looks as much like a dragon as a horse—a sign, some might say, of the unquenchable forces that the Christians tried to suppress.

The common characteristic in nearly all these legends is the dragon's guardianship of mysterious and symbolic treasure. The nature of this treasure may have become misty and distorted with the passing of time, but clues can still be detected both in the folklore of megalithic sites and in pagan mythology. Thus the dragon that flew around Cadbury Camp in Devonshire (on the Lands End–Bury St. Edmunds alignment), guarded a treasure that may have been the lost secret of crop fertility—an early piece of doggerel about the camp reads:

Spirals and linked zigzags at Newgrange.

Dragon inscribed by Vikings at
Maeshowe, Orkney Islands.

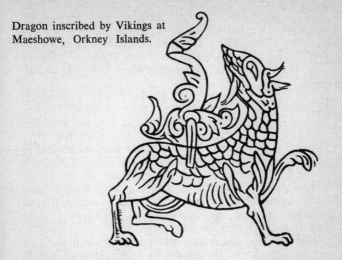

If Cadbury camp, & Dolbery Hill down delved were;
Then Denshire might plow with a golden Coulter,
& care with a guilded shere.

A *coulter* being part of a plow, and a *shere* being a
sickle or scythe, this medieval verse can only mean that
the causewayed camps at both Cadbury and Dolbury
(some five miles away) were thought locally to contain a
hidden power that could bring riches to the surrounding
countryside. Wagner's *Ring,* drawn from the remotest
depths of ancient myth, has Siegfried kill the dragon which
guards the treasured ring itself; as soon as he has done so,
and tasted the blood of the dragon on his lips, he becomes
at one with nature and is able to understand the song of
the birds.

So the meaning of the serpent dragon became altered
or forgotten, obscured by myth and legend, as did the
spiral which represented it. But in one curious form, the
markings of megalithic times have retained their power
right up until today. For as well as the spiral, it has been
noted earlier in this book how megalithic man's concentric
circles with linking lines—his "cup and ring" markings—
seem also to have been a universal symbol. And when
these two symbols are combined, you get a labyrinth or a

maze: a spiral that turns back on itself. The identical appearance of the maze in countries all over the world is one of the most compelling pieces of evidence we have for the theory of a kind of psychic unity that linked all races of early man as he sought answers to the puzzles of the universe.

The earliest one that can be dated with certainty is Egyptian, from the middle of the nineteenth century B.C., and the best known is the maze at Knossos, in Crete, where Theseus legendarily slew the Minotaur. But when identical mazes appear in places as far apart as Madras in India; on an uninhabited island off the coast of Finland; as the basic symbol for the Hopi Indians; set out as the central pattern in the floors of European cathedrals; and on medieval village greens all over England—then, it must represent a deep unconscious truth. (Curiously, these English mazes were known as "troys.")

Like leys and old stones, mazes still have a power that can be felt, almost obsessively, by some people. Geoffrey Russell, who ran a substantial financial and insurance business in Ceylon for twenty-five years, dreamed one night of a mazelike shape. He says the dream was so compelling that he was certain it held, for him at least, some visionary content. He drew the outline as accurately as possible on a piece of paper, and kept it in the top drawer of his desk where, occasionally, he would glance at it. "I never told anybody about it," he says. "I knew it had an immense personal significance for me, but it wasn't the kind of thing that it seemed possible to describe to anyone else."

So far as he knows, he had never at that time seen a labyrinth either in pictorial shape or on the ground, but in 1962, idly glancing through a copy of his wife's *Country Life,* he saw one which was instantly recognizable as the shape he had dreamed and drawn—a photograph of a maze cut out on a rock at Tintagel in Cornwall. The comparison with his own sketch of eighteen years before was so astonishingly exact, and the impression on him so revelationary in its impact, that within a short time he had wound up his business and dedicated his life to the investigation of the meaning of labyrinth patterns.

His most interesting discovery has been to show, with the help of aerial photographs taken by the Royal Air Force, that the meandering ridges etched out on the sides

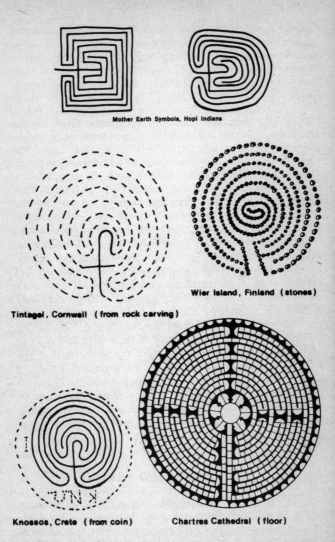

Mother Earth Symbols, Hopi Indians

Tintagel, Cornwall (from rock carving)

Wier Island, Finland (stones)

Knossos, Crete (from coin)

Chartres Cathedral (floor)

Mazes from different eras and countries. Compare megalithic carvings and cup-and-ring markings on pages 27 and 229.

of Glastonbury Tor seem to form the same universal maze
pattern—the only three-dimensional labyrinth known. He
believes it was put there for early Christian pilgrims or
initiates to tread a path from Hell—the entrance to the
maze—to Heaven—the summit, where the ruined chapel
of St. Michael now stands. It would have taken them
seven full circuits, and covered every part of the maze.
"Unlike the game of Snakes and Ladders, there are no
short cuts," he says. "Each part of each track of the labyrinth represents a different kind of experience, and I believe that to cross over the paths in an attempt to get to
the heart quickly was wrong and even dangerous."

Nowadays, of course, the vast majority of tourists who
climb the Tor do just that, by climbing directly up the
spine of the hill, and most of them feel nothing unto-
ward. At the same time, there are numerous local stories
of people who feel an inexplicable drain of energy on
certain points of the Tor. Subjective though the experiences are, to the people who have felt them they are real
enough—"as if an irresistible current was sucking away
part of your life energy," was how one of them explained
it. Similarly, and again it is impossible to prove objectively
one way or the other, those who walk the labyrinthine
tracks say they feel a lightening of their steps and a surge
of received power as they approach the final stretch. "The
journey through the maze is for the regeneration of the
soul," says Geoffrey Russell, echoing what the Hopi Indians believe of their own maze. According to their chronicler, Frank Waters: "All the lines and passages within
the maze form the universal plan of the Creator which
man must follow on his Road of Life."

SUN, MOON AND STARS

If the spiral represented the cosmic forces of creation
which megalithic man could sense but not see, his other
preoccupation was to capture and symbolize the influence
of the heavenly bodies on his life—the stars, particularly
the sun, and the planets. Sun-worship was recognized by
the early archaeologists as something that all primitive
races underwent at a certain stage of their development.
R. A. Courtney wrote in *The Hill and the Circle* (1912):

Amongst all nations there arises a desire to possess some symbol reminding them of their god, and as the deity was originally the sun, naturally it would be something in shape similar to that power. Daily they saw the sun rise, roll through the sky, till at eve it set, and as its motion suggested a wheel the divine symbol was made in that shape. It appears in Thibet among the Lamas. In Buddhist sculptures the sacred symbol is always represented as the wheel of a vehicle; this was with them not original, for they borrowed it from the Brahmans in whose ceremonies the wheel was a conspicuous feature. . . . In the north of Europe, among the Scandinavians, the sun was called a wheel; in the Eddas it is spoken of as the shining wheel, the beautiful wheel; and in some Runic calendars, the winter solstice is figured by a wheel.

There were other symbols for the sun, too. All over the world, archaeologists have found small discs, some with holes in them, which have been interpreted as being an attempt to capture the power of the sun and put it to some curative use. Numerous barrows and graves have revealed discs from two to six inches in diameter. Beneath the dolmens of Japan, archaeologists dug up radially striped discs which they dubbed "wagon-wheel stones." Egyptians and Babylonians wore amulets of bronze or gold discs. Cherokee Indian medicine men used circular beads to drop in the hole made when pulling up a root, in order to compensate the earth for the plant pulled out —and in this may be a clue to the reason for all this sun-worship.

Looking at the evidence of megalithic man's fascination with astronomy, one gets the impression that it cannot have had just an abstract purpose; that, instead, it had a mystical yet practical significance far deeper and more mysterious than even Alexander Thom has suggested. The minutely careful positioning of the light box at the entrance to Newgrange so that it fleetingly caught the midwinter sunrise; the alignment of Stonehenge and so many other circles to the midsummer sunrise; the massive alignment of southern English sites on the May Day sunrise; the meticulous care that he took to work out the solstices and the times of future eclipses—all these can be interpreted to say that he was trying to trap and harness some powerful force by means of an unthinkably complicated but accurate pattern laid out over the face of the earth. That the sun could warm the ground and make the crops grow was obvious. But could it—with the other heavenly bodies—provide some other power as well?

There is an astronomical concept known as declination, which like all similar terms is extremely difficult to put in words, since it defines a moving three-dimensional relationship between the center of the earth, the tilt of the earth ("true" north), and the sun, as both bodies orbit through space. A dictionary definition is "the angle of the sun above the equator as measured from the earth's center," but without a working model of the firmament on which to demonstrate this, it is perhaps best just to think of it as one of the fundamentals of modern astronomy, without which it is impossible to work out how the universe rotates. The astronomer Douglas Heggie called it "the most important astronomical concept." The *Encyclopaedia Britannica* says the angle of declination is "an unexplained mystery originating in the past history of the Earth."

Slight changes in the orbit of the earth caused by shifting gravitational pulls from outer space cause small changes in the angle, but it has a mean average over the last few thousand years of about 23½°. John Williams is convinced that megalithic man both knew the angle and discovered that when his mark stones and other sites were laid out in this relationship, their power was magnified in some way that is not now known to science.

Now this is a controversial discovery, and one that Professor Richard Atkinson thought was not worth considering. But John Williams is convinced it can be proved—indeed, that a computer-based analysis of his work in an American university has already proved it. Like ley hunters, his findings are based on tracing relationships of ancient sites on one-inch or 1:50,000 Ordnance Survey maps; but unlike them, he rigorously excludes anything of post-Roman origin. He has named his alignments "Scemb" lines by using the initials of the types of sites involved:

Standing stones and stone circles
Camps (pre-Roman) and cairns
Earthworks (such as causewayed camps)

Mounds (e.g. Silbury Hill) and pre-Roman moats
Barrows, including dolmens and rocking stones

Williams is nothing if not thorough, and he has catalogued and analyzed more than 3,000 sites over a period
of more than twenty-five years. "I have found that every
standing stone in the British Isles is positioned in direct
alignment with two or more other prehistoric sites," he
says. "I have also found that the angle of 23½° or its
multiples of 47°, 70½°, and 94°, occur repeatedly. By
the law of averages, this should happen only about 4 times
in 180. But when I sent one of my maps to be checked
in America, I received the answer that as many as 60
percent of the angles were declination angles."

To an outsider, Williams's maps are so crisscrossed with
lines (statistically, on most maps it is more likely than
not that three scemb-line points will occur in alignment)
that they become extremely difficult to interpret. But
Williams is sure that ultimately his research will be justified, and will take its place within our increasing awareness of ancient astronomy. "What worried me for many
years was, even if the astronomers of those days knew the
angle of declination, how their surveyors and engineers
could have worked out how to plan it so exactly on the
ground. Then one day I suddenly realized that 23½°
is exactly the angle formed when you draw a diagonal line
across a 9 × 4 rectangle. So if they wanted to lay out
the angle, and I'm convinced they did, they had an easy
way of doing it."

Although it is hard to see how, by observation alone,
megalithic man could have discovered the angle of declination, Professor Thom's discoveries about his astronomical abilities make it different to put a limit on his
achievements in this direction. Another concept that
John Williams believes he may have understood and used
—although it must have involved observations over thousands of years—is known as the precession of the
equinoxes. As it spins, the earth wobbles slightly, rather
like a spinning top as it starts to run down. It means that
the star toward which the North Pole points appears to
move very gradually across the sky until after some thousands of years it is replaced by another, and so on until
after about 26,000 years the cycle repeats itself. Our
present north star, Polaris, will not in fact be exactly due

north until A.D. 2100, and about 10,000 years after that it will apparently have drifted away until its place has been taken by the star Vega.

That megalithic man knew this, in spite of the enormous time scale concerned, seems likely as a result of further detective work by John Williams. In the millennia during which the stones and circles were being built, Polaris and its constellation the Great Bear were steadily moving toward the North Pole in place of two stars contained in the constellation Draco (the Dragon). In Welsh, and phonetically in Celtic, the Great Bear is *Arth Vawr*. Scattered over Great Britain and Ireland are more than 100 sites with the almost indistinguishable name "Arthur," many of them megalithic sites such as Arthur's Stone, Arthur's Seat, Arthur's Quoit, and so on. The great majority of the latter lie within a north-south aligned scemb line.

In the connection between these ancient megaliths and the pole star may hide the origins of the Arthurian legends. Scholars have always been puzzled why such a large amount of early medieval European literature—some estimates put it as high as one-quarter of the total—is devoted to Arthur; for not only has he never been proved to be a king of England but, even if he were, it is difficult to see why European clerics should have been so fascinated by him. If, however, they were writing about a supremely important prehistoric god of the pole star, whose powers were at one time essential to the workings of pagan religion and were then fancifully Christianized, it would fit in with the general pattern whereby the old pagan gods and beliefs were transformed and assimilated into the traditions of the Church.

The relevant prehistoric phase in the precession of the equinoxes, when Arth Vawr, the Great Bear, succeeded Draco, the Dragon, supplies additional evidence of the theory. Arthur's father has come down in fable and legend as Pendragon—in Welsh, Head of the Dragon—and his grandfather as Uthyr or Uter Pendragon, or Wonderful Head of the Dragon. In Arthurian legends, Merlin has many stories about fighting dragons, and Williams sees in these a symbolic account of the changeover of successive generations of pole stars.

As with the spiral and the disc, the importance of the pole star—perhaps for worship, perhaps for something more powerful—seems to be universal as man emerged everywhere into civilization, and to symbolize it he mostly used a triangle. In Egypt, Set and Horus were gods of the north star; entrances into the Pyramids were always made on the north side. In early China, their supreme god was known as T'ien; his symbol was a triangle with a slight extension of the downward arms, not unlike the capital letter A, and in his time the principal objects of worship were the pole star and the Great Bear. In Japan in this century, where the Ainu people were studied because it was believed they were direct descendants of the original inhabitants, the bear was worshipped above all gods. In India, the sacred and mythical mountain Meru is supposed to be at the North Pole, where the gods reside. Many of the polar-aligned megalithic sites incorporate a stone in an upturned V-shape, echoing the triangular symbol used elsewhere.

The spiral and the serpent for unseen forces; the disc and the angle of declination for the sun; the triangular pointer to the pole star—together these symbols may indicate that megalithic man was searching toward an understanding of the infinitely subtle universal forces that only today is science able to measure in its own fashion. What he must have realized, for instance, in his observations of the perturbation of the moon's orbit, is that all things are subject to minute and almost undetectable changes of influence, and live within cycles and rhythms that are largely dictated by this.

The lunar cycle is an obvious example, and its gravitational pull on the tides is there for all to see. But scientists have now developed instruments so sensitive that they can measure the tidal effects in a teacup full of water, and monthly distortions in the rock formations of Pennine caves. The world itself is a far from stable place even within these shifting forces of life. The theory of continental drift is now respectable: millions of years ago, America and Africa were joined, and satellites can detect minute, constant land movements at a rate of perhaps five millimeters a year. Geologists have discovered that on several occasions in the world's history, there has been a remarkable and so far unexplained change of direction of the earth's magnetic field—a complete reversal of its polarity. Over a period of about 10,000 years the field gradually weakens to a very small intensity and then reestablishes itself with equal intensity in exactly the opposite direction. The present field of polarity has been as now for most of the last 700,000 years—approximately the time since earliest man—but had two periods of 10,000–20,000 years within that time when it was reversed. Geneticists think that such periods accelerate the evolutionary process, by causing widespread extinctions and increasing the rate of mutations.

Equally mysteriously, the center of magnetic north wanders over the world's surface. In the distant past, it has probably been as far south as the equator, and many astronomers think this has caused substantial changes in the earth's orbit. Within the time between early megalithic man and ourselves it has been between 20° and 30° on either side of its mean average, true north. Nobody knows why this should be, nor where the magnetic field of the earth is derived. Probably, it comes about as a result of the electric currents near the earth's core, which magnetize the crust of the earth that is free from such currents; but there is no unarguably correct theory.

Living amid these subtle, shifting pressures and rhythms, megalithic man seems to have realized that the earth and the heavens were linked in such a way that the forces of one affected the other. His interest in astronomy, in other words, was much more an investigation of astrology: how much did the configuration of the sun, moon, stars and planets influence his life? and how were they connected with the spiral power that he had discovered?

Certainly, some people believe that he knew and practiced the principles of astrology, and that he laid out on the ground, in areas covering several square miles, pictorial representations of the signs of the zodiac—and did it long before the system was formalized by the Egyptians or the Greeks. The most famous of these terrestrial zodiacs is in the gently rolling landscape of the hills, woods and fields south of Glastonbury. First mapped in the late sixteenth century by John Dee, one of the physicians and astrologers to Queen Elizabeth I, its outline is marked by modern hedges, ditches and roads, as well as by more ancient contours. It was rediscovered in the late 1920s by Mrs. Katherine Maltwood, a scholarly researcher who was tracing the journeys of the knights of King Arthur as revealed by the medieval French romance *Perlesvaus*. Looking at one-inch Ordnance Survey maps of the area,

she noticed that the River Cary, between Charlton
Mackrell and Somerton, seemed to form the shape of an
animal. Looking more closely, she found that paths and
roads completed the picture of a lion, and discussing this
later with friends, she wondered if she had discovered one
of the great prehistoric zodiacs, which were rumored by
legend to have been laid out in the Andes and the Gobi
Desert as well as in Britain. Further map and field work
convinced her, and she completed a plan on which, when
the major stars and constellations are superimposed, a
zodiac pattern emerges. By her own account:

> It has been computed that the chance of such a pat-
> tern being found on the ground to harmonize with
> the sky so closely is of the order of 149,000,000 to
> 1 against. It must also be pointed out that both pat-
> terns correspond as to their north and south points;
> the signs of long ascension are also correctly larger
> for the most part than those of short ascension in the
> northern hemisphere.

Many people feel she overstated her case. It is not so
much that megalithic man would have been incapable of
landscaping the countryside to this degree; nor that the
design is invalidated by roads and hedges of medieval date
—they may well have followed the line of earlier tracks
and enclosures. It is that his obsession with accuracy in
other ways—his stone circle geometry, his alignments of
megaliths—leads one to expect a more effective zodiac
than it is. For not only are important stars excluded, but
many of the figures seem arbitrarily outlined: walking the
perimeter of the signs, it is difficult to know why a certain
field should be inside the design, and the next, indistinguishable in character, outside.

Nevertheless, there are those who are deeply convinced,
among them Rollo Maughling, who has run a Society for
the Preservation of the Glastonbury Zodiac. "Either you
see it or you don't," he says. "There is a very big element
of personal discovery in it. It's impossible to say how
much was created and how much was there naturally. I'm
convinced it was used to try to understand and harness
the planetary forces." Certainly, parts of the pattern
must have been put down as part of a conscious pattern of
design on a very large scale. Next to Leo is Virgo, part of

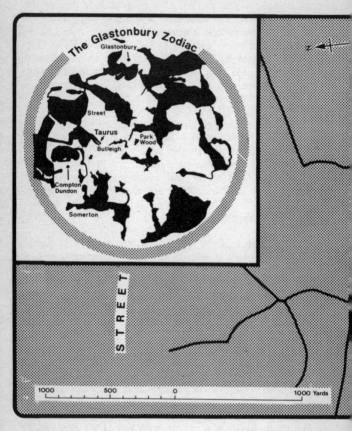

Circular silhouette of Glastonbury Zodiac, with large-scale outline of Taurus figure: unconvincing to geographers.

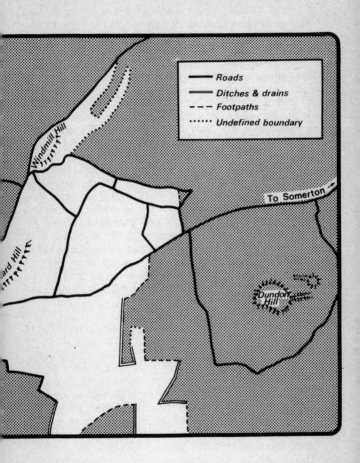

Roads
Ditches & drains
Footpaths
Undefined boundary

Windmill Hill

ard Hill

To Somerton

Dundon Hill

her outline formed by an inexplicable kink in an otherwise dead straight Fosse Way.

A similar mysterious deviation from a so-called Roman Road near Nuthampstead, Hertfordshire, led the young Cambridge biophysicist Nigel Pennick to trace out another Virgo figure there, and ultimately a complete zodiac on the borders of Essex, Hertfordshire and Cambridgeshire. It lies within an area as rich in prehistory, in its own way, as the more generally known Avebury and Glastonbury; and interestingly, it is crossed by the Lands End–Bury St. Edmunds southern dragon path. Other zodiacs have been seen by their discoverers at Ffarmers and Pumpsaint in Wales; at Kingston-on-Thames, Surrey; at Holderness, Yorkshire; and have been sketched in outline in Durham, Edinburgh, Glasgow, Banbury and elsewhere.

What unites those who believe in ancient terrestrial zodiacs with other researchers who are still doubtful, is a shared conviction that megalithic man had a fascination and understanding of the stars and planets that went far beyond basic astronomy. He wasn't just lying on his back with nothing to do on a warm summer's night but gaze at the firmament wondering what went on up there. He was using its mysteries for his own purpose, as an integral and inescapable part of his life. Nigel Pennick, writing about his zodiac, put the view at its extreme:

A system of advanced surveying, draughtsmanship and engineering was carried out by the arts of the Geomancers in charge of the project. The magnitude of such an undertaking makes work on it today vastly difficult, but accurate maps can show us the configurations of the effigies extant in these zones. Underlying the pictorial effigies is the universal mathematical structure of all things, microcosmic and macrocosmic, from subatomic particles to galaxies, from microscopic algae to interstellar cosmic dust-clouds.

CHAPTER

SEERS AND SPIRALS

Man's mind, when it is most intent upon any work, through its passion, and effects, is joyned with the mind of the stars, and intelligences, and being so joyned is the cause that some wonderful virtue be infused into our works and things.

—HENRY CORNELIUS AGRIPPA, COUNSELLOR TO CHARLES THE FIFTH, EMPEROR OF GERMANY, WRITING IN *Occult Philosophy, c.* 1530

DURING ALL THIS CENTURY, THERE HAS BEEN A CONFLICT between the metaphysical theorizing of those who believe in an idyllic lost civilization that once lived on earth in peace and plenty, and the evidence of the broken, dusty remnants of this supposed past that has been dug up and catalogued in museums. But it is possible to trace, however faintly, a pattern of development in which the two—one magical and the other practical—can live together. Much of the outline is sketchy and speculative, for as the stones and mounds left behind by megalithic man slowly yield up more information about their purpose, their nature is revealed as both complex and profound; and in an age of science, it is difficult to slip backward into the minds of a people who lived as much by instinct as by reason. So what follows is a broad concept of what might have been—a framework of prehistory that includes the supernatural and the mundane, and the paradox of great works being achieved from the primitive beginnings of an untamed earth.

The starting point would be about 15,000 years ago, when the world first felt the effects of an event of cataclysmic violence somewhere in the universe. Astronomers know that these happen all the time: in the vastness of the cosmos, stars explode, planets collide, galaxies collapse. As they occur, infinitesimally distant waves and forces touch the rhythms of life on earth, usually so faintly as to be unnoticeable. But on this occasion, as on others in the earth's history, it was enough to trigger off one of the changes in the climate that happen periodically.

Perhaps the earth's orbit, or the angle of the earth's axis, was altered slightly; perhaps a change in the constitution of the upper atmosphere allowed different sorts of radiations to come on to the earth's crust from the sun—scientists do not know. Whatever happened, the cumula-

tive effect allowed the great glaciers to retreat toward the
pole, and the earth to become accustomed to a new set of
vibrations and gravitational pulls that resulted from its
subtly changed place in the universe. At other times, during the millions of years when life was evolving, such
changes had accelerated genetic development. This time,
as man edged his way northward behind the retreating
ice, the conditions were right for him to achieve an advance that was qualitatively different from anything that
had happened before: to organize himself and his fellows
into a society that created and controlled, where before it
had merely survived.

Some people think that the cataclysm happened here on
earth. From this theory derive many of the stories of the
lost civilization of Atlantis, whose survivors are then said
to have sailed to various countries and, with their wisdom
and knowledge, helped the emerging civilizations on
their way. Certainly, scientists accept more readily nowadays that there may occasionally have been gigantic and
unexplained upheavals, which interrupted the process of
evolution. Mammoths, which lived in temperate climates
as late as 12,000 B.C. before their mysterious extinction,
have been found in Siberia frozen solid, standing upright,
the food in their stomachs still undigested; and this has
been alleged by some people to "prove" the extraordinary
suddenness of climatic change. No country in the world
is without its legend of the deluge or the flood.

But the weight of geological and other evidence is on
balance against either very early lost civilizations, or
worldwide climatic calamities. Plato's description of Atlantis, on which all Atlantean theories are based, can
readily be assigned to the Mediterranean island of Crete,
wrecked by an earthquake that happened on the nearby
island of Thera. Sudden catastrophes such as floods and
earthquakes also seem much more likely to have local
explanations, rather than tying together neatly into one
great event that reshaped the history of the world. In any
case, climatologists now have a range of techniques that
has let them plot in great detail the slow disappearance of
the glaciers from the northern hemisphere, and a worldwide flood does not fit in with the pattern that has
emerged. What can be seen is a gradual warming over
several thousand years, reaching its peak around 6000
B.C. It was not uninterrupted: for several hundred years

at a time, the glaciers would encroach back southward again.

Other writers are convinced that the spark which moved mankind along the path to civilization came from outer space. They point to another more or less universal myth, of fiery chariots and the sons of gods who came from the skies, and of ancient drawings of supposed spacemen and spaceships. Many megalithic researchers see dragons as descriptions of flying saucers, and ley lines as the magnetic paths to which they are attracted and down which they are guided. But as with Atlantis, there are other, equally probable explanations. The Biblical references, so often quoted in support of men from outer space who fathered the human race, are understood by all Hebrew scholars as part of a more conventional mythology of deities. The pictorial symbols, viewed alongside other art of the time, seem much less like spacemen or spaceships than when taken out of their context.

This is not to say that space is uninhabited by intelligent beings, since the probability of this is enormously high; nor that unidentified flying objects have not appeared throughout history, because, as J. Allen Hynek convincingly points out in *The UFO Experience*, they have been seen by too many reliable people too often for their existence to be denied. But it is a very big jump to go on from this and say that these were piloted by superhumans who decided to civilize the world. If they did so, they chose an odd way to do it, appearing in different forms at different times in different civilizations, leaving absolutely no physical trace whatsoever that they had been there, and teaching man skills that he was perfectly capable of developing on his own.

What man needed to ease his way toward an ordered society was for the times and conditions to be right, and for there to be enough gifted people to show him the path. He was not, after all, starting from nothing. By the end of the Palaeolithic period, when the ice started to retreat, many tribes had their own methods of marking a detailed calendar on bones, so that the seasons of the year, the phases of the moon, the annual migration of animals, birds and fish could be foreseen. The cave dwellings that spread across southern Europe were particularly rich in these, and other evidence of the time such as the burial ceremonies and the symbolic art shows that these small families of hunting peoples, spread over areas where food was plentiful, had progressed well beyond the confines of their day-to-day needs. But it was still a world in which most people's lives were bounded by the horizon around them, and in which, globally, progress was so slow that during hundreds of years a map of the population would show almost unnoticeable changes. Generations of cave dwellers stayed in the same place, living the same lives as their forefathers. In the inhospitable north of Europe and Asia, bands of nomadic hunters moved haphazardly from territory to territory, straggled thinly along the lands just below the snow line.

Then came the gathering warmth.

All life on the earth's surface stirred into giant patterns of movement on a scale and tempo that it had not known for 70,000 years. The snow melted on the mountain tops, and arid streams became deep rivers and cascading water-falls. Warm, damp winds blew from the Atlantic, carrying before them the pollen of lakeside trees that began to turn the grassy plains into forests thick with undergrowth. Animal life had to adapt or become extinct. The pools and rivers became abundant with fish. Wild boar rummaged in the woods. Reindeer, sheep and cattle moved north to forage for the grazing they needed. Everywhere nature was on the move.

Man had two choices. He could stay where he was, and come to terms with the new, strange conditions. Or he could move northward with the snow line, following the prey that he hunted. He did both. Those who stayed behind, the forests closing in around them and their food harder to find and kill, had a powerful reason to herd and domesticate livestock, and to grow crops on which to feed. Those who went northward found that they were treading in the footsteps of the nomadic hunters of the sub-Arctic north, some of whom in their turn had stayed put instead of following the ice. The areas where the migrating Mediterranean cave dwellers and the northern hunters met would have been in the great sweep of the northwest Atlantic coast from the Bay of Biscay up and around to the Baltic Sea, and the date of the earliest meetings some time around 10,000 B.C. It was this fusion that marked the misty beginnings of the megalithic complex.

Nobody will ever know how the first active stone was put up, or where. But there is a way in which, in the changed conditions of a postglacial climate, it could have happened naturally and been discovered accidentally. For it was not only on the face of the earth that the floods of melting snow were altering the landscape; underground, too, the great mass of newly released water was forcing its way through canyons and crevices, creating a vast and unfathomable labyrinth of rivers and streams. Then, as now, its movement within the earth's crust would have caused murmuring, unseen vibrations. At the same time above ground, on the slopes of hills and mountains where the ice receded, boulders of rock became unstable, and from time to time fell out of their formation and rolled away. All that needed to happen was for one rock of the right sort to finish up one day in the right place—above a crossing of underground streams, or some other geological fault that emitted the same mysterious force—and the conditions would be suitable for it to become an active standing stone, giving off an unmistakable surge of energy to anyone touching the point on its surface where the spiral force emerged.

Such natural menhirs can be found today, and their power felt. A few dowsers can identify them from distances of half a mile or more, their rods vibrating or swinging in the direction of the stone.

John Roberts, a Welsh hill farmer from the mountains above Harlech Castle, told how he had accidentally discovered one: "It must have been twenty or thirty years ago. I was sitting resting my back against a rock, watching my sheep in the valley below. Suddenly I had the strangest feeling. The rock began to shake from side to side, about three or four inches either way. That's how it felt through my spine, although it couldn't really have been the rock, which was absolutely solid. It was the strangest sensation—I thought I was going to pass out. I had to stand up and move away." Subsequently a dowser traced the rock's position, and found it exactly where John Roberts had described it, still emitting power. Precisely beneath was the crossing of two underground streams.

Similarly in America, a young dowser from Flagstaff, Arizona, showed how he could track down the sites of early man on the Navajo and Hopi Indian reservations. By question-and-answer dowsing techniques, he picked out two likely places, one near the main road to Oraibi, the other on an unmapped mesa that could only be reached on foot. At the first, he found a cache of five great boulders, each weighing more than a ton, scattered without pattern on the ground as if by a giant hand. In the arid desert scrub around, as far as the eye could see, there was nothing like them. Again on the second site, after climbing high onto the plateau of the mesa, there were unmistakable signs of man's presence in some distant time: where a burning wind had swept the bedrock clear of all but an inch of sand, so that the surface remained as it had been thousands of years before, a symmetrical, triangular rock some two feet high stood out; it was of a kind totally different from any others in the area, wedged upright in the center of a natural platform.

Less capable of proof, but widely believed by many dowsers, is the existence of natural "leys" since early times—not the old straight tracks of Alfred Watkins, but bands of force two or three yards wide, and extending twenty to thirty feet above and below the surface of the earth. Sometimes they seem to begin and end on unmarked sites—a hill with a past history of volcanic disturbance, a pond, or a spring. But often, the places where they are found by dowsers to intersect are precisely the ley points noted by Watkins and his successors: ancient stone temples, near altars in churches, sacred burial sites, menhirs, dolmens. This interpretation of leys has many adherents now, particularly in the United States, where the lack of information from maps makes classical ley hunting impossible. A vice-president of the American Society of Dowsers, T. Edward Ross II, has traced by dowsing many such leys, including four that originate at Mystery Hill. Stephen Bosbach thinks their points of intersection are the basis of a pattern that will one day be understood again through mysticism, and calls them "co-ordination points of Reality." Discussion about these intangible, seemingly immeasurable lines of force is conducted almost entirely in a metaphysical framework, so that it is extremely difficult to place them in a scientific context. Yet Jim Mello, a Rhode Island electrical engineer, believes he has detected and recorded electromagnetic anomalies on the path of leys. And Russian scientists, whose work on the nature of dowsing is the most comprehensive in the world, are seriously discussing, in technical papers, the possibility of a universal, crystal-shaped grid that underlies the surface of the world, and whose intersection points mark significant places in the earth's history.

If the likely explanation of megaliths is that they were placed to fix or amplify such lines of force and their sources, one has to assume that at least some of the hunters and travelers emerging from the Ice Age were able to identify the same sensations. It seems likely. The gifts shared by dowsers and other sensitive people are strangely unintellectual, and directly responsive to the forces of nature. All creatures from animals to insects seem to possess instincts about unseen currents that lead them along migratory paths, or give them a homing instinct, or sometimes what seems like precognition of danger or pain or death. It is impossible that man alone evolved without this capability in some degree, and probable, from the evidence of primitive tribes investigated in recent times, that at a certain stage of his development it is automatic to "know" and "feel" things without the need to rationalize them.

So common sense (almost a synonym for instinct) suggests that at some point in the thousand years or more that it might have happened, the right man felt drawn to the right place to discover a stone such as that felt by John Roberts in Wales. It must have been an awesome and magical experience, for although he would have been sensitive enough to recognize the earth forces, the stone would mystifyingly amplify them. Just how this happens is as much of a mystery now as then—perhaps more so. It is a force that seems to be linked with electromagnetism, although it is certainly not yet fully understood. It may have something to do with the unique qualities of quartz, which in a white crystal form seems to be a constituent of every active stone. The molecular structure of quartz is spiral, and may be left-handed or right-handed just as on the carved decorations at Newgrange. It is also piezoelectric: that is, it expands slightly if given a slight charge of electricity. If placed under pressure—as it would be if charged while inside another stone—alternate edges of its prism give off positive and negative voltages on what can reach a dramatic scale: a force of 1,000 lb. applied on each face of a half-inch crystal of quartz creates 25,000 volts. Perhaps, in a similar way, it is able to act as an amplifier of forces other than electricity, and this is how people have been able to feel the power in the stones.

Quartz-bearing rocks are common enough. The next step would perhaps have been for the discoverer of a naturally active stone to try and find out if the same force could be intentionally duplicated elsewhere. As a "seer," he readily sensed sites where the underground forces were capable of being tapped, and on one of these he and his tribe manhandled into position a lump of stone—granite, say—the quartz in the middle emitting minute vibrations which he could also feel. For a few days, perhaps, the stone would be apparently inactive, as the invisible charge built up within it. But once the force was there, and could be felt, the beginnings of a megalithic network had been created. Because with first two, and then gradually more, magically powerful sites, the seer would begin to notice some other characteristics of active stones: that the same forces which activated them also linked them; that the direction or polarity of force could be left-handed or right-handed, and that it usually changed monthly; that the sun and moon were involved in the activation and the effect; that the physical mass of certain hills or natural rock formations could be linked into the network; and that the power could be concentrated by artificial earthworks and stone circles.

We do not know in what order these discoveries were made, nor how many tribes or people independently discovered that there was some natural magic to be released from the earth's surface, nor how long it took. But a theory of the experimental, haphazard and scattered evolution of the megalithic system from simple beginnings fits more comfortably into the known prehistoric background than a theory of it coming ready-made from China, Atlantis or outer space. All over the world, but more especially in the northern hemisphere from the Far East through Asia and Europe to North America, different peoples found their own way of discovering and using this magic. Historically, it happened at different times; but each people were at a psychically parallel stage in their development—before they could read or write, and while they were still living close enough to nature to be able to sense unconsciously its hidden powers.

It was along the northwest Atlantic coast of Europe, by an accident of climate, geography, and the movement of population, that the discovery happened first and lasted longest. Archaeological dating currently puts the megalithic culture in a period from around 5000 B.C. to 1500 B.C. But this is for the network of vast and imposing mega- liths that we can still see and photograph today, which represent the culture at its most complex, preceded by thousands of years of continuing observation and practical experience. We know that many of the sites were rede- signed many times—Stonehenge at least five times, pos- sibly more—and that beneath the stones that remain are sometimes the vestiges of earlier circles and monuments. Each year, too, excavations reveal that mesolithic man in the postglacial period lived a more advanced life than had previously been thought. So it is not unreasonable to sug- gest that perhaps as early as 10,000 B.C., scattered experi- ments were going on in the positioning of stones and circles.

Scientifically, this is very difficult to prove, because isolated pieces of stone do not lend themselves to conven- tional dating techniques, and in any case, the original stones may not be there. But the story of archaeological dating is to discover an ever-greater antiquity in prehis- tory; and a time span of some 8,000 years is long enough both for the immense physical reshaping of the landscape that went on, and for the observations needed to acquire such deep astronomical and mathematical knowledge. More important than the exact date is to place these first tentative encounters with earth magic in the context of an underpopulated and largely nomadic society; for it is by envisaging how those people used the force in the stones that we can trace how the great megaliths later came to be built.

THE USE OF ACTIVE SITES

A community in those times was small and vulnerable. Perhaps twenty or thirty people, mostly of the same fam- ily, lived precariously at the mercy of the weather, illness, the availability of food, the potency of the men and the fertility of the women. How much fighting there was be- tween one tribe and another is uncertain. Logically, there was no need for it—with so few people, many square miles of land were there for each family to live off. But the territorial imperative that seems to be part of all animal life probably led to bloody skirmishes—part of the capri-

cious and unpredictable dealings of fortune that as often
led to hardship and death as to plenty and good health.
Tribal life, whether day to day or year to year, was determined by incomprehensible physical facts: lightning that
struck down a tree near their camp; mist and rain that
swept over the open moors as they hunted, and made the
way back treacherous with marshes; bitter snowstorms
that drove down from the north and made their living
places uninhabitable with cold.

Amid this, the newly discovered power in the stones
was both magical and practical. On the one hand it was a
force like warmth, running water, or wind, that could be
felt on the body. To a certain degree, also, it could be
manufactured, rather as fires could be kindled. But it was
different from anything else. It was sensed not with the
eyes or nose or ears; but rather as imminent danger was
sensed, or the heightened visions of a fevered mind, or
vertigo on the edge of a high ravine—feelings both in-
voluntary and inexplicable. Like other elements in a dangerous and often hostile world, it was there to be
harnessed and used.

On a practical level, one of the earliest functions of an
activated standing stone must have been its potential as a
beacon. If some people can find their way nowadays to
the power centers on leys, so then could seers, and probably most others in the community too. It was an age of
few people, the pathways scarcely trodden except where
animals laid their tracks. In these conditions, especially
where shrubland and woods grew up to obscure the view,
the line between one stone and another would have performed the same function as a compass. Here, perhaps,
they laid down the foundations of Alfred Watkins's
straight tracks, which so often skirt the "camps" built
around the power centers on the highest hills. The natural
place for men to live and move would have been in the
sheltered and protected valleys; but in the high places
they built their network of beacons, like psychic trans-
mitters.

At about the same time came the realization that some
wells of water and some stones, drunk or touched or em-
braced in a certain way, could be used to regenerate and
revitalize. For most people in the tribe, probably no special gifts were needed. Nowadays, such power as there is
in the stones seems too unpredictable to be used in this

way. Either people have lost the ability to absorb the power consistently, or the force has changed in character. But as recently as the 1880s, a traveler in America, reporting to the U. S. Bureau of Ethnology about his observations on the medicine men of the Apache Indians, gave a vivid and precise summary of what was presumably felt originally. He said the medicine men seemed to be subject to "a gradual decadence of their abilities, which can only be rejuvenated by rubbing the back against a sacred stone projecting from the ground in the country of the Walapai on the Atlantic and Pacific railroad." Another stone of the same kind was used by the medicine men of the Pueblos of Laguna and Acoma. The Sioux at Standing Rock, South Dakota, had a sacred medicine stone, and the medicine men of Tusayan "a great stone around which they marched in solemn procession in their snake-dance."

The American writer Alan Landsburg's book *In Search of Ancient Mysteries* contains an account of an apparently natural rock cleft in the wall of the fortress city of Sacsahuaman in the Andes, which was believed to contain magical powers. Before going into battle, warriors thrust their fists into the crevice, supposedly so obtaining a supernatural strength and courage to overcome their enemies. In a striking echo of the megaliths of western Europe, the crevice appears in the shape of a snake standing on its tail. And inside, there is an electromagnetic anomaly so powerful that if a compass is placed there, the needle swings wildly.

As well as revitalizing, the stones were found to heal— a faculty well documented, from the early edicts of the Christian church, through folklore, to modern accounts of primitive societies. As late as Victorian times, writers noted practices that still existed in Europe. In Germany, many churches contained stones with cup-markings, into which sick people "blew, as it were, the disease into the cavities." In a French church near Bourg, a large stone was preserved "into which the sick and impotent grind holes, and drink the pulverised matter, which, as they believe, cures the fever and renews the vital strength."

That "as they believe" is important, because there is no scientific basis whatsoever for the curative properties of stones, and little enough for healing waters. Yet the power that comes from contacting an active stone is real enough, at least to some people, and the cure and effort of erecting

them over such an extraordinarily long period suggest
that they must have worked some kind of wonders, or
people would simply have stopped bothering. Perhaps
what happened was that the surge of spiral energy from
the stone, reinforced by tradition and ritual, was enough
to induce the changed mental attitude that brings about
so-called miraculous cures. For the earliest communities,
the power in a stone or circle would have been invoked to
increase fertility, cure sickness, and prolong life. If these
things happened successfully, the power would be seen to
have worked; if they didn't, then the power had been used
wrongly—but was still there for another attempt.

Doubtless, the stones and their sites took on a primitive
spiritual significance. In ancient Germany, gravestones
were supposed to contain the spirits of the person buried
beneath. Hindu travelers left stones by the roadside to
represent the *lingam,* the symbol of creativity. Australian
aborigines still treasure small "sacred stones," which they
believe to contain the spirits of their ancestors. In other
ways, too, study of Australian aborigines suggests ways in
which the rituals that grew up in circles and standing
stones might have parallels with the decorated aboriginal
totem poles which are surrounded by circles in the sand.
The lines from these circles, so similar to the lines of megalithic cup-and-ring markings, represent the pathways
trodden by ancestors. Spirals represent sacred springs
from which spirits could travel to and from the under-
world.

Probably the force in the stones in earliest megalithic
years, as now, was mysterious and erratic, and not fully
understood by those who were using it. In any case, the
same motivation that led to the erection of the first artificial standing stone would have driven the communities on
to explore and amplify its powers—to find out if its effects
could be made more certain, more efficient, and more
readily obtainable. Quite soon, the link between the activation of the power and the influence of the heavenly
bodies would have been felt and noticed. As the moon
waned, the polarity of the spiral force altered—and
study of the moon's orbit became a vital part of the community's education. Before long, too, there may have
been the inspired discovery that placing stones with an
angle of 23½° between them seemed somehow to increase
their energy, and that this angle could be simply laid out

on the ground by bisecting a 9 × 4 rectangle. Gradually, the primitive lunar markings on bones were replaced by the more permanent record of stones arranged on the landscape to form a calendar that could be used by all. In this way, by trial and error over the millennia, the first tentative rules of astronomy and mathematics were worked out, and a spider's web of interlocking lines of force grew up over the face of the earth.

The fixed points of the stones and power centers also helped give rise to the settled farming communities that replaced the nomadic hunters. By about 4000 B.C., from the evidence of the earthworks that were beginning to be built, many of them must by now have contained more than 100 people, one group sharing with its neighbor a common knowledge of the earth magic. By now the network was grander in scale. Hilltops were shaped with mounds of earth and turves, or raised artificially like Silbury Hill, perhaps to act within the force lines like condensers in an electrical circuit. Dolmens were built, their capstones carefully aligned so as to concentrate the force beneath them. Rocking stones—more than twenty have been found in Britain today, and they have been noted in North America, France and Greece—were set in place on the leys, perhaps to help generate energy as they were tilted up and down. Barrows were built to contain stone chambers that mysteriously trapped and concentrated the power. Across the surface of northwest Europe, vibrant lines of psychic force shimmered ceaselessly.

Since what is left of this force is now fragmented and uncertain, it is impossible to do more than speculate about how it was used when the network was reaching its most powerful. Some people are sure that a degree of levitation, the defeat of gravity, was obtainable, and that this was how at least some of the great stones were maneuvered so exactly into position. This is not so unlikely as it at first seems. There is a well-documented ceremony that still takes place in the village of Shivapur near Poona in central India where eleven men link arms and dance around a heavy, sacred boulder of stone, chanting the words *quama ali dervish.* After a few minutes of this, they merely touch the stone with their fingertips and it rises, apparently unaided, to shoulder level. Whatever the cause of this, it does not exclusively have to be the villagers who achieve the effect. Many tourists have tried it successfully. The common factors are that it must be exactly eleven people, and they must circle and chant.

Many people are sure, too, that the network of force was used for communication, particularly between the major power centers. Bill Lewis, in his dowsing investigations, has carried out successful experiments on this, by standing alongside an active stone and inducing clockwise and anticlockwise movements in a pendulum held by an independent observer at another standing stone more than a mile away. Iris Campbell, a Devonshire psychic healer who has investigated many of Britain's megalithic sites, says she felt the ability to communicate over long distances in the stone circle known as Long Meg and her Daughters in Cumberland: "I felt people used to tap out a message through the stones, and that each stone vibrated in a certain way that had its counterpart in circles elsewhere." Bill Lewis thinks that Avebury was the most important center of all, and that from there it was possible to contact the other major centers, from Callanish in the north to Carnac in the south. If this is indeed the case, it would help solve one of the riddles of prehistory—how relatively small and scattered megalithic communities could have organized the labor force needed for such giant operations as, for instance, Stonehenge. It could, quite simply, have been recruited from all over the country, the manpower willingly made available as part of the unceasing urge to improve and expand the network.

RITUAL AND THE UNIVERSE

Viewed from the standpoint that megaliths had practical day-to-day functions, which could only happen if they were activated in conjunction with the heavens, the reason for the baffling astronomical and mathematical sophistication, documented by Alexander Thom, becomes plain. Megalithic man needed to know about eclipses, solstices, equinoxes, and high geometry because, in some way that we do not now understand, he felt these were vital to the proper working of the stones. He wasn't just building observatories, although they could be used as these. The reverse was more important: he was constantly experimenting, placing all his stones so that at certain key moments in the rhythms of the cosmos, his magical sites were imbued with a supernatural energy that renewed and enhanced life on earth.

Although we can guess at something of the way in which he achieved this, if for instance we measure all the possible sight lines from Stonehenge, or work out the calendrical dates contained within the design of a stone circle, there must have been a much more important metaphysical element which is now lost. Philosophers and occultists from Aristotle onward have believed that there is an endless source of psychic energy in the universe, which must be renewed at the same time as it is drawn upon. Cornelius Agrippa summed up in the sixteenth century a view of worship and magic that can be traced right back to Celtic times:

> When anyone by binding or bewitching doth call upon the Sun or other stars, praying them to be helpful to the work desired, the Sun and other Stars do not heare his words, but are moved after a certain manner by a certain conjunction, and mutual series; whereby parts of the world are mutually subordinate the one to the other, and have a mutual consent, by reason of their great union. As in one man's body one member is moved by perceiving the motion of another—so, when any one moves any part of the world, other parts are moved by the perceiving of the motion of that. The knowledge therefore of the dependence of things following one the other, is the foundation of all wonderfull operation, which is necessarily required to the exercising the power of attracting superior vertues.

This concept of the inseparable unity of all things, one drawing strength from another, and at the same time having to return it in a different form, is the basis of much primitive religion. A Victorian anthropological survey published in 1901, which is valuable because the field work was done before missionaries were working in the areas concerned, summarized the religious and magical beliefs of recently discovered tribes in Australia, Africa, Asia, Siberia, North and South America, and New Guinea, and found a common groundwork of ideas:

1. The thought that all nature shares a common life, and that all things—rocks and stones, plants and trees, birds and beasts and men—are interchangeable one with the other, under certain conditions.
2. The earth, sea and sky were inhabited by myriads of spirits, who animate each separate object.
3. The spirit world transcends man, and can be good or bad.

This leads on the one hand to sacrifice—giving away a life force—and on the other to the widely held belief that inanimate objects—stones, or poles, or altars—can be given a sacred power through the force of human worship. It explains why many people, even today, believe that stones, and to a lesser extent trees, can somehow absorb the psychic energy given off by human emotion. According to this belief, it is why so many people can immediately sense "good" or "bad" vibrations in an old house, and also why ghosts appear—they are formed in the fabric of a building when people give off the extreme emotions of terror or anguish or even joy, and periodically reappear before other people sensitive enough to see or feel them.

In a similar sort of way, the stone circles would not have been fully activated unless the calendrical events were accompanied by human rituals that focused the forces and fixed them in the stones, and at the same time, by pouring out man's own life force, replaced and balanced the psychic energy drawn from the universe. A Yorkshire painter, Monica English, by drawing on some uncanny subconscious memory, is able to visualize scenes "as if I'm watching short lengths of scratched black and white film, seen through the wrong end of a telescope." To achieve this, she needs to undergo a trancelike effort of concentration. "But I think it is genuinely like a broadcast from the past, not imagination. As a painter, I know what it feels like to visualize and imagine scenes, and what I see of the ceremonies round the megaliths isn't like that at all."

She sees that there was noise, feasting and commotion for three days at each of the four major festivals in each year, with complicated processional movements, sacred chants, music, and many fires. "The idea was deliberately to make the circle powerful by pouring out their own emotions, and they did it so efficiently that you can still feel it there now. But at the time it was all to do with preparation for the entrance of the Goddess Queen. The reverence in which she was held was enormous. The circle protected her, but somehow at the same time allowed the life force to enter her and be concentrated in her. All the ritual was to lead up to the great moment when she was possessed and made her pronouncements, like an oracle. It was to do with the fertility of nature, the safety of the cattle, the welfare of the people, that sort of thing—the original witchcraft, the natural sort, not all the invented witchcraft which is around today."

Echoes of those Bronze Age ceremonies can still be heard even now—in the celebration of May Day, midsummer, Halloween and even Christmas, which was once at the winter solstice. The Beltane fires, the rolling of fiery discs of straw down dragon hills that took place right up to this century, the yule fire, and even the blazing Christmas pudding are all remnants of this pagan past. There is archaeological evidence in hundreds of barrows and circles of fires and feasts—usually attributed to funerals, but just as readily explicable in terms of calendar ceremonies and rituals. Many of the legends of the megaliths involve dancing maidens who are turned to stone, and throughout Christian times there have been edicts against people dancing around ancient sites or the churchyards that replaced them. Without doubt, the rituals seen by Monica English, or something very like them, took place.

Similarly, there are countless traditions which have come down into modern times that hark back to the importance of ritual movements, both in their direction and in the magic numbers used. The "sun-wise" turn around sacred places was a Celtic custom discovered by the early Christians; it survives today in the way playing cards are dealt, or wine is passed around at table, or by the sanctified progression of the bishop and clergy whenever a new church or churchyard is consecrated. Dr. William Borlase gave many examples of the three-times circle: "The islanders of Skye turn three times round their cairns; round the persons they intended to bless, three times; three times they make round St. Barr's church; and three times round the well—all sun-ways; so that the number three was a necessary part of the ceremony." In the Middle Ages there was a widespread belief that if anybody was to place an object on the capstone of a dolmen and walk three times around on the night of a full moon, it would disappear. Many of the circles became known in recorded history as the "Nine Stones," a memory of the healing ceremonies that were supposedly made possible by the number nine—nine times through the holed stone at Men-an-Tol in Cornwall, for instance.

So, probably at some time in the third millennium B.C., the megalithic civilization reached its height with the fusion and interaction of the three elements necessary for the generation of earth magic: the underground forces, the influence of the cosmos, and the power of man's mind. Together, in varying proportions and mixtures, they were used by all ancient societies in different ways and at different times—by the Chinese geomancers, by the Indian dolmen builders, by Australian aborigines, by the Mayan priests, by North American Indians—at a time in their progress when this magic was used confidently as a part of everyday life. But at some time the peak was reached, and on the way downward, the monuments fell into disuse and the knowledge became dissipated. What was undoubtedly the most powerful metaphysical factor in man's life became forgotten and fragmented, until today it requires a conscious imaginative effort to recognize that it was there at all. There are many explanations why.

For instance, there is a widely held belief that the knowledge was not in fact lost, but was handed down through the ages, known to a handful of people in secret societies, by means of mathematical codes and ciphers. According to this theory, the geometry of the circles and the geomancy of the siting of the ancient power centers, and their relationship one to another, contain the key to the fundamental workings of the universe, expressed by a harmony of numbers that was understood by initiates, and can be interpreted today. This knowledge was taken abroad and taught to Pythagoras in Greece in the sixth century B.C., who combined it with similar mathematical knowledge that was secretly enshrined in the measurements of the Egyptian Pyramids, and hidden in the sacred books of the Babylonians and Indians. The findings and teachings of Pythagoras were never written down in his lifetime, but later became embodied in the works of Plato and Euclid, and thus became part of the mainstream of classical philosophy and mathematics.

In northwest Europe, the last people to know these secrets, and use them ceremonially, were the Druid priests. But like the Magi of Persia, the Gymnosophists of India, the High Priests of Egypt, the Chaldeans of Assyria, and similar sects, they had two sets of doctrines and opinions: one written and spoken at ceremonies; the other communicated only to the initiated, who were solemnly sworn to keep it secret from the rest of mankind. In time, the Druids were slaughtered by the troops of Caesar and his successors. But their knowledge was passed on through oral tradition, and expressed in the sacred geometry of abbeys, churches and cathedrals. Thus Glastonbury Abbey and Stonehenge can be shown to have the same internal geometry. The secret was known to certain Freemasons, who incorporated the magic numbers in all their most important buildings. In the same way as the Egyptian architects of the Pyramids were supposed to have hidden within their dimensions eternal truths about the relationship of the sun, earth and other planets, builders in medieval times and even later did the same, leaving clues for others to follow up in future generations. By this reasoning, it is no coincidence that the height of St. Paul's Cathedral, at 365 feet, is the same number as days in the year; it was built like this deliberately, to encourage further investigation of its mathematical mysteries. According to one of the most respected academic researchers on this continuing tradition of geomancy, Keith Critchlow: "Ecclesiastical architecture is a hieroglyph which all except the blind could read."

The trouble with this theory is that so many things can be "proved" with an abstract selection of numbers and dimensions. While there may be hidden truths in the geometric formulae of Pythagoras, or the Pyramids, their interpretation has been argued ever since they were first proposed, and probably will continue to be. For the fact is that they are too complex and profound to be understood by any single man, and if indeed they contain some of the knowledge discovered in megalithic times, this itself may be a clue to why the megalithic civilization declined: it became too complicated to be supported by the power of mind and memory alone.

What had been, in earlier times, relatively simple centers of psychic power, became, by the completion of Stonehenge around 1600 B.C., both unwieldy and complex.

Millennia of sacred power fused in one site: menhir with spirals and Christian cross (from Blight's *Ancient Crosses of East Cornwall*, 1856).

There is some evidence, too, that the forces generated may have been, occasionally, uncontrollably powerful. In Scotland, there are said to be so-called "hill-forts" on scemb lines set at the declination angle of 23½°, in which the base of the stones used in their construction has, at some time after they were put there, become vitrified, or molten. It is a phenomenon that can very occasionally be found in other standing stones, and a number of the stones at Avebury are discolored as if they had undergone intense heat. The archaeological explanation, of brushwood fires lit around the hill forts to incinerate the defenders, is inadequate. Something between 2,000° C and 3,000° C would be needed to melt the rock, and this is quite outside the range of burning wood. There are a number of people, too, who feel that Stonehenge collapsed as a result of an unrecorded catastrophe.

Another problem for megalithic man was the almost impossible weight of intellectual knowledge that had to be transmitted, almost certainly without writing, from generation to generation. It involved astronomy, geometry, pure mathematics, and numerology on the one hand, and lengthy ritual and ceremonial magic on the other. To a certain degree, and in some individuals, we know that memory can be trained to an exceptional level. Professor Stuart Piggott, comparing the astronomical abilities of the Druids with the calendrical knowledge of the Tamil people in southern India, reported the case of one man "who did not understand a word of the theories of Hindu mathematics, but was endowed with a retentive memory which enabled him to arrange very distinctly his operations in his mind and on the ground," and who predicted by this means a lunar eclipse within four minutes of its true time. But Julius Caesar, reporting in *De Bello Gallica* on his observations of Druid learning, gives a clear description of the immense amount of effort involved in achieving this without breaking the chain of ever-increasing knowledge:

> Their priesthood was taught to repeat a great number of verses by heart, and often spend twenty years on this institution; for it is deemed unlawful to commit their statutes to writing . . . for two reasons: to hide their mysteries from the knowledge of the vulgar, and to exercise the memory of their scholars, which would be apt to lie neglected, had they letters to trust to, as we find is often the case.

And finally, there is the view of history which says that great civilizations, like everything else in the universe, have a rhythm which causes them to end as mysteriously as they began. When the megalithic age declined, there is no event so cataclysmic as the post-Ice Age climatic changes which can be suggested as a cause. It is just that the conditions for man's advancement, which swaddled northwest Europe for so many thousand years, seem to have become concentrated elsewhere: China, for the growth of the dragon emperors; the Middle East and Egypt, where the arts of writing and architecture cradled the modern world; some thousand years later, in India; and after that, in central America.

By 2000 B.C., when the Beaker People arrived in England from Europe to infuse society with new traditions of aggrandizement and aggression, represented by their gold and their bronze, it may be that the power in the stones was already waning, and that Stonehenge represented one last attempt to amplify and concentrate it by a race that had not grown up with the same tradition of earth magic. Certainly, from now on the megaliths themselves seem to have become, as a whole, of less and less importance. The rituals of burial were more significant than ceremonies to enhance life; and later, the Druids retreated for their most sacred ceremonies into the shaded secrecy of oak groves, neglecting the stones and the network of psychic energy that perhaps had once formed the basis of an entire culture.

They had been years of great wonder. They had seen, for the first time, the emergence of men and women with whom we today could readily communicate and discuss matters of common interest: farming, the weather, health —in fact, the stable gossip of rural life. But we have lost something which those people had. If we tried to create a stone circle today, we wouldn't know how to make it work. A dowser could find us a new site with the right underground forces, or a place where there had once been a circle; an archaeologist could excavate and show us the original position of the stones; an astronomer could show us where to replace them so as to take account of the changed conditions in the heavens; and a geologist could take us to the right sort of rocks. But even if a power might then be generated, it would be a different sort of power. Our knowledge of how to amplify and use it wouldn't be there, as if we were passengers getting into a bus in a strange country with the engine idling—but without a driver. So perhaps there is one basic lesson to be learned as we look into this lost age: that man achieved his advance through conditions that were puzzling, hostile and confusing by the combined use of his instinct and his intellect, his mind and his brain. It was by this blend that, for a while, he moved forward in harmony with nature.

APPENDIX

Consider a one-inch Ordnance Survey map of area A square miles, upon which is drawn a thick line representing a ley of length y miles and breadth x miles. If a random point is dropped on the map, the probability that it will fall in the line will be the fraction (f) of the area of the map that the line occupies.

i.e. Probability $= f = xy/A$

Similarly, the probability that m such points fall in the line is f^m.

Now: if we scatter n points on the map, the probability that exactly m of these will fall in the line is given by:

$$P(n, m) = f^m (1-f)^{n-m} \frac{n}{m}$$

where $(1 - f)^{n-m}$ represents the probability that the remaining $(n-m)$ points do not fall in the line, and (n/m) is the number of ways of selecting m points out of n.

It can be shown that

$$\frac{n}{m} = \frac{n!}{m!(n-m)!}$$

where $n!$ denotes the product of all the numbers from n down to one; i.e. $3! = 3 \times 2 \times 1 = 6$.

If the line is first fixed on the map by two points (the method used in ley hunting), the probability of getting an exact alignment of m points becomes:

$$P(n,m) = \left(\frac{n-2}{m-2} \right) f^{m-2} (1-f)^{n-m} \quad \text{(Equation 1)}$$

If there is a total of W alignments in the n points (including two-point lines) then the number $N(m)$ of m point lines to be expected by chance is given by:

$$N(m) = WP(n, m) \qquad \text{(Equation 2)}$$

It can be shown that

$$W = \left(\frac{n}{2}\right) - \sum_{3}^{n}\left[\left(\frac{m}{2}\right) - 1\right]P(n,m)W$$

rearranging:

$$W = \frac{(n/2)}{1 + \sum_{3}^{n}[(m/2) - 1]P(n, m)}$$

$$\text{(Equation 3)}$$

If we assume that ley points are random, we can find n for a particular map of area A. If the length of the ley is y miles, what can we reasonably take as its width x? The ultimate minimum for this is the breadth of the pencil or ink line representing the ley, but inaccuracies in drawing, in symbolism on the map itself, make it reasonable to take x to be 1/100 of a mile or 17.6 yards.

The following are results of calculations performed using a typical one-inch Ordnance Survey map.

Counting gave the number of good ley points as 200. The area of land A of the map was 625 square miles. The length of a typical ley on this map was taken to be 30 miles.

From equations 1 and 3, $W = 16,500$

From equation 2, $N(3) = 1,570$, i.e. 1,570 3-point leys by chance.

Similarly $\qquad N(4) = 72$, i.e. 72 4-point leys by chance.

Similarly $\qquad N(5) = 2$

Similarly $\qquad N(6) = 0.05$

Similarly $\qquad N(7) = 0.001$

SELECTED BIBLIOGRAPHY

The following books are suggested for further reading because most of them were still in print in 1976, or are standard texts normally obtainable through public libraries. Further evidence for *Earth Magic* was, and can still be, found in proceedings of local archaeological and natural history societies, and the references contained there.

Part One

Chapters One to Three

Anderson, J. R. L. *The Oldest Road: The Ridgeway*. British Book Center, 1976.

Ashbee, Paul. *The Bronze Age Round Barrow in Britain*. Phoenix House, 1960.

———. *The Earthen Long Barrow in Britain*. University of Toronto Press, 1970.

Atkinson, R. J. C. *Stonehenge*. Pelican, 1960.

Ceram, C. W. *The First American*. Harcourt Brace Jovanovich, 1971.

Childe, V. G. *Prehistoric Communities of the British Isles*. Benjamin Blom, Inc., 1940.

———. *The Dawn of European Civilization*. Knopf, 1958.

Clark, J. G. D. *World Prehistory, A New Outline*. Cambridge University Press, 1969.

———. *Excavations at Star Carr*. Cambridge University Press, 1954.

————. *The Stone Age Hunters*. Thames and Hudson, 1957.

Coles, John (ed.). "Contributions to Prehistory offered to Grahame Clark." *Proceedings of the Prehistoric Society,* December 1971.

Coles, John. *Field Archaeology in Britain*. Methuen, 1972.

————. *Archaeology By Experiment*. Scribner, 1974.

Coles, J. M., and Simpson, D. D. A. (eds.). *Studies in Ancient Europe*. Humanities Press, 1968.

Cornwall, I. W. *The World of Ancient Man*. Dent, 1964.

————. *Prehistoric Animals and their Hunters*. Faber and Faber, 1968.

————. *Ice Ages—Their Nature and Effect*. Humanities Press, 1970.

Daniel, G. E. *The Megalith Builders of Western Europe*. Pelican, 1958.

————. *The First Civilizations*. Apollo Editions, 1970.

Farb, Peter. *Man's Rise to Civilization*. Avon, 1969.

Gimbutas, Marija. *The Gods and Goddesses of Old Europe 7000-3000 B.C.* University of California Press, 1974.

Giot, P. R. *Brittany*. Thames and Hudson, 1960.

Gordon, Cyrus H. *Before Columbus*. Crown, 1971.

Hawkes, C. F. C. *The Prehistoric Foundations of Europe*. Barnes & Noble, 1973.

Hawkes, Jacquetta. *A Guide to Prehistoric and Roman Monuments in England and Wales*. Sphere, 1973.

Hawkins, Gerald S. *Stonehenge Decoded*. Dell, 1966.

————. *Beyond Stonehenge*. Harper Trade Books, 1973.

Kendrick, Sir Thomas. *British Antiquity*. Methuen reprint, 1970.

Lethbridge, T. C. *The Legend of the Sons of God*. Routledge and Kegan Paul, 1972.

MacNeish, Richard S. (ed.). *Early Man in America*. W. H. Freeman and Company, 1973. (Readings from *Scientific American*)

Murray, Jacqueline. *The First European Agriculture: A Study*. Aldine, 1970.

Piggott, Stuart. *Neolithic Cultures of the British Isles*. Cambridge University Press, 1954.

———— (ed). *The Dawn of Civilization*. Thames and Hudson, 1961.

————. *Ancient Europe*. Aldine, 1966.

Powell, T. G. E. *The Celts*. Thames and Hudson, 1958.

Power, T. G. E., et al. *Megalithic Enquiries in the West of Britain: a Liverpool symposium.* Liverpool, 1969.

Renfrew, Colin. *The Art of the First Farmers.* Sheffield, 1969.

————. *Before Civilization.* Jonathan Cape, 1973.

———— (ed.). *British Prehistory: A New Outline.* Noyes Press, 1975.

Roe, Derek. *Prehistory.* University of California Press, 1970.

Silverberg, Robert. *The Mound Builders.* Ballantine, 1974.

Simpson, D. D. A. (ed.). *Economy and Settlement in Neolithic and Early Bronze Age Britain and Europe.* Humanities Press, 1972.

Starr, Chester G. *Early Man.* Oxford University Press, 1973.

Stern, Philip van Doren and Lillian. *Prehistoric Europe.* Norton, 1969.

Stone, J. F. S. *Wessex.* Frederick A. Praeger, 1960.

Wernick, R. *The Monument Builders.* Time-Life Publications, 1973.

Willey, Gordon R., and Sabloff, Jeremy A. *A History of American Archaeology.* W. H. Freeman and Company, 1974.

Wood, E. S. *Collins Field Guide to Archaeology.* Collins, 1968.

Zeuner, F. E. *Dating the Past.* Hafner Press, 1970.

Zubrow, Ezra B. W., et al. (ed.). *New World Archaeology.* W. H. Freeman and Company, 1974. (Readings from *Scientific American*)

Chapter Four

Ivimy, John. *The Sphinx and the Megaliths.* Harper Trade Books, 1975.

Lockyer, Sir J. N. *Stonehenge and other British Stone Monuments Astronomically Considered.* Macmillan, 1909.

Proceedings of the Royal Society, 1972. *The Place of Astronomy in the Ancient World.* Oxford University Press, 1974.

Thom, Alexander. *Megalithic Sites in Britain.* Oxford University Press, 1967.

————. *Megalithic Lunar Observatories.* Oxford University Press, 1971.

Chapter Five
Greed, John A. *Glastonbury Tales*. St. Trillo Publications, 1975.
Michell, John. *The Old Stones of Lands End*. Garnstone Press, 1974.
Watkins, Alfred. *The Old Straight Track*. Ballantine, 1973.

Part Two—*General Reading*

Bord, Colin and Janet. *Mysterious Britain*. Doubleday, 1973.
Graves, Robert. *The White Goddess*. Octagon, 1972.
Lethbridge, T. C. *A Step in the Dark*. Routledge and Kegan Paul, 1967.
———. *The Monkey's Tail*. Routledge and Kegan Paul, 1969.
———. *E.S.P.—Beyond Time and Distance*. Routledge and Kegan Paul, 1965.
Marshack. Alexander. *Roots of Civilization*. McGraw-Hill, 1972.
Michell, John. *The View Over Atlantis*. Ballantine, 1972.
———. *City of Revelation*. Ballantine, 1973.
Screeton, Paul. *Quicksilver Heritage*. British Book Center, 1976.

Chapters Six and Seven
Allcroft, A. Hadrian. *The Circle and the Cross*. Macmillan, 1930.
Anderson, M. D. *Looking for History in British Churches*. John Murray, 1951.
Eitel, E. J. *Feng-Shui: or the Rudiments of Natural Science in China*. Cockaygne, 1973.
Grinsell, L. V. *The Ancient Burial Mounds of England*. Greenwood Press, 1975.
James, E. O. *Prehistoric Religion*. Thames and Hudson, 1957.
Johnson, Walter. *Byways in British Archaeology*. Cambridge University Press, 1917.
Underwood, Guy. *Pattern of the Past*. Abelard-Schuman, 1973.

Chapters Eight and Nine
Castle, E. W., and Thiering, B. B. (eds.). *Some Trust in*

Chariots! Popular Library, 1974.

Gauquelin, Michel. *Astrology and Science.* Peter Davies, 1970.

Holiday, F. W. *The Dragon and the Disc.* Norton, 1973.

Hynek, J. Allen. *The UFO Experience.* Ballantine, 1974.

Koestler, A. *The Roots of Coincidence.* Random House, 1972.

Matthews, W. H. *Mazes and Labyrinths.* Dover Publications, Inc., 1970.

Michell, John. *The Flying Saucer.* Abacus, 1974.

Pennick, Nigel. *The Nuthampstead Zodiac.* Endsville Press, 1972.

———. *Geomancy.* Cockaygne, 1973.

Purce, Jill. *The Mystic Spiral.* Avon, 1974.

Roberts, Anthony. *Atlantean Traditions in Ancient Britain.* Unicorn, 1974.

Rocard, Y. *Le Signal du sourcier.* Dunod, Paris, 1962.

Smith, Sir G. Elliot. *The Evolution of the Dragon.* Manchester University Press, 1919.

Spence, Lewis. *The Magic Arts of Celtic Britain.* Aquarian Press, 1970.

Taylor, John. *Superminds.* Viking Press, 1975.

Velikovsky, I. *Worlds in Collision.* Doubleday, 1950.

Waters, Frank. *Book of the Hopi.* Viking/Compass, 1963.

Watson, Lyall. *Supernature.* Bantam, 1974.

Williams, Mary (ed.). *Glastonbury—a Study in Patterns.* RILKO, 1969.

——— (ed.). *Britain—a Study in Patterns.* RILKO, 1969.

INDEX